Prolog Programming

D1710051

Prolog Programming

Applications for Database Systems, Expert Systems, and Natural Language Systems

Claudia Marcus, Arity Corporation

Addison-Wesley Publishing Company, Inc.
Reading, Massachusetts   Menlo Park, California
Don Mills, Ontario   Wokingham, England   Amsterdam   Bonn
Sydney   Singapore   Tokyo   Madrid   Bogotá
Santiago   San Juan

Many of the designations used by manufacturers and sellers to distinguish their products are claimed as trademarks. Where those designations appear in this book, and Addison-Wesley was aware of a trademark claim, the designations have been printed in initial caps or all caps.

Arity and Arity/Prolog are registered trademarks of Arity Corporation.

Libary of Congress Cataloging-in-Publication Data

Marcus, Claudia.
  Prolog programming.

  Bibliography: p.
  Includes index.
  1. Prolog (Computer program language)   2. Data base
management.   3. Expert systems (Computer science)
4. Linguistics–Data processing.   I. Title.
QA76.73.P76M37   1986   005.13 ′3   86–17287
ISBN 0-201-14647-9

Copyright © 1986 by Arity Corporation

All rights reserved. No part of this publication may be reproduced, stored in a retrieval system, or transmitted, in any form or by any means, electronic, mechanical, photocopying, recording, or otherwise, without the prior written permission of Addison-Wesley. Printed in the United States of America. Published simultaneously in Canada.

Cover design by Steve Snider.
Printed from repro supplied by the author.

 BCDEFGHIJ–AL–89876

2nd Printing, November 1986

Contents

Figures

Acknowledgments

No book is the result of a single person's effort, particularly a book about a technical subject area such as this. Although my name appears on the cover, this book could not have been written without the assistance of the staff at Arity Corporation.

I would first like to thank Peter Gabel, who put the company's resources behind me and allowed me to put my other responsibilities aside so that I could work on the book full time.

I thank the technical staff for contributing their technical expertise throughout the project. In particular, I want to thank Steven Huberman for his help in the area of the Prolog database and the database applications, and for his contribution of the Rock Climbing expert. I thank David Drager for his assistance in the area of expert systems and natural language. I also want to thank Paul Weiss for his contribution of the expert system shell and for his suggestions for the overall programming "style" used throughout the book.

Finally, I would like to thank all the people who carefully reviewed the manuscript, especially Meredith Bartlett and Greg Closter. Without each of these people, the book would not have been possible.

Preface

This book is written primarily for programmers. They may be new to Prolog or to the applications areas listed in the somewhat lengthy subtitle of this book, but they share one desire — to start writing applications without too much delay. With this in mind, the smallest part of the book is devoted to the Prolog language itself, and the majority deals with applications. It is also assumed that most readers are at least somewhat familiar with languages such as C and Pascal.

A Pascal or C program defines the procedures that the program must follow to arrive at a solution or perform some task. In Prolog, on the other hand, a program is not defined as a series of steps but as a description of the relationship between objects. From these descriptions, Prolog derives solutions to questions. Programmers must conceptualize a program within a different frame of reference, thinking not so much about the steps that the program must follow as about the objects that are involved and how they interact in different situations.

In many ways, however, Prolog is like other programming languages. Programmers can trace the steps that Prolog takes to find an answer, and the language gives them mechanisms for controlling the execution path. It provides a library of built-in functions, called evaluable predicates, that can be invoked to produce "side effects." That is, these evaluable predicates perform input and output to the terminal and to files, calculate the answers to arithmetic expressions, and perform the operations that programmers would expect to find in any programming language. For readers who have had no exposure to Prolog, chapters 1 and 2 provide an overview of the language.

Prolog is unique as a programming language in that it provides a built-in database in which to store information. When used within an interpreted environment, the database stores the program as well as any information required by the user or the program at run time. When used within a compiled application, the program is no longer stored in the database, but the database is still available for storing information required by the user or the program at run time.

Prolog provides access methods into the database and enough evaluable predicates to allow alternate access methods to be built as well. Chapter 3 discusses the features of Prolog's internal database, including some more recent enhancements to its design. It also presents some methods for accessing information stored in hash tables, binary trees, and balanced trees.

Its built-in database makes Prolog well suited for writing database applications, especially relational database management systems. Information is represented by the language in a way that closely resembles relational tables, and access to the information in Prolog resembles access by relational database queries. Chapter 4 describes the basic features of a relational database management system, using SQL as the query language. The chapter shows how SQL queries can be transformed into Prolog questions.

Another area in which Prolog has proven its applicability is in the development of expert systems. Expert systems derive solutions to problems using many of the same inference techniques that people use. Because many of the concepts used in expert system technology may be new to readers, chapter 5 gives an introduction to expert system concepts. This chapter illustrates how to write two expert-like systems, using some of the more common techniques for knowledge representation and inference.

Expert systems are usually written with an expert system shell rather than a programming language such as Prolog. A shell defines how knowledge is represented internally and how solutions are derived. To build an expert system with a shell, programmers define the expertise required by the system using a very high-level language. Expert system shells can be written in Prolog; a simple shell is described in chapter 6.

Prolog is also an excellent language in which to implement other language processors. Two parsing techniques are built into the language: one for operator precedence grammars, the other for definite clause grammars. In chapter 7, the operator precedence grammars are used for writing a Prolog interpreter and for writing an object definition language such as might be found in an expert system shell. The definite clause grammars are used for writing a parser for arithmetic expressions. Chapter 8 uses definite clause grammars for building a natural language system.

Many Prolog systems are now commercially available, running on a variety of computers. There is no formal standard for the language, but most implementations conform to the language and evaluable predicates described in the book *Programming in Prolog* by Clocksin and Mellish (Springer-Verlag, 1984). Many also provide the additional predicates defined by ''DEC-10'' or ''Edinburgh'' Prolog. The language syntax and the set of predicates used throughout the body of the book conform to the DEC-10 Prolog de facto standard. A summary of Arity/Prolog, a superset of this standard, is given in appendix A.

Each of the major topics in this book — the Prolog language, database management systems, expert systems, and language processors — is a major area of study. Volumes of information are written about each topic. The breadth of subject matter in this book has therefore imposed a limit on depth. The emphasis in this book is on the practical application of Prolog, not on the theories upon which the applications are based. To fully understand these application areas, the reader should refer to other readings. A bibliography is provided in the back of this book.

Prolog Programming

1

Introduction to Prolog

If you are a programmer new to Prolog, you probably have questions like these:

1. What are the tokens recognized by the language, such as its reserved words, constants, and identifiers?

2. What are the language's data types? How do you define objects of those types?

3. What are the operators of the language and how do you form expressions that use these operators?

4. What statements does the language provide for assignment and for program control?

5. How are procedures defined? How are they called by other procedures?

For the conventional programming languages, there is a fairly predictable set of answers, too. Languages such as C, BASIC, or Pascal define a similar set of data types that map directly to the machine architecture. Integers and characters, for example, occupy a specific number of bits. Each language has a similar set of statements to describe the steps the machine must take in order to solve a problem. FOR, WHILE, and DO loops set up specific execution paths; IF...THEN...ELSE statements set up conditional branches of execution. Because a program must describe how to solve a problem, these languages are said to be "prescriptive."

Prolog does not fit neatly within the bounds of these questions because its roots are different from those of conventional languages. Prolog evolved out of the branch of logic called predicate calculus, which is used by mathematicians and logicians to make assertions about the world. They then use these assertions to prove theorems. For example, by asserting that "Socrates is a man" and that "All men are mortal," it is possible to prove that "Socrates is mortal." Although you do not need to know predicate calculus before you begin learning Prolog, you may find it interesting to know that you will learn something about this field as you learn Prolog.

Like predicate calculus, Prolog defines a way to make logical assertions and to prove theorems based on those assertions. Stated quite simply:

- You describe the problem in terms of "facts" and "rules." Facts are statements that are simply true. They are analogous to logical assertions. Rules, similar to theorem proofs, tell Prolog how to prove whether something is true.
- You access facts or set a rule into action by asking questions.

Thus, Prolog allows you to concentrate on the problem at hand rather than concern yourself with the machine's solution of the problem. Because a program describes the problem rather than the steps taken to solve the problem, Prolog is said to be "descriptive" rather than prescriptive.

What constitutes a program, then? In conventional languages, a program is a collection of procedures that are executed in a specific order. In Prolog, a program is a collection of facts and rules. You do not need to concern yourself with the details of how these facts and rules are executed. To a large degree, Prolog defines the order in which they are executed.

This chapter describes the basic features of the Prolog language, including how facts and rules are defined and how Prolog answers questions based on these facts and rules. Also described are the basic data types defined by the language and how arbitrary data structures are built from these types. Finally, the chapter introduces the evaluable predicates provided by the language to perform arithmetic operations.

Facts and the Prolog Database

At the heart of the Prolog language lies a built-in database where facts and rules are stored. This database shares many of the characteristics of the relational database model. One shared characteristic is its method of storing facts.

Relational databases store information in tables consisting of rows and columns. A row, called an "instance" of the relation, contains an individual fact. An instance consists of one or more columns, called "attributes." All instances in the same relation have the same number of attributes and similar information is placed in the same attribute position of each of the rows.

The distance from the sun to the planets in the solar system is an example of information that fits nicely into a table. Figure 1-1 shows how a relational database would store this information. *Distance* is the name of the relation. It has two attributes. Each instance gives the name of one planet and that planet's distance (in millions of miles) from the sun.

Attributes

Planet	Millions of Miles
Mercury	36
Venus	67
Earth	93
Mars	141
Jupiter	484
Saturn	886
Uranus	1,790
Neptune	2,800
Pluto	4,600

Instances

Figure 1-1: The *Distance* Relation

Prolog's representation of this information is similar to the relational table, though its syntax differs. Because of its roots in predicate calculus, Prolog facts are expressed as "clauses" rather than table entries, and a collection of related clauses is called a "predicate." Like a relational table, a predicate provides a consistent way to group similar facts. The same qualities that make a table meaningful also make Prolog facts meaningful. That is, each related clause has the same number of "arguments." Like the columns of a table, related arguments in each clause hold the same type of information. If these arguments were not consistent, it would be very difficult to evaluate the information in the database.

One type of Prolog clause is the unit clause, which is used for writing facts. The formal syntax of a unit clause is as follows:

A functor, which gives the name of the predicate, followed by a parenthesized list of arguments, followed by a period.

The following predicate shows how the distance from the sun to each planet would be written as unit clauses. The functor is equivalent to the relation name, the arguments to the functor are like the attributes of the table, and each unit clause relates directly to one instance of the table.

```
distance(mercury,36).
distance(venus,67).
distance(earth,93).
distance(mars,141).
distance(jupiter,484).
distance(saturn,886).
distance(uranus,1790).
distance(neptune,2800).
distance(pluto,4600).
```

Prolog stores the clauses in the database in the same order in which you enter them. If you enter the planets in the order that they appear around the sun, Prolog will retrieve them in that order. Therefore, the ordering of clauses in the database can be as significant as the facts themselves. In this example, the order is merely interesting. At other times, such as when you define rules, the order can ensure that your program executes properly.

Prolog Data Types

In many conventional languages, data is highly typed; information must have a specific format. The typing of information is carried over into the applications written in those languages. For example, a customer name may be constrained to an arbitrary number of characters. As a result, to define a new kind of object often requires a great deal of effort. For example, if a program were designed to accept customer information, it would be difficult to add information about the planets in the solar system.

Consider the following C representation of the solar system information. In C, the solar system information is defined as an array of structures, where the planet name is an array of 10 characters and the number of miles is an integer. Initialized, as it is here, the array of structures is fixed at compile time. There is no space to add more elements to this structure or more structures to this array at run time.

```
struct {
    char name[10];
    int miles;
    } distance[9]  =
        { { "mercury",36 },
          { "venus",67 },
          { "earth",93 },
          { "mars",141 },
          { "jupiter",484 },
          { "saturn",886 },
          { "uranus",1790 },
          { "neptune",2800 },
          { "pluto",4600 }
        } ;
```

In Prolog, data is neither highly typed nor constrained to a predefined set of objects. It is always possible to add new *distance* clauses to the database. If you want to add other kinds of information, you simply add facts to express the new information.

For instance, you could add information about the planets that have satellites:

```
satellites(uranus,5).
satellites(earth,1).
satellites(saturn,9).
```

Alternatively, you could add information about the atmosphere of Earth:

```
atmosphere(earth,[hydrogen,oxygen,nitrogen,carbon_dioxide]).
```

Prolog gives you a systematic and simple way to define complex objects from a few atomic types. The language encourages you to represent data the way humans think rather than the way the computer should store the data.

Variables

A variable is an object that can take on any value. Variables can replace arguments to a functor when you want Prolog to return the value of the argument. They can also replace entire goals when you want to determine at run time what goal to execute. A variable name must begin with an uppercase letter or an underscore. It cannot be surrounded by quotes.

A single underscore is referred to as an ''anonymous'' variable. Each anonymous variable is unique. Each is treated like an ordinary variable except that Prolog does not return its value. Anonymous variables are useful when you do not want to return the value of a particular argument to a functor.

Atoms

Atoms are unique strings of characters representing a single object. Atoms can be quoted or unquoted. Unquoted atoms must begin with a lowercase letter. They can contain dollar signs and underscores but they cannot contain spaces. Atoms are quoted when they are surrounded by single quotes. Quoted atoms can begin with an uppercase letter or a symbolic character, they can contain spaces, and they can contain any special character. Within a quoted atom, a single quote is written as two single quotes.

Thus, atoms can be used to represent vastly different kinds of information, such as the names of planets or the address or phone number of a customer. Each of the following is a valid atom:

'358 Baker Avenue, Concord, Massachusetts'

earth

'(617) 371-1243'

Integers

An integer is any positive or negative whole number. The range of integers that Prolog can handle is determined by the hardware on which it runs. The range for 16-bit computers is -32768 to 32767. Many implementations of Prolog also supply a floating-point data type, which can handle very large and very small numbers.

Structures

Structures allow you to manipulate complex data as a single object rather than as separate objects. For example, you can collect the elements of the atmosphere together in the structure:

air(hydrogen,oxygen,nitrogen,carbon__dioxide).

The elements of a structure can be of any data type or a combination of data types. This means that structures can represent very complex data objects. For example:

```
customer(name(smith,john),
     address(street(1,main),
          city(concord),
          state(massachusetts),
          zip(01742)),
          phone(617,371,1234))
```

Like unit clauses, structures consist of a functor followed by a parenthesized list of arguments. Although structures and unit clauses may look the same, they are different. Unit clauses have meaning procedurally. Structures do not; they are data objects.

Lists

Lists are a special form of structure. Unlike regular structures, which you name, lists have the predefined functor name '.' (dot). Lists consist of nested structures, each having two elements referred to as a "head" and a "tail." For example, the elements in the Earth's atomosphere could be written as a list:

.(hydrogen,.(oxygen,.(nitrogen,.(carbon__dioxide,[]))))

Dot notation illustrates the special head/tail form of lists. The outermost structure holds the element *hydrogen* plus the structure forming the rest of the list. The second structure holds the element *oxygen* plus the structure forming the rest of that list, and so on. The innermost structure holds the last element plus the empty list, written as [].

Although the dot notation most accurately shows the internal representation of a list, working with it can be awkward. Therefore, Prolog provides a more convenient notation. A list can also be written as the elements enclosed in square brackets. Using this notation, the atmosphere of Earth can be written as follows:

[hydrogen,oxygen,nitrogen,carbon__dioxide]

Notice that in this notation, the square brackets ([]) that mark the end of the list are not needed.

When using list notation, you can separate the head and tail with a vertical bar, as shown below:

[a|b,c]

or

[a,b|c]

Lists can contain variables, or a combination of variables and nonvariables:

[a|T]

and

[H|T]

The list *[a|T]* represents all lists that begin with the letter *a* and have any elements as the tail; the list *[H|T]* represents all lists.

Another form of list notation is used for character strings. A character string is text that is enclosed in quotation marks. For example:

''abc''

Internally, this string is treated as the list of ASCII character codes:

[97,98,99]

In chapter 4, when lists and structures are discussed in more detail, you will see when one representation may be better than another. Because it is simple to convert lists to structures and structures to lists, choosing one type over the other is a matter of convenience and does not restrict the data to that type.

Questions, Matching, and Unification

As discussed earlier, Prolog facts resemble relational tables. Another characteristic of a relational database that is shared by Prolog is the ability to handle *ad hoc* queries. Once you have learned a general purpose query language, you control what information is retrieved, as well as how and when it is retrieved. Query languages for relational database systems allow you to choose the data you want returned by selecting attributes from tables. For example, a relational database query to generate the table in figure 1-1 might look like this:

SELECT *
FROM DISTANCE

Prolog also gives you the ability to retrieve information in an *ad hoc* manner. This is done by forming Prolog questions. A question has the syntax:

A question mark and hyphen followed by a functor, followed by a parenthesized list of arguments, followed by a period.

A question looks much like a unit clause, except that it begins with the question mark and hyphen symbol (?-). The ?- symbol is used as a prompt by many Prolog interpreters to indicate that the system is ready to accept questions from the user.

Prolog answers questions by performing "matching" and "unification." Matching is the way Prolog locates the correct clause in the database. In order for a question and a clause to match, they must have the same functor and the same number of arguments. Unification is similar to the assignment performed by conventional languages. However, assignment is specific to a computer address that probably has a certain size and a specific data type. Unification is more general. Prolog data types unify according to the following rules:

- Variables always unify with other variables. If one variable becomes unified with a value — "instantiated" — any other matching variables also become instantiated to the same value.

- A variable always unifies with a matching atom, integer, or structure. When the variable and the data object are unified, the variable is instantiated to that value.

- Atoms unify with other atoms if they match. For example, the atom *star* can unify with another atom *star*, but not with the atom *sun*.

- Structures unify with other structures if they have the same name and number of arguments and if the arguments of one structure unify with the arguments of the other structure.

Prolog returns values from the database by unifying variables with objects of other data types. At one time, a variable can be unified with an integer; at another, the same variable can be unified with a structure or an atom. A unified variable, therefore, represents only one instance among possibly many valid instances of the variable.

In conventional languages, it is possible to assign new values to variables. Again, Prolog is less specific. Prolog can "uninstantiate" a variable if further processing proves the previous instantiation to be incorrect. It then backs up to look for another possible value for the variable. This process is called "backtracking."

If a question matches a clause in the database and if the arguments unify, the question succeeds. If a question does not match a clause in the database or if the arguments do not unify, it fails. All questions either succeed or fail. When a variable has been unified, Prolog instantiates the variable to that value.

The rest of this chapter provides examples showing how Prolog performs matching and unification. In these examples, a goal is matched against a clause in the database. The goal is written in regular type and the database clause is in italics. Arrows from the goal to a database clause show how Prolog determines whether the arguments match. Arrows from the database clause to the goal show how variables are instantiated. Finally, each attempt at matching and unification has a status showing whether the goals succeeded or failed. The status is "yes" for success and "no" for failure. The status is shown in bold. For instance, the following question asks whether Earth is 93 million miles from the sun. Prolog can match the question with a clause in the database, so it responds to this question with *yes*.

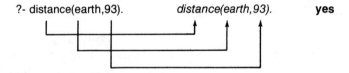

?- distance(earth,93).   *distance(earth,93).*   **yes**

You can ask Prolog to return the distance from the sun to Mars, supplying a variable in place of the number of miles:

?- distance(mars,X).

The answer is found in this way:

1. *distance* is matched with *distance* in the database to locate the correct predicate:

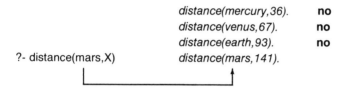

2. The database is searched for a distance clause containing *mars* as the first argument.

	distance(mercury,36).	**no**
	distance(venus,67).	**no**
	distance(earth,93).	**no**
?- distance(mars,X)	*distance(mars,141).*	

3. A variable matches any value in the corresponding position within the clause, as long as the rest of the clause also matches. Therefore, *X* matches *141*.

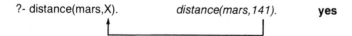

4. After the correct clause is found, the value from the database is unified with the variable in the question, and the goal succeeds.

?- distance(mars,X).   *distance(mars,141).*   **yes**

X is instantiated to *141* million miles.

Prolog provides a consistent syntax for both defining and retrieving information. The unit clause defines a new fact for the database; the question returns information from the database. Both the unit clause and the question are written as a functor followed by a series of arguments.

Contrast this to C, where retrieving information is very different from defining that information. For example, to access the array of structures defined earlier, you must know the structure's offset into the array (in this case, an integer between 0 and 8) and you must know the name of the structure element that you want to reference. Thus, to reference Earth's distance from the sun, you would write in C:

distance[2].miles

To reference the name of the fifth planet from the sun, you would write:

distance[4].name

In addition, you must write a separate C function to handle each of the different types of questions that you may want to ask. Prolog, on the other hand, provides a simple framework in which you can formulate many different questions.

Finding Multiple Answers to a Question

The following question asks for the distance from the sun to any planet. In this question, both the name and the number of miles are variables. Because they represent different values, the two variables must have different names, such as *X* and *Y*.

?- distance(X,Y).

Because variables will unify with any type of object, the question succeeds at the very first *distance* clause and Prolog unifies *X* with *mercury* and *Y* with *36*.

One answer to the question may be adequate, but you may want to see whether Prolog can find other answers. Prolog interpreters allow you to do either. When the interpreter has successfully located an answer to a question, it first displays the values of any variables that have become instantiated. Then it displays what is called a "continuation prompt." You can press the enter key to indicate that no more answers are needed, causing Prolog to stop searching the database for answers. You can also press the semicolon key to force Prolog to search for another answer.

When you press the semicolon key, any instantiated variables are uninstantiated. That is, Prolog throws out the previous values for the variables. It then looks for the next matching clause in the database. When it finds another match, Prolog unifies the variables with the new values. This process can be repeated to return all possible values. When no more matching clauses can be found, the question fails.

In the Arity/Prolog interpreter, all answers to the question *distance(X, Y)* can be found by repeatedly pressing the semicolon key at the continuation prompt —>. The *no* returned at the end of the display shown below indicates that no more matching clauses were found.

```
?- distance(X,Y).

X  =  mercury
Y  =  36 —> ;

X  =  venus
Y  =  67 —> ;

X  =  earth
Y  =  93 —> ;

X  =  mars
Y  =  141 —> ;

X  =  jupiter
Y  =  484 —> ;

X  =  saturn
Y  =  886 —> ;

X  =  uranus
Y  =  1790 —> ;

X  =  neptune
Y  =  2800 —> ;

X  =  pluto
Y  =  4600 —>

no
```

Although other interpreters may display the results differently, they all perform the same internal steps. Here is how Prolog goes about finding the answers.

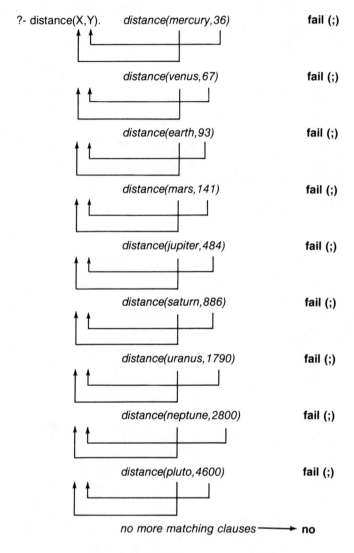

It is important to remember that a database is a finite entity. The success or failure of a Prolog question means only that the requested information cannot be found within the bounds of the database. Scientists suspect that there is a tenth planet beyond Pluto. If this database cannot return the distance from the sun to that planet, it neither proves nor disproves the existence of the planet.

Conjunctions

The questions asked so far involve only one goal at a time. It is also possible to ask questions that involve more than one goal. This is done by separating the two goals with a comma (,). All goals must succeed for the entire question to succeed. A question that requires all its goals to succeed is called a "conjunction." For instance, you can ask Prolog to return the name of the planet that has both a satellite and an atmosphere. To keep Prolog from returning the number of satellites or the composition of the atmosphere, you can place an underscore in the position of those two arguments.

   ?- satellite(X,__), atmosphere(X,__).

Given the database thus far, Prolog answers the question in this way:

1. Prolog begins by trying to satisfy the first goal. It searches for a planet with satellites and finds *uranus*. It instantiates *X* to *uranus*.

2. With *X* instantiated to *uranus*, Prolog then tries to determine whether *uranus* has an atmosphere. This goal fails.

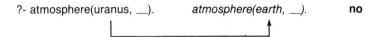

3. Prolog then backtracks to the first goal. It uninstantiates *X* and tries to find the next planet that has a satellite. It unifies *X* with *earth*.

4. Again, it tries to satisfy the second goal. This time, *X* is instantiated to *earth*.

Both goals succeed with *X* equal to *earth*.

Disjunctions

It is also possible to ask a question in which either one or another goal must succeed. This kind of question is called a "disjunction." Disjunctions are formed by separating the goals with a semicolon (;), as in:

?- atmosphere(X,＿) ; satellites(X,＿).

This question finds the planets that have either an atmosphere or a satellite.

1. To solve this question, Prolog tries to satisfy the first goal. If it finds a value for *X*, the question succeeds without trying the second goal.

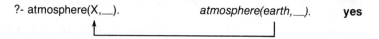

2. If the first goal fails, Prolog tries to satisfy the second goal.

Rules

Not all information must (or can) be represented by facts. Some facts imply other facts. For example, distance must be measured between two points. In the *distance* predicate, only one point is given; the other point, the sun, is implied. Facts and rules, therefore, must operate on the same assumptions.

Information can also be inferred. For example, if it were possible to determine that life requires oxygen, nitrogen, and carbon dioxide (and that those were the only requirements), then it would be possible to infer that a planet could support life if it has those elements. Rules can define the process by which such inferences are made.

Other information can be calculated. In these cases, you can save space in the database by storing a formula as a rule rather than storing the individual results of the formula as facts.

Rules state that:

The conclusion is true if
 Condition 1 is true and
 Condition 2 is true and

 ...
 Condition n is true.

In Prolog, rules have the following syntax:

A functor and its arguments, followed by a colon and hyphen symbol (:-), followed by one or more goals, followed by a period and carriage return.

The functor and its arguments are often called the "head," which states the conclusion to be proved. The colon/dash symbol (:-) is referred to as the "neck." It separates the head from the rest of the clause. The goals make up what is called the "body" of the rule. They define the conditions that must be satisfied in order for the head to be proven true. These goals are just like Prolog questions, except that instead of being preceded by the ?- symbol, they are collected into one clause.

Unit clauses are the simplest form of rule. They state that some conclusion is true. Therefore, the unit clauses in the *distance* predicate are equivalent to the rules:

```
distance(mercury,36) :- true.
distance(venus,67) :- true.
distance(earth,93) :- true.
distance(mars,141) :- true.
distance(jupiter,484) :- true.
distance(saturn,886) :- true.
distance(uranus,1790) :- true.
distance(neptune,2800) :- true.
distance(pluto,4600) :- true.
```

More complicated statements such as the following can also be written as Prolog rules:

A planet can support life if
    It is 93 million miles from a sun and
    It has an atmosphere and
    It has one satellite.

In Prolog, this rule is written:

```
supports_life(Planet) :-
    distance(Planet,93),
    atmosphere(Planet,_),
    satellites(Planet,1).
```

Unlike questions, rules are stored in the database. Once you have defined a rule, you can invoke it at any time by using the head of the clause as a question. When you ask the question, "What planet supports life?", Prolog uses matching and unification to find the planet that satisfies all three conditions. The question in Prolog is written like this:

```
?- supports_life(X).
```

To answer the question, Prolog must prove that each of the subgoals of the predicate *supports_life* can be proven. This is done by following these steps:

1. It first finds the planet whose distance is 93 million miles from the sun and instantiates X to *earth*.

	distance(mercury,36).	no
	distance(venus,67).	no
distance(X,93),	distance(earth,93).	yes

2. It then proves that *earth* has an atmosphere.

atmosphere(earth,_).	atmosphere(earth,_).	yes

3. Finally, it proves that *earth* has one satellite.

Because each of its subgoals succeeds with *X* instantiated to *earth*, the entire predicate succeeds.

Rules That Generate Multiple Answers

As shown earlier, typing a semicolon at the interpreter's continuation prompt forces a goal to fail and causes Prolog to find alternate solutions to a question. If you want Prolog to find alternate solutions without prompting you first, you can use a predicate called *fail* as the last goal in the rule.

Prolog can generate the relational database table in figure 1-1 by finding each *distance* clause stored in the database. The *fail* goal causes *distance(X, Y)* to fail automatically and proceed to the next matching clause in the database. To write the table to the screen or to a file requires the use of input and output routines, discussed in chapter 2. For now, it is enough to make Prolog find all possible answers to the question without writing them:

```
find_all :-
    distance(X,Y),
    fail.
```

When you ask Prolog to find all planets and their distances, Prolog returns *no*.

```
?- find_all.
```

no

By stepping through the solution, you can see why.

1. Prolog satisfies the first goal and instantiates *X* to *mercury* and *Y* to *36*.

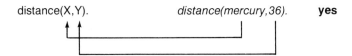

2. The second goal (*fail*) causes *distance(X, Y)* to backtrack. *X* and *Y* are uninstantiated and Prolog attempts to resatisfy the question.

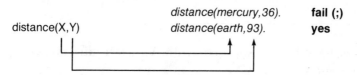

distance(X,Y)

distance(mercury,36).   **fail (;)**
distance(earth,93).   **yes**

3. It repeats these two steps for each matching clause in the database, first instantiating *X* and *Y*, then failing and uninstantiating the variables again.

distance(venus,67).	**fail (;)**
distance(earth,93).	**fail (;)**
distance(mars,141).	**fail (;)**
distance(jupiter,484).	**fail (;)**
distance(saturn,886).	**fail (;)**
distance(uranus,1790).	**fail (;)**
distance(neptune,2800).	**fail (;)**
distance(pluto,4600).	**fail (;)**
distance(X,Y)———————→ No more matching clauses.	**no**

When no more clauses can be found, the *distance(X, Y)* goal fails, causing the entire question to fail.

To make *find_all* succeed, you would need to add another clause to the predicate. A predicate can be made up of many clauses with the same name and number of arguments. Prolog tries to satisfy each clause in the order in which it appears in the database. Therefore, the *find_all* predicate should contain these two clauses:

```
find_all :-
      distance(X,Y),
      fail.
find_all.
```

Prolog will find each matching clause in the database when it executes the first clause. When no more matching *distance* clauses can be found, the first *find_all* clause fails. Then, Prolog tries to satisfy the second *find_all* clause. In this example, the second clause is a unit clause, which succeeds. Now when you ask the same question, *find_all* succeeds:

?- find__all.

yes

When writing rules that consist of more than one clause, you must make sure that the clauses are in the correct order. For example, if the *find__all* clauses were written in the reverse order, the predicate would never find the names and miles of the planets. The first clause would immediately succeed and the second clause would never be executed.

Rules That Perform Calculations

Arithmetic is performed by combining an arithmetic expression with an arithmetic evaluable predicate. Arithmetic expressions are structures such as the following:

+(1,4)

*(824,3)

/(3,2)

The arithmetic operators (+ , − , *, and /) are predefined, or built-in, functors that take two arguments.

The result of an arithmetic expression is not computed, however, until the expression is used as an argument to an arithmetic evaluable predicate, such as *is*. An evaluable predicate is a built-in rule. Evaluable predicates can perform I/O, they can directly access the database, and they can perform arithmetic computations. All of these operations are outside of the logic of the language. However, evaluable predicates perform very valuable functions for practical programming.

To calculate the answers to the three expressions above, you would combine the expression with the evaluable predicate called *is*. When Prolog encounters these goals, it computes the answer and returns the result to the variables, X, Y, and Z.

is(X, +(1, 4))

is(Y, *(824, 3))

is(Z, /(3, 2))

In addition to *is*, Prolog defines these other arithmetic evaluable predicates to compare arithmetic expressions for the following conditions:

>   Greater than
<   Less than
> =   Greater than or equal to
= <   Less than or equal to
= : =   Equality
= / =   Inequality

In each of these cases, the operator precedes its operands. This notation is called Prefix Polish notation. Prefix Polish notation is the way that Prolog handles data structures, facts, rules, and questions. Arithmetic expressions and arithmetic calculations are no exception. People, on the other hand, are not taught arithmetic in Prefix Polish notation. Because it is more natural to think of arithmetic in infix notation, Prolog allows you to write arithmetic in either infix or Prefix Polish form. In infix notation, the arithmetic expressions are written as:

1 + 4

824 * 3

3 / 2

Evaluation with the *is* predicate is written like this:

X is 1 + 4

Y is 824 * 3

Z is 3 / 2

Knowing this about arithmetic, you can use the solar system database to calculate the distance between the orbits of two planets. To do this, you need to find out how far each planet is from the sun and subtract the smaller from the larger distance. The first clause handles the case where the first argument is the further planet.

```
how__far(Planet1,Planet2,Distance) :-
    distance(Planet1,X),
    distance(Planet2,Y),
    Distance is X - Y,
    Distance > = 0.
```

A second clause handles the case where the first argument is the nearer planet.

```
how__far(Planet1,Planet2,Distance) :-
    distance(Planet1,X),
    distance(Planet2,Y),
    Distance is Y - X.
```

Of course, you could store all the distances from one orbit to the other as facts in the database. However, if you did you would need to store 81 different facts, such as:

```
        .
        .
        .
how__far(mercury,neptune,2764)
how__far(mercury,pluto,4564)
how__far(venus,venus,0)
how__far(venus,earth,26)
        .
        .
        .
```

In this way, rules can help save space.

Summary

Conventional programming languages are prescriptive; a program written in a conventional language must describe the steps required to solve a problem. Prolog, on the other hand, is a descriptive language; a program written in Prolog describes the problem more than the procedures for solving the problem. In this way, the language defines a general approach to problem-solving that can be applied to a wide variety of problems.

Using Prolog, you define the information needed by the program. This chapter described how to define information with unit clauses, which state facts that are always true within the context of the program. To define the data objects stored by facts, Prolog provides a few general data types. These are variables, atoms, integers, structures, and lists.

In addition, you define general rules for solving a particular type of problem. This chapter showed how rules describe relationships between objects and how these relationships must be true in order for a conclusion to be true. Rules can also call evaluable predicates to perform operations such as arithmetic. In this way, rules can produce "side effects," or results.

Facts and rules are collected in Prolog's built-in database. This chapter described some of the ways in which Prolog's database resembles a relational database. This resemblance will be disucussed further in chapter 4.

You ask questions to request the solution to a specific problem. Prolog answers questions by executing the facts and rules, using a few simple mechanisms. Matching and unification search forward through the database to find an answer to a question. A question succeeds when it matches a clause in the database; it fails when no match is found. Backtracking lets Prolog search for alternate solutions.

Facts, rules, and questions, matching and unification, success, failure, and backtracking all have a basis in logic and predicate calculus; they are the same mechanisms by which logical assertions are proven. However, logic alone falls short of solving all programming problems. Therefore, Prolog also has a procedural side, which is the topic of the next chapter.

2
The Procedural Side of Prolog

Often in a conventional programming language, there is a large gap between the statement of a problem and its solution. Suppose, for example, you want to write a program to determine whether one person is an ancestor of another person. Your solution in C or Pascal would have to include steps to:

1. Define persons A, B, and C by allocating space for them as objects having one of the language's data types.
2. Locate the persons A and B in an external database or file.
3. If they cannot be found, exit with a failure status.
4. Locate the parent of B. Call that person C.
5. Test to see if person A is equal to person C.
6. If they are equal, return a status value indicating success.
7. If they are not equal, reinvoke the procedure with new arguments to see if person A is the ancestor of person C.

The solution includes steps to allocate space in memory, to perform database look ups and arithmetic operations, and to maintain status values. None of these operations relate to the true nature of the problem.

The Prolog definition of the ancestor relationship comes much closer to the relationship between grandparents, parents, and children. The definition of *ancestor* is as straight-forward as stating that:

"A is the ancestor of B if A is B's parent or if A is the ancestor of B's parent."

At the same time that this statement defines the relationship between people and their ancestors, it also defines a method for determining whether any person *A* is the ancestor of a person *B*. The procedures are inferred from the statement by the Prolog system rather than described by the program itself. The mechanisms of matching and unification, success, failure, and backtracking define how the Prolog description is executed. In this way, Prolog is not just a descriptive language; it is also a procedural language.

Prolog programs often require more control than matching, unification, and backtracking allow. In order for many programs to execute properly, some "extra-logical" aspects of the language have been developed. *Cut*, written as *!*, allows you to control when backtracking should and should not occur. Input and output evaluable predicates make it possible to communicate with the user. Other evaluable predicates allow you to maintain the program database or perform some traditional programming activities, such as incrementing or decrementing a counter. None of these fall within the realm of logic, but they make Prolog suitable for writing practical applications.

When dealing with the procedural side of Prolog, as with any programming language, it is helpful to draw a map of the program's execution path. For conventional programming languages, this is done with flow charts. Although flow charts map the decision points and alternate execution paths for the program, the program flow is always "forward." Flow charts are not adequate for describing the execution path of a Prolog program because a Prolog program can proceed forward or backward through a series of goals. Therefore, for Prolog, other methods of representing the execution path are needed.

The procedure box model, whose development is credited to Lawrence Byrd, a colleague of Clocksin and Mellish, describes a program's execution path through goals both when they succeed and when they fail. Many Prolog debuggers use the procedure box model because it can illustrate why a program follows a certain execution path. For the purposes of this chapter, procedure boxes provide a graphical representation of a program, much as a flow chart provides for programs written in conventional programming languages.

The Procedure Box Model

To create a procedure box model for a Prolog program, you represent each goal in the program with a box. A predicate is made up of a series of goals and it is executed when called as a goal from other predicates. Therefore, you place procedure boxes for goals within the procedure boxes for the predicate that calls those goals.

Every procedure box has four "ports," which connect the boxes. A program can either enter or exit a procedure box through one of the four ports at different times during the program. Each port has a different purpose:

- A goal passes through the "call" port when it is invoked normally.
- A goal passes through the "exit" port upon successful completion.
- A goal is entered through the "redo" port when it is reactivated during backtracking.
- A goal exits through the "fail" port when it fails.

You link a series of goals so that the exit port of one goal is linked to the call port of the succeeding goal and so that the fail port of one goal is linked to the redo port of the preceding goal.

For example, look again at the *find_all* predicate from chapter 1, which uses a *fail* loop to locate the distance from the sun to each planet in the solar system.

```
find_all :-
      distance(X,Y),
      fail.
find_all.
```

The procedure box model shown in figure 2-1 illustrates how Prolog executes this predicate.

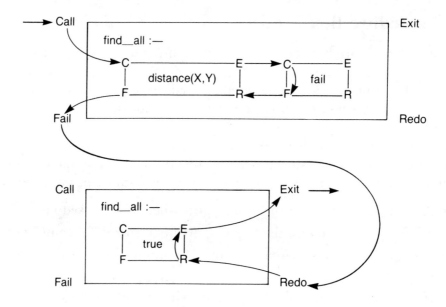

Figure 2-1: The Linking of Procedure Boxes

You can trace the steps the program takes through the procedure boxes, as follows:

1. The call port of the *find__all* predicate is linked to the call port of the *distance(X, Y)* goal. Therefore, when *find__all* is invoked, control passes immediately to *distance(X, Y)*.

2. This goal locates the first *distance* fact stored in the database, instantiates *X* and *Y*, and exits through the exit port.

3. The *fail* goal is invoked. It exits through the fail port.

4. The *distance(X, Y)* goal is then reentered through the redo port. It uninstantiates *X* and *Y* and looks for the next instance in the database.

5. The program repeats steps 3 and 4 until no more matching *distance* clauses can be found.

6. Then, *distance(X, Y)* exits through the fail port and proceeds to the redo port of the procedure box for *find__all*. At this point, the program executes the second *find__all* clause.

7. Because a unit clause simply succeeds, the flow of control passes immediately from the redo port to the exit port and the predicate exits successfully.

As this example shows, procedure boxes can give a concise representation of the behavior of a Prolog program. The procedure box model will be used to illustrate how the *cut* affects the flow of control and to illustrate the behavior of recursive predicates written in Prolog.

Using Cut

One of the stumbling blocks for the new Prolog programmer is learning when to use the *cut*. A missing or misplaced *cut* can produce strange behaviors in a program or incorrect results. It can be frustrating to track down a *cut*-related problem unless you understand how and when to use the *cut* properly.

The *cut* symbol is an exclamation point (!) and it is used just like any other goal in a predicate. The effect of the *cut* is to control and limit backtracking within that predicate. There are three instances when a *cut* is necessary:

- When you want to execute only one clause of a predicate. This use of the *cut* makes the predicate behave like an if-then-else construct.
- When you want to limit a program's search through facts in the database.
- When you must handle exception conditions. In this case, you use the *cut* in conjunction with *fail*.

Wherever it appears, the *cut* makes a predicate "deterministic" rather than "non-deterministic." Deterministic predicates do not backtrack, they are executed only once, and do not produce alternate solutions. Non-deterministic predicates backtrack. They can and should produce alternate solutions if necessary. All routines written in conventional programming languages are deterministic because these languages do not operate on the concepts of matching, unification, and backtracking.

Implementing If-Then-Else

Most conventional programming languages provide an if-then-else construct, which defines alternate paths that the program can take. The *if* statement tests a condition within the program; the *then* statement defines one path the program may take; the *else* statement defines another. You can define many alternate paths with additional *else* statements. However, the choice of one path excludes any other paths from being taken.

In Prolog, alternate paths are defined by multiple clauses having the same name and number of arguments. However, if a failure occurs after the choice of a clause is made, backtracking can cause a different path to be taken. To exclude other paths, each clause within the predicate must contain the *cut* as one of its goals.

A program that simulates the operation of a thermostat can illustrate the use of *cut*. A thermostat defines a set of actions to take when the temperature is out of a certain range. The actions can be expressed as a set of if-then-else statements like these:

- *If* the temperature is too high, *then* turn off the heat.
- *Else if* the temperature is too low, *then* turn on the heat.
- *Else*, take no action.

For any temperature, the thermostat takes only one of the three possible actions.

The thermostat simulator can be written in Prolog. First, the program stores some sample temperatures to act upon. These temperatures will be stored as facts in the database, although a real-time application would read this information from a file or from another device.

```
temp(81).
temp(69).
temp(75).
```

Next, a *thermostat* predicate controls the overall execution of the program. It finds a temperature and passes the temperature to a predicate called *action*. When the *action* predicate completes, *thermostat* displays what action was taken by writing a message to the screen. A *fail* goal is included to make the program find all possible solutions.

```
thermostat(Action) :-
      temp(X),
      action(X,Action),
      write('Action': Action), nl,
      fail.
```

Finally, the *action* predicate performs the if-then-else function. It contains three clauses. The first states that if the temperature is greater than 80, turn off the heat. The second states that if the temperature is less than 70, turn on the heat. The third clause executes if the temperature is between 70 and 80; it takes no action. The first and second clauses include a *cut* so that the program takes one, and only one, action for any temperature.

```
action(X,'Turn off heat') :-
    X > 80, !.
action(X,'Turn on heat') :-
    X < 70, !.
action(__,'Take no action').
```

When you execute the thermostat program, three solutions are found — one for each temperature:

```
?- thermostat(X).
```

Action : Turn off heat
Action : Turn on heat
Action : Take no action

If you remove the *cut*s from the *action* predicate, a different set of solutions is found. The program takes two actions for the temperature value 81, two for the value 69, and one for the value 75:

```
?- thermostat(X).
```

Action : Turn off heat
Action : Take no action
Action : Turn on heat
Action : Take no action
Action : Take no action

By comparing the procedure boxes, you can see why the two versions of the program behave differently. Figure 2-2 shows the execution path of the *thermostat* program when no *cut*s are present. By following the links between the boxes, you can trace the flow of control back through the redo port of the *action* predicate. Thus, a failure causes the program to look for other valid actions for each temperature before looking for other temperatures. This produces erroneous results, because the *no__action* clause can apply to any temperature that also conforms to the "heat on" or the "heat off" clauses.

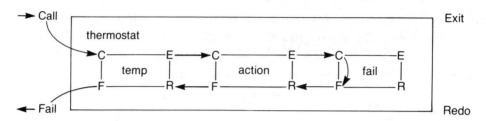

Figure 2-2: Thermostat Procedure Boxes without *Cut*

The *cut* changes the flow of control so that the goal containing the *cut* is bypassed during backtracking, as shown in figure 2-3. Within *action*, the redo port for the *cut* goal goes directly to the fail port of the entire *action* predicate. When *action* fails, the *temp* goal within *thermostat* is reentered through its redo port. The program looks for another temperature and applies the *action* predicates to that new temperature rather than applying a new clause to the same temperature.

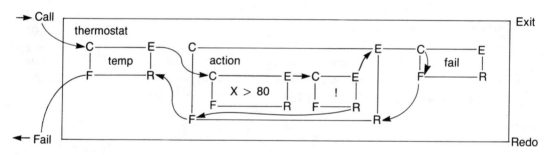

Figure 2-3: Using *Cut* for If-Then-Else

Limiting Facts

The second use of *cut* limits the facts that are considered by the program. You use the *cut* in this way when you want to take some action for any instance of a certain fact. It does not matter how many valid instances may exist and none but the first instance is considered by the program.

Suppose you want the *thermostat* program to look in the database for only one temperature. This is done by adding a *cut* immediately after the goal *temp(X)*, as shown here. The rest of the program remains the same.

```
thermostat(Action) :-
    temp(X), !,
    action(X,Action),
    fail.
```

The program now produces one result:

?- thermostat(X).

Action = Turn off heat

Procedurally, this use of *cut* has the same effect as the if-then-else construct; predicates containing the *cut* fail immediately on backtracking. Figure 2-4 shows how the *cut* alters the links between the procedure boxes. A failure in this chain of goals bypasses both the *action* and the *temp* goals. No additional actions are taken and no additional temperatures are found. Backtracking proceeds to the redo port of the *thermostat* predicate. What happens then? Prolog looks for another *thermostat* clause. If one is found, it is executed. Otherwise, *thermostat* fails.

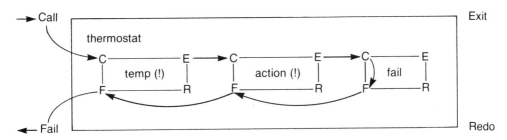

Figure 2-4: Using *Cut* to Limit Solutions

Confirming Failure

All the goals up to now attempt to prove that something is true. However, sometimes it is desirable to find out whether something is not true. For example, to avoid redundant actions, the *thermostat* program should check that the heat is not already on before turning it on.

Prolog defines the built-in predicate *not* which succeeds if some goal fails and which fails if the goal succeeds. The *not* predicate can be implemented with the cut/fail combination and it is worth looking at its definition now:

```
not(Goal) :-
      call(Goal), !, fail.
not(Goal).
```

The first clause, illustrated in figure 2-5, attempts to invoke a goal using the evaluable predicate named *call*. If the goal succeeds, then *not* fails. The *cut* ensures that the redo port of *call* is bypassed during backtracking; the fail makes the *not* exit through the fail port. The second clause is excecuted if the call to the goal fails. It simply succeeds. Thus, the failure of the goal causes *not* to succeed and the success of the goal causes *not* to fail.

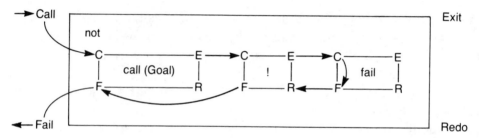

Figure 2-5: The *Not* Predicate

In order to add the appropriate tests to *thermostat* so that the predicate does not attempt to do unnecessary work, you first need to add a fact to the database stating that the heat is on:

```
heat(on).
```

Then, you need to make the *action* predicate check that the temperature is over 70 degrees and that the heat is not already on. Because both conditions determine whether to turn on the heat, the *cut* must follow the second test.

```
action(X,'Turn on heat') :-
      X < 70,
      not(heat(on)), !.
```

As the temperature changes, you need a way to dynamically update the database each time the heater is turned on or off. A later section of the chapter will present a method for doing this.

Cut/fail can also be included in a program to handle exception conditions. For example, suppose you are studying the living things found in a pond. Your samples, however, cannot contain algae. The presence of algae is an exception condition as it disqualifies the entire sample.

A program can be written to test pond samples. First, some facts are defined, representing three samples:

```
sample([frog,turtle,salamander]).
sample([tadpole,catfish,algae]).
sample([turtle,salamander,trout]).
```

The main predicate, *study_sample*, controls the overall execution of the program. It finds a sample in the database, tests the sample for algae, and fails so that it will find the next sample in the database:

```
study_sample :-
    sample(X),
    test_sample(X),
    fail.
study_sample.
```

The *test_sample* predicate looks to see if *algae* is in the sample, using a predicate called *member*. (*Member* will be defined later in this chapter.) If algae is found, the cut/fail disqualifies the sample. That is, *cut* makes sure that the predicate is not reentered on backtracking; the *fail* makes the predicate exit with a failure status.

```
test_sample(X) :-
    member(algae,X), !, fail.
test_sample(X) :-
    write('Valid Sample':X), nl.
```

When you run this program, it finds that only two of the three lists are valid samples:

```
?- study_samples.

Valid Sample : [frog,turtle,salamander]
Valid Sample : [turtle,salamander,trout]
```

You can replace most instances of cut/fail by a call to *not* and often improve the readability of your program. For example, the *test_sample* predicate is much simpler when it uses *not*.

```
test_sample(X) :-
    not(member(algae,X)),
    write('Valid sample':X), nl.
```

Recursion

Recursion is a common programming technique used in Prolog as well as in many conventional programming languages. Recursion is a form of loop, as are *fail* (discussed in chapter 1) and repeat/fail (discussed later in this chapter). Whereas *fail* backtracks to cause the next iteration of the loop to occur, a recursive predicate calls itself.

In recursion, the result of one invocation of a procedure is needed by the next invocation of the same procedure, and the result of that invocation, in turn, is needed by the next. When the last invocation exits, the calling invocations can also exit. Therefore, procedure boxes for recursive predicates are nested.

The ancestor relationship and the factorial predicate are two common examples of recursion.

Family Relationships

The *ancestor* predicate is part of a larger group of predicates that describe family relationships. The definition of family relationships is a common Prolog programming example because it very clearly demonstrates the descriptive nature of the language. For example, if you know that Paul, Monroe, and Aaron are males, and that Susan and Barbara are females, you can write the facts as follows:

```
male(paul).
male(monroe).
male(aaron).

female(susan).
female(barbara).
```

Next, a set of facts can describe the relationship between the males and females in the database — for example, that Paul's parents are Monroe and Susan.

```
parent(paul,monroe).
parent(paul,susan).
parent(barbara,monroe).
parent(barbara,susan).
parent(monroe,aaron).
```

Other predicates can be added to determine who are the mothers and who are the fathers in this database. Such predicates state that "A mother is a female parent" and "A father is a male parent."

```
mother(X,Y) :- parent(X,Y), female(Y).
father(X,Y) :- parent(X,Y), male(Y).
```

Finally, the *ancestor* predicate shows how predicates can be defined recursively. The *ancestor* predicate states that "An ancestor is a parent" or "An ancestor is an ancestor of a parent."

```
ancestor(X,Y) :- parent(X,Y).
ancestor(X,Z) :- parent(X,Y), ancestor(Y,Z).
```

To find all of Paul's ancestors, you ask the following question and fail until no more solutions are found.

```
?- ancestor(paul, X).

X = monroe —> ;

X = susan —> ;

X = aaron —>
```

The first two solutions are found by the nonrecursive *ancestor* clause because Monroe and Susan are Paul's parents. The third solution is found by the recursive clause, because Aaron is the ancestor of Paul's parent.

Figure 2-6 shows the procedure box representation of the recursive *ancestor* clause. When a value for the ancestor is found, it is passed back to the calling invocation, which passes the value to its calling invocation.

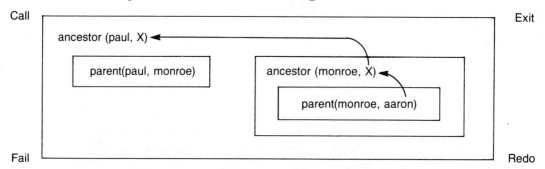

Figure 2-6: The *Ancestor* Predicate

The *Factorial* Predicate

The *factorial* predicate is another example of a recursive predicate, though its definition is less descriptive.

```
fact(0,Factorial,Factorial).
fact(Count,Intermediate,Factorial) :-
      C1 is Count – 1,
      I1 is Intermediate * Count,
      fact(C1,I1,Factorial).
```

In this definition, the number for which the factorial is calculated is the argument that counts the number of iterations remaining. The first *fact* clause looks for the terminating condition, where the counter has been decremented to 0. The second clause performs the calculation:

1. Subtract 1 from the count argument.

2. Calculate the intermediate result, which is the count times the result of the previous iteration of *fact*.

3. Pass the new counter and intermediate values to the next iteration.

You call *fact* as shown here to calculate the factorial of 3, supplying an initial intermediate value of 1:

?- fact(3,1,X).

X = 6

Figure 2-7 shows the procedure box representation of *fact*. That is, the first invocation multiplies 3 times 1; the second multiplies 2 times 3; the third multiplies 1 times 6. The fourth iteration locates the terminating condition and passes the result back through each calling invocation's third argument.

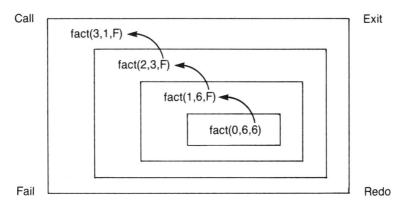

Figure 2-7: The *Factorial* Predicate

List Handling

As discussed in chapter 1, lists are a special form of structure in which the first argument of the structure is the head of the list and the second argument is the tail of the list. The head contains the first element and the tail is a structure containing the remaining elements; this structure also has a head and a tail. The list is like a recursive data type, with the head and tail structures nested within each other as invocations of a recursive predicate are nested.

Its recursive structure and special notation make the list a convenient data type to manipulate. Lists lend themselves to recursive handling, as this section will show using the two most common list operations, *member* and *append*.

The *Member* Predicate

The *member* predicate determines whether a value is contained in a list by recursively comparing that value with the head of the list. The *member* predicate is defined by two clauses. The first states that "*X* is a member of a list if it is at the head of the list."

> member(X,[X|__]).

The second clause states that "*X* is a member of a list if it is a member of the tail of the list."

> member(X,[__|Y]) :- member(X,Y).

Each invocation of *member* compares the value with succeeding elements of the list. For example, to determine whether the number 3 is a member of the list [1,2,3], the *member* predicate is called three times, as shown in the procedure boxes in figure 2-8. When it is proven that 3 is a member of the list [3|[]], then it is also proven that 3 is a member of the list [2|3] and the list [1,2,3].

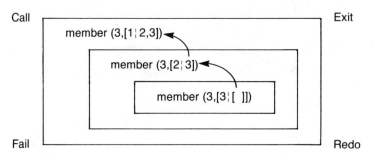

Call | Exit

member (3,[1|2,3])

member (3,[2|3])

member (3,[3|[ ]])

Fail | Redo

Figure 2-8: The *Member* Predicate

The *member* predicate simply succeeds or fails. It does not pass back a value. Look now at *append*, which does.

The *Append* Predicate

The *append* predicate creates a single list from two lists by recursively tacking the elements of the first list onto the beginning of the second list.

The append operation is defined by two clauses. The first clause states that the result of appending an empty list to a list *L* is the list *L*. It defines the condition that terminates the append operation.

append([],L,L).

The second clause is not as straightforward:

append([H|T],L,[H|T1]) :- append(T,L,T1).

This clause places the head of the first list (*H*) at the beginning of a variable list (*T1*) and calls *append* to perform the append operation on the tail of the list (*T*). The third argument builds an intermediate list until the first *append* clause is satisfied. Then, *T1* becomes instantiated and this value is passed back through the calling iterations. Figure 2-9 shows how the list *[a,b,c,d]* is constructed from the two lists *[a,b]* and *[c,d]*.

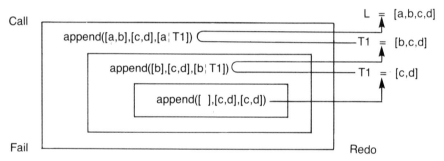

Figure 2-9: The *Append* Predicate

Input and Output Evaluable Predicates

Evaluable predicates are the built-in functions supplied by the Prolog system. Various implementations of Prolog differ most in the evaluable predicates that they supply. For example, some implementations of Prolog define the predicates *see*, *seeing*, *telling*, and *told* to perform input and output to files. Others define predicates such as *open*, *close*, *seek*, and *dup* to perform file operations. In the area of character and term I/O, the most conformance is found. These evaluable predicates, also referred to as the "standard I/O" predicates, perform I/O on characters and on Prolog terms typed at the keyboard and displayed on the monitor.

Performing Character I/O

The character I/O predicates accept single characters from the keyboard and send single characters to the terminal. Printing characters have ASCII codes in the range of 32 to 126. However, character I/O can also be performed on control characters, which have codes from 0 to 31, and on extended ASCII characters, which have codes from 127 to 256. So, you can use these predicates to ring the terminal bell (ASCII code 07), for example, in addition to reading and writing printing characters.

The following character I/O predicates are common to most Prolog implementations:

- *get0(Char)* accepts the next character from the keyboard.
- *get(Char)* accepts the next character from the keyboard, but skips spaces, tabs, and newlines.
- *put(Char)* writes a character to the terminal.
- *tab(N)* writes to the terminal the number of spaces specified by the argument.
- *nl* writes a single newline character to the terminal.

The *get*, *get0*, and *put* predicates take an ASCII character as an argument. This argument can be written as the ASCII code or, in some versions of Prolog, as the character itself preceded by a backquote. Thus, the ASCII code 97 and the sequence 'a both represent the letter *a*.

Menu-driven systems or help systems can make good use of the character I/O predicates because they frequently operate on single character input. Consider the following example, which calls *get0* until the user types either *y*, *n*, or *e*. If the user types *y* or *n*, then the predicate calls the appropriate processing predicate. If the user types the letter *e*, then the program exits. Any other letter is ignored and another character is read from the terminal.

```
yes__no :-
    repeat,
    get0(X),
    test(X),
    X = 'e.

test('y) :- tab(1), process__yes, nl.
test('n) :- tab(1), process__no, nl.
test(__).
```

A repeat/fail loop controls the *yes_no* predicate's execution path by defining a series of actions to perform until a specific condition is found. You place the *repeat* goal at the beginning of the loop and place the condition to be tested at the end. Prolog executes the goals between the *repeat* and the test until the test succeeds.

The *repeat* predicate is an evaluable predicate, defined like this:

```
repeat.
repeat :- repeat.
```

When a program encounters a repeat/fail loop, the first *repeat* clause is executed. This clause simply succeeds and the program proceeds through any number of goals until it encounters a failure. At that time, the program backtracks through the fail and redo ports, as shown in figure 2-10. When it reenters the *repeat* procedure box, the second *repeat* clause is executed. Because the *repeat* is called recursively, subsequent goals are reinvoked through the call ports rather then the redo ports.

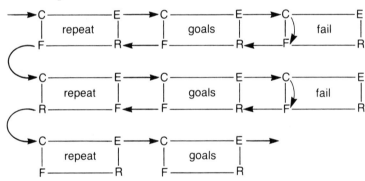

Figure 2-10: The Repeat/Fail Loop

A repeat/fail loop differs from the fail loop in the way that the database is accessed. A fail loop steps through subsequent matching clause in the database. When no more clauses are found, then the loop terminates. This is because subsequent invocations of the goals are reentered through the redo port. Goals that follow a *repeat* are always entered through the call port. Each invocation of a goal locates the first matching clause in the database. Thus, repeat/fail loops do not sequentially step through clauses in the database.

In a repeat/fail loop, it is important that you define a successful condition that can be achieved. Otherwise, the loop will never terminate. For instance, when the following clause is executed, it goes into an infinite loop:

```
infinity :-
    repeat,
    write('Hello world'), nl,
    fail.
```

Performing Term I/O

A "term" is any atom, integer, structure, or clause. Because the term I/O predicates operate only on valid Prolog terms, atoms that contain spaces must be placed in quotes and end with a period and carriage return.

Four term I/O predicates are common to most Prolog implementations:

- *read(Term)* accepts a term from the keyboard, using the operator definitions to translate terms from infix notation to Prefix Polish notation.

- *write(Term)* outputs a term to the terminal, using operator definitions to translate terms from Prefix Polish notation to infix notation. You have seen *write* used in previous program examples to print messages at the terminal.

- *writeq(Term)* outputs a term to the terminal. The *writeq* predicate differs from *write* in that it places quotes around symbolic characters and atoms that contain spaces.

- *display(Term)* outputs a term to the terminal. It quotes quotable atoms and does not use the operator definitions. Therefore, all terms output with *display* are in Prefix Polish notation.

Table 2-1 shows how *write*, *writeq*, and *display* each handle quoted atoms and operators.

Table 2-1: Writing Atoms and Operators

Operators	Predicate	Quoted Atom
write	This is a quoted atom	1 + 1 is 2
writeq	'This is a quoted atom'	1 + 1 is 2
display	'This is a quoted atom'	is(+(1,1))

The following program reads Prolog terms from the keyboard and identifies the type of the term until *exit* is entered. It uses *read* to accept the term and *write* to report the type of the term. Reading and checking the type of the term is performed by a repeat/fail loop defined in the predicate called *term*. The *fail* portion of the loop, however, is not in the same predicate as the *repeat* portion.

```
term :-
    repeat,
    nl,
    write('Term : '),
    read(X),
    check(X).
```

The *check* predicate determines whether the loop terminates. The first *check* clause does not contain a *fail* goal; it looks for the term *exit*. When this clause succeeds, the loop terminates. This clause contains a *cut* so that the repeat/fail loop cannot be reentered on backtracking. For this program, which stands alone here, it is not important to include the *cut*. However, if the repeat/fail loop were part of a larger program, the *cut* would be very important.

```
check(exit) :- !.
```

The second *check* clause executes when any term other than *exit* is read; it looks for the type of the term. This second *check* clause contains the *fail*, which causes the program to return to the *repeat* goal.

```
check(X) :-
    type(X,Type),
    write(Type:X), nl,
    fail.
```

The *type* predicate checks to see if the term is an atom, integer, rule, list, or structure. The first two clauses use some evaluable predicates that perform data type checking. A more complete list of data type checking predicates is included in appendix A. The ones used here are *atom(X)*, which succeeds if X is an atom, and *integer(X)*, which succeeds if X is an integer.

```
type(X,atom) :- atom(X), !.
type(X,integer) :- integer(X), !.
```

The predicate also checks the type of a term in the head of the clause. A rule has the form *X :- Y* and a list has the form *[H|T]*. If the term has one of these forms, no other type checking is required.

```
type((__ :- __), rule) :- !.
type([__|__],list).
```

The only remaining type is the structure. The program assumes that if the type of the term is not discovered by any of the preceding clauses, then it is a structure.

```
type(__,structure).
```

Some of the *type* clauses contain *cuts* after the data type of the term is discovered. The *cuts* ensure that, once its type is discoverd, no term is tested twice. Since a list is also a structure, however, the clause that looks for the list does not contain a *cut*. When a list is entered, the program reports that it is both a list and a structure.

The program is invoked by asking the question *?- term*. The following shows how it responds to a sample set of terms.

```
?- term.

Term : apples.
Atom : apples

Term : 256.
Integer : 256

Term : infinity :- repeat, write('hello world'), fail.
Rule : infinity :- repeat, write('hello world'), fail

Term : [a,b,c].
List : [a,b,c]
Structure : [a,b,c]

Term : .(a,.(b,.(c,nil))).
List : [a,b,c]
Structure : [a,b,c]
```

Term : air(hydrogen,oxygen,nitrogen,carbon__dioxide).
Structure : air(hydorgen,oxygen,nitrogen,carbon__dioxide)

Term : exit.

Using the Prolog Database

All the examples in this book have assumed that you are interacting with a Prolog interpreter. These examples have shown how to add clauses to the database from what is called the interpreter ''top level'' and how to access these clauses by asking questions or invoking rules from the top level. (See the manual that comes with your Prolog interpreter for specific instructions about interacting with the interpreter at the top level.) In all these instances, adding clauses to the database is a separate activity from accessing those clauses at run time.

It is also possible to add and remove clauses at run time, using the following evaluable predicates:

- *asserta(Clause)* adds a clause to the beginning of the database.
- *assertz(Clause)* adds a clause to the end of the database.
- *retract(Clause)* removes a clause from the database.

Clauses you add at run time with these predicates can be accessed in the same way as clauses you add from the interpreter top level. That is, you call them as goals or questions.

In addition, everything that the program examples have stored in the database has been a procedure. Even unit clauses are procedures, because they are defined to have a body of *true*. When accessing the Prolog database at run time, however, it is important for program efficiency to distinguish between procedures and data.

Every fact that can be represented by a unit clause can also be represented by a data object. Data objects are atoms, integers, or structures that you store in the database. Each is stored under a name, known as the ''key,'' and each has a unique identifier to distinguish one object from another object stored under the same key. The identifier is call the ''ref.''

The following predicates add data objects to the database:

- *recorda(Key, Term, Ref)* adds an object to the beginning of the database.
- *recordz(Key, Term, Ref)* adds an object to the end of the database.

Whereas you access clauses by asking questions, you access data objects with the following predicates:

- *recorded(Key, Term, Ref)* returns a specific data object.
- *erase(Ref)* removes a specific object from the database.
- *eraseall(Key)* removes a group of related data objects.
- *instance(Ref, Term)* returns the object associated with a given ref.
- *replace(Ref, Term)* replaces the object identified by a particular ref with the object specified by *Term*.

To understand why you would want to separate data from procedures, you need to understand how each is stored in the database and accessed by Prolog.

Clauses, including unit clauses, are stored in the database in the order in which you enter them. Clauses with the same functor and number of arguments are grouped together. When you ask a question, or invoke a procedure as a goal within a rule, Prolog sequentially searches through the database to locate the clause whose functor matches the goal and whose arguments unify with the arguments in the goal.

Data objects are stored under a key, which groups related objects together. Like clauses, the objects are stored in the order in which they are added. Unlike the way it handles clauses, Prolog assigns a unique ref to each data object. With the ref, you can access any object directly, without sequentially searching the entire database. Thus, data objects can be accessed more efficiently than clauses.

You will find that you rarely need to use the *assert* predicates. It is not common to add clauses at run time. Adding clauses with the *assert* predicates changes the program itself at run time. This can create all kinds of problems. For instance, these predicates make it possible for the user to throw your program into an infinite loop. The *assert* predicates are used by Prolog interpreters to add clauses to the database from the top level. This is the kind of application for which they are best suited.

The *record* predicates are useful for a broader range of applications. They can, for example, gather information from the user, as in a database application. They make it possible for a program to adjust its behavior to specific situations or to the needs of particular users. Expert systems make use of this ability to update their knowledge bases as information is supplied by the user. The *record* predicates can also be used by the program for more traditional programming functions. For example, you can create a data object to contain status values, such as *on* and *off* or *0* and *1*, or to maintain program counters.

Storing Run Time Information in the Database

In an earlier section of this chapter, the *thermostat* program was changed so that it would check that the heat is not already on before turning it on. However, that version of the program did not update the database. Each time the heat is turned on or off, the program needs to update the database to reflect the change. Here is a new version of the program, using the database predicates.

Before starting up the program, you need to record the initial status of the heater. This is done with *recordz*.

```
?- recordz(heat,on,__).
```

In addition, this version of *thermostat* will operate over a larger set of temperatures. The temperatures can be stored in the database as facts:

```
temp(81).
temp(69).
temp(75).
temp(90).
temp(80).
temp(60).
```

The *thermostat* predicate remains unchanged:

```
thermostat :-
    temp(X),
    action(X),
    fail.
```

However, the *action* predicate must now use the database predicates to maintain the current status of the heater (*on* or *off*).

```
action(X) :-
     X > 80, !,
     recorded(heat,Status,Ref),
     ( Status = = off ;
        replace(Ref,off) ),
     write('Heat is off.'), nl.
action(X) :-
     X < 70, !,
     recorded(heat,Status,Ref),
     ( Status = = on ;
        replace(Ref,on) ),
     write('Heater on.'), nl.
action(__) :-
     recorded(heat,Status,__),
     write('Heat':Status), nl.
```

The first two *action* clauses each contain a disjunction of goals (enclosed in parentheses and separated by the semicolon). The goals appearing outside of the parentheses are common to both parts of the disjunction. The disjunction is yet another way to write an if-then-else construct in Prolog.

The disjunction in the first *action* clause states that if the temperature is greater than 80 degrees and the heater is off, then simply display the message "Heat is off." If the temperature is greater than 80 degrees and the heater is on, then the second part of the disjunction is executed. The *replace* predicate removes the current *heat* status from the database and replaces it with the new status. Then, the "Heat is off" message is displayed.

The *action* clauses could have been written as two clauses each rather than one. For example, the disjunction to handle the heater status *off* could be written in the following manner. These two clauses follow the if-then-else construct discussed at the beginning of the chapter:

```
action(X) :-
     X > 80,
     recorded(heat,off,__), !,
     write('Heat is off.'), nl.
action(X) :-
     X > 80,
     recorded(heat,on,Ref),
     replace(Ref,off),
     write('Heat is off.'), nl.
```

Some may find the program easier to read when each condition is contained in a separate clause. Others may find the disjunction preferable because it reduces the number of database look-ups performed on the status value.

Incrementing and Decrementing Counters

Many common programming problems are handled with counters. The *factorial* predicate, for example, uses the number for which it calculates the factorial to count the number of iterations of the predicate. That is, the number is decremented at each iteration of the predicate. When it is decremented to 0, the loop terminates.

Counters work quite well in recursive procedures because the new counter value can be passed to the next iteration. However, not all problems that require a counter may be recursive. For example, if you need to add a counter to a repeat/fail loop, the counter reverts to its original value at the beginning of each iteration. To handle this programming problem, you need to store the counter value in the database. Each iteration of the loop looks up the value, increments or decrements the value, and replaces the old value with the new.

There are four general-purpose counter operations that you can define, if they are not already defined as evaluable predicates by the Prolog system that you use:

- *Ctr__set* initializes a counter.

```
ctr__set(Counter,Value) :-
    recorded(Counter,__,Ref),
    replace(Ref,Value).
ctr__set(Counter,Value) :-
    recorda(Counter,Value,__).
```

- *Ctr__is* returns the current value of a counter.

```
ctr__is(Counter,Value) :-
    recorded(Counter,Value,__).
```

- *Ctr__inc* increments a counter and returns the counter's previous value.

```
ctr__inc(Counter,Value) :-
    recorded(Counter,Value,Ref),
    C1 is Counter + 1,
    replace(Ref,C1).
```

- *Ctr__dec* decrements a counter and returns the counter's previous value.

```
ctr__dec(Counter,Value) :-
        recorded(Counter,Value,Ref),
        C1 is Counter - 1,
        replace(Ref,C1).
```

By defining these predicates, you can separate the counter operations from the rest of the program, making the program clearer. For example, a predicate to count the number of spaces typed at the keyboard uses the counter predicates in a repeat/fail loop:

```
count__spaces(X) :-
        ctr__set(c,0),
        repeat,
        get0(C),
        count(C),
        C = 13,
        ctr__is(c,X).

        count(32) :- ctr__inc(c,__), !.
        count(__).
```

Notice that goals appear both before and after the repeating portion of the clause. These goals are not part of the loop. The first initializes the counter to 0 and the second returns the value of the counter after the loop terminates.

Compiled Prolog

Early versions of Prolog were run in interpreted environments only. Over time, the trend has shifted toward Prolog compilers. Compiling Prolog code has some obvious advantages, not the least of which is the increased efficiency and speed of execution. Compiled Prolog code can be highly optimized; speed of execution can be ten or more times faster than interpreted Prolog code.

The less obvious advantage is the program's ability to continue to use the Prolog database. Unlike other interpreted languages that take away the space for loading and editing programs when they are compiled, compiled Prolog continues to give programs access to its built-in database. Predicates that are procedural in nature can be placed in the compiled portion of the program. These predicates can take advantage of increased speeds provided by the compiler. Predicates that are dynamic, such as program and user data, can be kept in the Prolog database.

The *thermostat* program can be broken into compiled and interpreted sections. The temperatures and the current status of the heater (*on* or *off*) must change during the course of the program. Therefore, they are placed in the program database. The temperatures will be recorded as regular terms and the status of the heater will be asserted as a unit clause, to show how both clauses and data are handled by compiled code. These terms will be added to the database when the *init* predicate is invoked at run time.

```
init :-
     recordz(temp,81,__),
     recordz(temp,69,__),
     recordz(temp,75,__),
     recordz(temp,90,__),
     recordz(temp,80,__),
     recordz(temp,60,__),
     assertz(heat(off)).
```

The procedures for determining whether to turn the heater on or off are the same regardless of the temperature. Therefore, they can be compiled.

```
thermostat :-
     recorded(temp,X,__),
     action(X),
     fail.
thermostat.

action(X) :-
     X > 80,
     ( call(heat(off)) ;
        retract(heat(__)),
        assertz(heat(off)) ),
     !,
     write('Heat is off.'), nl.
```

```
action(X) :-
    X < 70,
    ( call(heat(on)) ;
        retract(heat(__)),
        assertz(heat(on)) ),
    !,
    write('Heat is on.'), nl.
action(__) :-
    call(heat(X)),
    write(heat : X), nl.
```

Finally, a *main* predicate invokes both the *init* procedure, to initialize the database, and the *thermostat* predicate, to process the temperatures in the database.

```
main :-
    init,
    thermostat.
```

Summary

Prolog is not just a descriptive language; it is also a procedural language. In Prolog, when you describe the relationship between objects, you also define an executable procedure. To build practical applications, however, additional facilities are necessary to control the program flow.

Prolog provides the *cut*, written as *!*, to exclude a predicate from backtracking. This chapter showed how the *cut* can implement if-then-else constructs and how it can limit the facts that are considered in the database. Finally, it showed how the *cut* in combination with *fail* can handle exception conditions.

Prolog's descriptive nature makes it well suited for writing recursive procedures. The list's nested head/tail structure, for instance, lends itself to recursive handling. Many programming problems, such as calculating the factorial of a number or determining whether an object is an element of a list, can be handled by recursion.

Evaluable predicates let you write predicates that produce "side effects." In this chapter, the input and output predicates were used to gather information from the user and to return information to the user. These kinds of operations have nothing to do with the descriptive nature of a program, but they are necessary for communicating with the user.

Evaluable predicates that access the Prolog database are also outside of the logic of the program. However, these evaluable predicates allow programs to manage information at run time. The examples in this chapter used the database to store program information, such as the status of a heater or the value of a counter. However, the database could also contain user information, such as a database application might store.

It is important to understand the nature of Prolog from both the logical and the procedural side. The logical aspect of the language makes it possible to describe a program most simply; the procedural side makes it possible to write practical applications. Given an understanding of these two aspects of the language, you can begin to write applications in Prolog.

3

A Closer Look at Prolog's Internal Database

Prolog is powerful because it is descriptive, because the description of a problem also describes the procedures for solving the problem, and because it has a built-in database. The descriptive and procedural aspects of Prolog have been covered in chapters 1 and 2; this chapter takes a closer look at the Prolog database. It discusses methods for improving a program's use of the database to increase efficiency and speed. Some of these improvements must be made by the Prolog system itself. Others can be made by the application's use of alternate storage and access methods.

As an application becomes more sophisticated, it requires a larger and larger program database. Therefore, an obvious way to increase Prolog's power is to increase the maximum size of the database. The Prolog system itself determines how large a database can be. When choosing which Prolog system to use, you should check that the database is large enough to fit your needs. One type of database design, called the "virtual database," allows the database to grow onto the disk when memory is exhausted.

Another enhancement, called "worlds," allows the database to be partitioned into separate areas, each of which can be as large as the maximum database size. Partitioning the database lets you build dramatically larger programs as it lets you make better use of the space that is available. Worlds must be provided by the Prolog system; they cannot be built on top of a system that does not provide them.

Whereas the time to search for one term among twenty-five is insignificant, searching through hundreds of terms can slow performance. When you have very large databases, then, speed of accessing the information becomes an important issue. You can use alternative storage and retrieval methods to increase your program's performance. These alternative methods, such as hash tables, binary trees, and balanced trees, let you access information in the database more efficiently.

Database Models

The first Prolog databases were placed in memory. The database size was therefore limited by the size of memory. On the large machines, where there is a large amount of memory, this database model is adequate. When Prolog migrated to smaller machines, memory size was prohibitive. It was necessary to develop other models so that larger databases could be handled. One such model is the "virtual database."

In a virtual database, disk space supplements memory. Prolog terms are stored in sections, called "pages." When pages in memory become full, Prolog swaps pages onto the disk. When information is needed from a page on the disk, Prolog swaps a page from memory to the disk so that it can then swap the page from disk to memory, as illustrated in figure 3-1. Terms with the same key are stored on the same page, if possible, to minimize the amount of swapping that occurs.

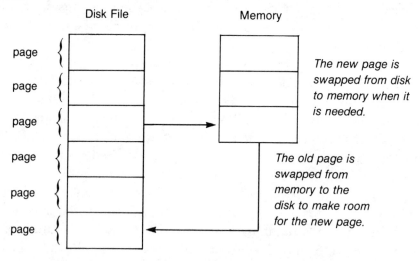

Figure 3-1: The Virtual Database Model

In a virtual database system, the database size is limited by the amount of disk storage on the machine. As memory sizes and storage capacities increase on the personal computers, they will compare more favorably with the large machines as vehicles on which to deliver Prolog applications. Furthermore, all virtual memory management can be performed by the Prolog system without any intervention from the program or programmer. Therefore, no extensions to the language are necessary to allow for a virtual database.

Multiple Worlds and Scoping

The "scope" of an object describes two characteristics. First, it defines when storage is allocated and deallocated for the object. Second, it defines which portions of the program can refer to the object. The scope of an object can be either "local" or "global." Objects that are local can be referenced only from within the function that defines them. Storage for the object is allocated when the function is invoked and that storage is deallocated when the function exits. Objects that are global are known throughout the program. Storage is allocated when the program is invoked and is not deallocated until the program exits.

Scope is a concept that is more common to conventional programming languages than it is to Prolog. For example, in the following C function, the integer *i* is local to the function that defines it:

```
funct()
{
    int i;
        .
        .
        .
}
```

No other function can reference the same integer *i* unless its value is passed to the function as an argument. In addition, each instance of a local object is unique within its defining function. Therefore, another function can define an integer *i* but each *i* is a unique object.

The C program called *distance* (see chapter 1) defined a static array of structures containing information about the planets. In that program, the structure is global because it is defined outside the function's curly braces. Global objects are known throughout the program and storage for the object is allocated for the duration of the program. Therefore, a function cannot define an object with the same name and any function can refer to the structure without declaring it.

```
/*
 * A global definition
 */
struct {
    char name[10];
    int miles;
    } distance[9]  =
                { { "mercury", 36 },
                  { "venus", 67 },
                  { "earth", 93 },
                  { "mars", 141 },
                  { "jupiter", 484 },
                  { "saturn", 886 },
                  { "uranus", 1790 },
                  { "neptune", 2800 },
                  { "pluto", 4600 }
                };
/*
 * References to the structure can occur within any
 * function
 */
main()
{
int i;
for( i = 0; i < 9; i + +)
    printf("%s\t%f\n", distance[i].name,
        distance[i].miles);
}
```

Scoping allows you to keep information hidden from other parts of the program. Not all functions need or should know about all data objects in a program. Scoping also allows the program to make good use of system resources because it can deallocate storage for an object when it is no longer needed by the program.

According to these definitions of local and global objects, all terms in a Prolog database are global because they can be accessed from all parts of a program. All objects that are defined within a rule, but not stored, are local. This includes variables and instantiations of variables that occur at run time only. They all disappear when the rule terminates.

Whereas it is easy to make an object global by simply adding it to the database, it is not as easy to make an object that resides in the database local. However, an extension to Prolog known as "worlds" makes this possible. Worlds are discussed by Hideyuki Nakashima of the Electrotechnical Laboratory, Ibaraki, Japan, in his paper entitled "Knowledge Representation in Prolog/KR" (*1984 International Symposium on Logic Programming Proceedings*, p. 126).

A world is a portion of the database that is exclusive of any other portion of the database. Terms that are stored in a world are local to that world. Suppose, for instance, that you want to have two definitions of a predicate with the same name but behaving differently from different parts of the program. You would define two worlds, each containing its own definition of the predicate.

Figure 3-2 shows two worlds containing slightly different definitions of a predicate called *hello*. When you are in *world1*, the *hello* predicate writes the message *hello world1*. When you are in *world2*, the predicate writes the message *hello world2*. The scope of *hello* is the world in which it is defined. Neither version of the predicate is known to the other world.

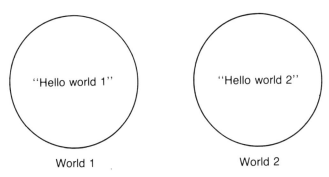

Figure 3-2: Defining Local Predicates in Worlds

Not all information should be local. All parts of a program need to access Prolog evaluable predicates or the standard operator definitions, for instance. These things should remain global. Thus, a default world stores all global information; additional worlds store local information.

Worlds were originated in order to create hierarchical data networks. Dividing information between the global world and the local worlds allows you to build the hierarchy. Imagine an application that is partitioned into *world1* through *world4* and the *default* world. Each world can access the terms in their local databases and in the *default* world. The relationship between the *default* world and the local worlds can be represented by the hierarchical tree in figure 3-3.

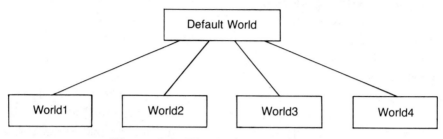

Figure 3-3: The Default Hierarchy

Worlds allow you to build applications that are substantially larger than applications built with non-partitioned databases. Each world is a separate database. Thus, the amount of database space that is available to a program is a multiple of the number of worlds the application defines. However, worlds require extensions to the language. In particular, Prolog must provide predicates to create or delete worlds and to save and restore the contents of those worlds.

The Sequential Database

By definition, the Prolog database stores and accesses terms sequentially. Terms with the same name and number of arguments are stored in the order in which they are added. Prolog also accesses terms sequentially. That is, matching and unification occur in the same order in which the terms appear in the database.

Sequential storage and retrieval is not only adequate for Prolog rules, it is essential for solving many programming problems. Rules often take advantage of the sequential database in order to execute properly. Because rules are usually made up of only a few clauses, sequential access does not affect a program's speed. Facts, on the other hand, can proliferate. For example, given the set of numbers from 1 to 100, you can record them in the database sequentially like this:

```
recordz(num,1,__),
recordz(num,2,__),
    .
    .
    .
recordz(num,100,__).
```

Prolog will need to access the database 100 times in order to find the last number stored. This kind of overhead presents a real performance problem. For facts, you may want to employ other storage and access methods.

Hash Tables

Wed

Hash tables provide one method for speeding up access into the database. A hash table lets you store information in groups, called "buckets." The hash table provides quick access to any particular bucket within the table. Once the correct bucket is found, searching for a specific object proceeds sequentially. By first locating a subset of objects in a hash table, you narrow the amount of searching that needs to be done.

A hash table stores information according to some hashing scheme. The numbers 1 to 100 can use a simple scheme because any number divided by 10 returns a remainder between 0 and 9. Three methods for handling hash tables will be presented here based on this hash scheme.

The Naive Hash Program

In the "naive" hash program, the hash table is made up of 10 buckets, numbered 0 through 9. This hashing example will store the numbers in the hash table directly, as shown in figure 3-4.

0	[10, 20, . . . 100]
1	[1, 11, . . . 91]
2	[2, 12, . . . 92]
3	[3, 13, . . . 93]
4	[4, 14, . . . 94]
5	[5, 15, . . . 95]
6	[6, 16, . . . 96]
7	[7, 17, . . . 97]
8	[8, 18, . . . 98]
9	[9, 19, . . . 99]

Figure 3-4: A Naive Hash Table

A hash table such as this is defined as a structure with ten arguments, one for each bucket. You can easily locate a specific bucket by using an evaluable predicate named *arg0*. The *arg0* predicate locates any argument in a structure, where arguments are numbered upward from zero. For example, the goal *arg0(1, capitol(ma, boston), X)* determines that *boston* is argument 1 of the structure *capitol(ma, boston)*. *Arg0* can locate a bucket directly without making repeated database queries.

Initially, the hash table contains ten empty lists, defined by the *make__hash* predicate:

```
make__nhash :-
     recorda(nhash,nhash([],[],[],[],[],[],[],[],[],[]),—).
```

To add a number to the hash table, the program must perform these steps:

1. Find which bucket the number belongs in by returning the remainder of the number divided by 10.
2. Locate the hash table in the database.
3. Get the currect bucket from the table, using the *arg0* predicate.
4. Append the new number to the bucket.
5. Reconstruct the new hash table to reflect the change.
6. Replace the old hash table with the new one.

These steps are performed by the *nhash* predicate:

```
nhash(H1) :-
     X is H1 mod 10,
     recorded(nhash,OldHash,Ref),
     arg0(X,OldHash,Y),
     append(Y,[H1],NewY),
     reconstruct(OldHash,NewHash,X,NewY),
     replace(Ref,NewHash).
```

The naive hash table may be an efficient method of storing the numbers but there is considerable overhead in reconstructing the hash table each time a number is added.

The *reconstruct* predicate uses an evaulable predicate named *functor* to create a new structure with the same functor and number of arguments as are present in the hash table. Given a structure, *functor* returns that structure's functor and number of arguments. Given a functor and the number of arguments, it returns a structure with that functor and the correct number of uninstantiated variables as its arguments. The *reconstruct* predicate creates this new structure and passes the structure to a predicate called *do_reconstruct*.

```
reconstruct(OldHash,NewHash,X,NewY) :-
    functor(OldHash,Func,N), functor(NewHash,Func,N),
    do_reconstruct(OldHash,NewHash,X,NewY,0).
```

The new structure is used by the *do_reconstruct* predicate, which goes through each argument in the hash table, instantiating each argument but one with its old value, and instantiating the changed argument with the new value. The first *do_reconstruct* clause handles the argument that changed; the second clause handles the arguments that did not change. The third clause handles the terminating condition — when there are no more arguments to the structure. Because it procedes argument by argument, reconstructing the hash table is a slow process.

```
do_reconstruct(OldHash,NewHash,X,NewY,X) :-
    X = Arg,
    arg0(X,NewHash,NewY), NewArg is Arg + 1,
    do_reconstruct(OldHash,NewHash,X,NewY,NewArg).
do_reconstruct(OldHash,NewHash,X,NewY,Arg) :-
    arg0(Arg,OldHash,Val),
    arg0(Arg,NewHash,Val),
    NewArg is Arg + 1,
    do_reconstruct(OldHash,NewHash,X,NewY,NewArg).
    do_reconstruct(_,_,_,_,_).
```

A Hash Table Using Refs

In the next version of the hash program, the hash table does not store the actual numbers. Instead, it stores pointers to lists of numbers, as shown in figure 3-5.

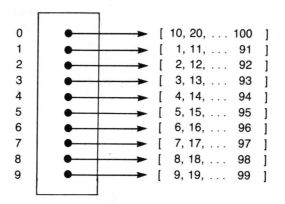

Figure 3-5: Hash Table with Reference Numbers

The *make_hash* predicate builds this hash table by recording ten empty lists in the database and using the database reference numbers returned by the *recordz* predicate as arguments to the hash table structure:

```
make_rhash :-
       recordz(lists,[],R0),
       recordz(lists,[],R1),
       recordz(lists,[],R2),
       recordz(lists,[],R3),
       recordz(lists,[],R4),
       recordz(lists,[],R5),
       recordz(lists,[],R6),
       recordz(lists,[],R7),
       recordz(lists,[],R8),
       recordz(lists,[],R9),
       recorda(rhash,rhash(R0,R1,R2,R3,R4,R5,R6,R7,R8,R9),_).
```

Adding a new number to this hash table requires these steps:

1. Determine which bucket points to the appropriate list for the number.

2. Retrieve the hash table from the database.

3. Locate the reference number for the list.

4. Append the number to the list.

5. Replace the old list with the new list.

6. Reconstruct the hash table so that it points to the new list rather than the old list.

7. Replace the hash table.

Although the hash table can simply be replaced, it must still be reconstructed each time a number is added.

```
rhash(Num):-
      X is Num mod 10,
      recorded(rhash,HashTable,Ref),
      arg0(X,HashTable,LRef),
      recorded(lists,List,LRef),
      append(List,[Num],NewList),
      replace(LRef,NewList),
      reconstruct(HashTable,NewTable,X,NewRef),
      replace(Ref,NewTable).
```

A Hash Table Using Linked Lists

The last method discussed here, and the best of these methods, creates a linked list of numbers for each of the buckets. A linked list is not to be confused with the Prolog list data type. Objects in a linked list are not physically stored together in the database. Instead, each object is a separate entity storing both the number and a pointer to the next number in the list, as shown in figure 3-6.

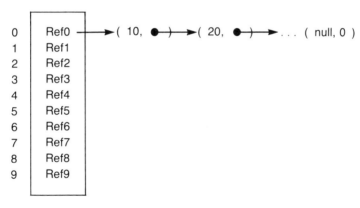

Figure 3-6: Hash Table with Linked Lists

Each entry in the linked list is a pair of values giving the number being added and a pointer to the next number in the list. Unlike the previous versions of the program, which appended new objects to the end of a list, this version places new entries at the beginning of the list. Thus, when a new number is added, only the first entry in the list and the reference to it from the hash table must change. The rest of the linked list remains intact. The end of a list con-

tains the entry *(null, 0)*. To create this hash table, you must create the initial
entries in the linked lists, return the reference numbers to those initial entries,
and store the reference numbers in the hash table.

```
make__hash :-
      recordz(chain,(null,0),R0),
      recordz(chain,(null,0),R1),
      recordz(chain,(null,0),R2),
      recordz(chain,(null,0),R3),
      recordz(chain,(null,0),R4),
      recordz(chain,(null,0),R5),
      recordz(chain,(null,0),R6),
      recordz(chain,(null,0),R7),
      recordz(chain,(null,0),R8),
      recordz(chain,(null,0),R9),
      recorda(hash,hash(R0,R1,R2,R3,R4,R5,R6,R7,R8,R9),__).
```

Adding a number to the linked list is much simpler than adding a number
in the previous versions of the hash program:

1. Find the bucket in which this number belongs.
2. Retrieve the hash table from the database.
3. Locate the reference number for the first entry in the list.
4. Get the first entry, using that reference number as an argument to the
   instance evaluable predicate.
5. Copy that entry to a new location.
6. Replace the old entry with a new one, which contains the new number
   and a pointer to the old entry.

The *hash* predicate defined here performs these steps.

```
hash(Num) :-
      X is Num mod 10,
      recorded(hash,HTable,__),
      arg0(X,HTable,Ref),
      recorded(chain,OldPr,Ref),
      recordz(chain,OldPr,Ref1),
      replace(Ref,(Num,Ref1)).
```

You can locate a number with a predicate such as *hash_get*, defined below. It finds the correct bucket within the hash table and then searches the linked list for the correct number:

```
hash_get(Num) :-
     X is Num mod 10,
     recorded(hash,Table,_),
     arg0(X,Table,Ref),
     recorded(chain,NumPr,Ref),
     walk(NumPr,Num).

walk((Num,_),Num).
walk((_,Ref),Num) :-
     instance(Ref,NewPr),
     walk(NewPr,Num).
```

These hash mechanisms can find a number in the database with fewer database accesses than the sequential method requires. Using sequential access, Prolog must make 100 database accesses to find the last number in a series of 100 numbers. A hash table accesses the database at most 11 times — once to retrieve the hash table, and 10 times to find the last number within the linked list.

Hash tables are good for increasing the speed of access to information in the database. They do not, however, store information in what might be considered a hierarchical or sorted order. Hashing schemes sometimes group information in a seemingly arbitrary way. If the information must be ordered in some way, you need to use trees instead of hash tables.

Binary Trees

Binary trees store information in a hierarchical order, although not necessarily in a sorted order such as alphabetical or numerical order. Because information is in a hierarchy, you can employ non-sequential search strategies. These strategies are more efficient than either Prolog's sequential search strategy or the modified sequential strategy of hash tables.

Binary trees are made up of nodes and branches. A node holds the information for the current location in the tree. The first node in a binary tree is called the "root node." Branches point to the nodes that are subordinate to the current node. In this way, the binary tree maintains its hierarchical structure.

In a binary tree, each node has exactly two branches. Nodes in a binary tree must therefore contain four pieces of information:

1. The contents of the node.

2. The node's identification, which is used as a pointer by the node's predecessor.

3. A pointer, or branch, to the left-hand node that is the successor to this node.

4. A pointer to the right-hand node that is the successor to this node.

For example, in the tree in figure 3-7, the nodes are numbered from 1 through 11. Node 1, at the top of the tree, is the root node. All nodes are subordinate to the root node.

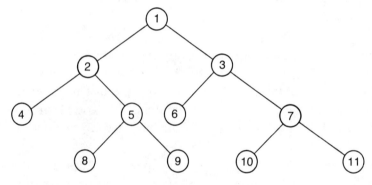

Figure 3-7: Tree-structured Information

Suppose one node holds an object called *cheese* and the remaining nodes hold an object called *nut*. You can represent such a tree with Prolog facts. Each node is written as a structure containing four arguments. The first is the contents of the node (either *nut* or *cheese*), the second is the current node number, the third is the left-hand successor's node number, and the fourth is the right-hand successor's node number. The atom *null* indicates that the node has no successors.

```
node(nut,1,2,3).
node(nut,2,4,5).
node(cheese,3,6,7).
node(nut,4,null,null).
node(nut,5,8,9).
node(nut,6,null,null).
```

node(nut,7,10,11).
node(nut,8,null,null).
node(nut,9,null,null).
node(nut,10,null,null).
node(nut,11,null,null).

Depth-first search and breadth-first search are two kinds of search strategies that you can employ to locate the *cheese* in this tree.

Depth-first Search

The depth-first search strategy searches all branches of a tree from left to right and from the bottom up. You are already familiar with depth-first search within the context of how Prolog solves a rule. Suppose A, B, C, D, and E are Prolog goals, such that A is defined in terms of B and C, B is defined in terms of D, and C is defined in terms of E, like this:

A :- B, C.
B :- D.
C :- E.

In order to prove goal A, Prolog must first prove goals B and C; in order to prove B and C, Prolog must prove D and E. The relationships between the goals can be illustrated in the tree structure of figure 3-8. The goals that are deepest in the tree must be proved first. Solutions to goal A rise up from the bottom of the tree. In addition, goals are proved from left to right. That is, Prolog proves the goals on the left-hand side of the tree before proving the goals on the right-hand side of the tree.

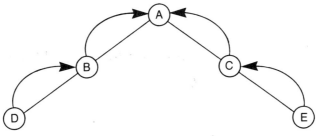

Figure 3-8: Tree Representation of a Rule

To apply this search strategy to facts in the database, you must write routines to search the tree in depth-first order. That is, the routine must search first left-hand nodes and then right-hand nodes from the bottom up. For example, to find the *cheese*, the routine would look at nodes 1, 2, 4, 5, 8, and 9 before finding the *cheese* at node 3.

Searching through the tree is a recursive procedure. The first clause states that "If *cheese* is found in the current node, then that node is the answer." This clause finds the terminating condition for the rule.

findcheese(node(cheese,Answer,__,__),Answer).

If the *cheese* is not found at the current node, then the next clause checks to see if the left-hand successor holds the *cheese*. It calls *findcheese* with this node as the new current node. In this way, all left-hand nodes are examined until the end of a branch is found.

findcheese(node(__,__,L,__),Answer) :-
    node(A,L,C,D),
    findcheese(node(A,L,C,D),Answer).

If the cheese is not found in a left-hand node, then *findcheese* must check the right-hand nodes.

findcheese(node(__,__,__,R),Answer) :-
    node(A,R,C,D),
    findcheese(node(A,R,C,D),Answer).

The *findcheese* rule operates within a larger program, which defines the initial node at which to begin the search. This rule is written as:

cheese(N,Ans) :-
    node(A,N,C,D),findcheese(node(A,N,C,D), Ans).
cheese(__,__) :- write('Cheese not found').

To start the search at node 1, you call *cheese* like this:

?- cheese(1, Ans).

Breadth-First Search

A breadth-first search examines all nodes at the same level from the left to right and from the root node downward. In the nut/cheese tree, a breadth-first search looks through the nodes in the order in which they are numbered: 1, 2, and 3.

Two advantages to breadth-first search make it preferable to depth-first search:

- When the object of the search is at a right-hand node near the top of the tree, breadth-first search locates the object more quickly than depth-first search.

- When infinite structures are involved, breadth-first search is guaranteed to find a solution if one exists. A depth-first search may never find an object in an infinite structure.

In any case, breadth-first search always finds the closest answer to the root of the tree.

In Prolog, the rule for breadth-first search describes the relationships between nodes in terms of *child* and *descendant* nodes. That is, a *child* is defined as either a left- or right-hand successor node:

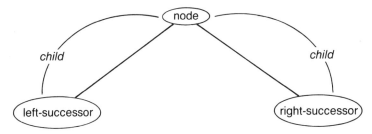

In Prolog, this rule is written as:

```
child(node(__,__,L,__),node(A,L,C,D)) :-
    node(A,L,C,D).
child(node(__,__,__,R),node(A,R,C,D)) :-
    node(A,R,C,D).
```

A *descendant* is defined as an immediate *child* or the *child* of a *descendant*:

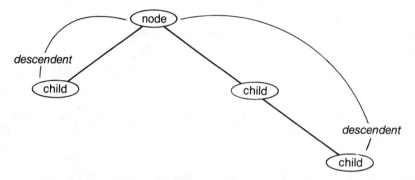

This translates into the Prolog predicate:

```
descendant(Node1,Node2) :- child(Node1,Node2).
descendand(Node1,Node2) :-
     descendant(Node1,Node3),
     child(Node3,Node2).
```

These rules operate within a *findcheese* rule that states that ''The *cheese* can be found on a *descendant* node that has *cheese*.''

```
findcheese(Node,N) :-
     descendant(node(nut,__,Node,null),node(cheese,N,__,__)).
```

You invoke this program by asking the question:

```
?- findcheese(1,N).
```

Search Strategies Using Lists

Both depth-first and breadth-first search strategies can be implemented with lists that control the order in which nodes are searched. This is the method commonly used in Lisp programs. As the program searches a node, it adds the right and left successor nodes to the search list. Depth-first and breadth-first searches differ only in whether the successors are placed at the beginning or at the end of the search list.

To implement a search strategy using lists, you must still write a clause to accept the starting node number. This clause then passes the number as a list to a predicate called *get__node*.

```
find(Node,N) :- get_node([Node],N).
```

When *get_node* locates the empty list, it means that the *cheese* was not found and *get_node* fails. A cut/fail handles this exception condition.

```
get_node([ ],__) :- !, fail.
```

The second *get_node* clause returns the node from the database and passes the node to a predicate called *search*.

```
get_node([H|T], N) :-
    node(X,H,L,R),
    search(node(X,H,L,R),T,N).
```

There are three *search* clauses. The first succeeds when the *cheese* is found in the current node. The second succeeds when the node has no successors. This clause simply continues the search by calling *get_node* with the tail of the list. The third clause succeeds when the node has successors. It adds the successors to the search list.

```
search(node(cheese,H,__,__),__,H).
search(node(__,H,null,null),T,N) :-
    get_node(T,N).
search(node(__,H,L,R),T,N) :-
    append([L,R],T,A),
    get_node(A,N).
```

The order in which nodes are appended to the search list determines whether the program performs a depth-first or a breadth-first search. For depth-first, the left and right successors of the current node are placed at the beginning of the search list. For breadth-first search, the left and right successors are placed at the end of the search list. The version of *search* shown above defines a depth-first search strategy. To define a breadth-first search, you simply change the order of the arguments to *append*, like this:

```
append(T,[L,R],A).
```

Balanced Trees

Another kind of tree, called the balanced tree, may also be used. A tree is balanced if all its branches extend to the same level. The nut/cheese tree is not balanced because nodes 5 and 7 extend one level deeper than nodes 4 and 6.

Information in a balanced tree can be accessed more directly. Using key values stored in the nodes of the tree, a program can locate an object by following one, and only one, path. The depth-first and breadth-first strategies must often backtrack to find the correct search path.

Creating and maintaining a balanced tree requires additional effort. Adding a new entry can affect all parts of the tree. If a new node is created at a level lower than the tree currently extends, then new branches need to be added to extend to this level from the rest of the tree as well. Sometimes a new root node must be created.

In addition, actual data would not be stored at every node of the tree. Just as the most efficient implementation of the hash table program did not store any data within the table itself, a tree structure is more efficient if it, too, stores only pointers to information. When the data is stored somewhere other than in the tree itself, it can be kept in sorted order.

Balanced trees are made up of nodes, branches, and leaves. The same number of branches extend from every node, pointing to the successor nodes. The nodes at the lowest level point to the leaves, which hold the information. In order to maintain an even distribution of information throughout the tree, each leaf can hold only a limited number of objects.

Each node also contains a "key." The key helps determine which branch to follow when searching for an object. It can be one of two values — either the maximum value contained in the left-hand branches of this node or the minimum value contained in the right-hand branches of this node.

Figure 3-9 shows a tree that stores information in alphabetical order. The root node contains the key n, the lowest letter stored on the right-hand side of the tree, and pointers to the nodes immediately below it. Below the root node is one node for the letters below n and one node for the letters between n and z.

Nodes at each level contain two branches each. Therefore, this tree is also a binary tree. However, it is not necessary for a balanced tree to be a binary tree.

At the bottom level of the tree, the nodes contain pointers not to other nodes, but rather to the data, or "leaves." For example, the node marked d contains pointers to leaves containing a, b, c and d, e, f, g. In this tree, each leaf can hold a maximum of four objects. The objects stored in the leaves have two parts: the letter that refers to the object (the key) and the word that begins with that letter.

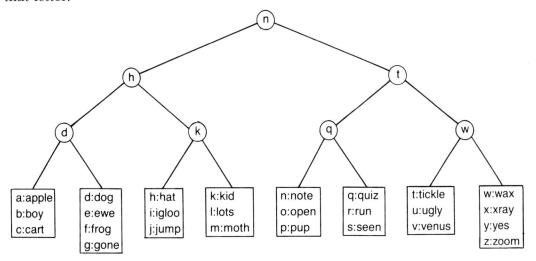

Figure 3-9: A Balanced Tree

The tree in figure 3-9 is complete, but how was it built? Given an initial entry of the word *m:moth*, the tree had only one level — a root node containing the object *m:moth*:

m:moth

When the words *apple*, *wax*, *little*, and *seen* were added, the tree grew in the following manner. The root level contained the key *s*, which was the lowest letter on the right side of the tree. In addition, when the initial leaf grew to over four objects, it split into two leaves.

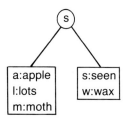

Next, the words *gone*, *boy*, *quiz*, and *hat* were added. Each time a list split, a new level was added to the tree so that at all times every branch extended to the same level.

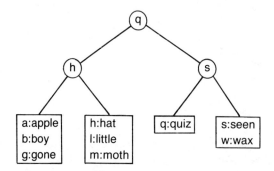

Inside the Prolog database, the tree is represented as a collection of *leaf* and *node* structures. The *leaf* structures hold the objects pointed to by the nodes. The *node* structures store the keys and pointers to the successor nodes. In this example, a key is the lowest value contained in the right-hand branch for that node; the pointers are the reference numbers returned by *recordz* or *recorda*. The reference numbers for the lower-level nodes are used as arguments to the *node* structures at the higher levels. Thus, the tree is built from the bottom up rather than from the top down.

You can see how the tree is stored in the database by looking through all the *node* and *leaf* structures with the *recorded* predicate. The hexadecimal numbers beginning with the tilde are the database refs that point to the right and left successor nodes in the tree.

```
?- recorded(node,X,__).

X = node(n,~0100403E~01003C3E) —> ;

X = node(t,~0100483E,~0100443E) —> ;

X = node(h,~0100503E,~01004C3E) —> ;

X = node(w,~01005C3E,~0100583E) —> ;

X = node(q,~0100643E,~0100603E) —> ;

X = node(k,~01006C3E,~0100683E) —> ;
```

X = node(d,∿0100743E,∿0100703E) —>

?- recorded(leaf,X,__).

X = leaf(a : apple,b : boy,c : cart,nil) —> ;

X = leaf(d : dog,e : ewe,f : frog,g : gone) —> ;

X = leaf(h : hat,i : igloo,j : jump,nil) —> ;

X = leaf(k : kid,l : little,m : moth,nil) —> ;

X = leaf(n : note,o : open,p : pup,nil) —> ;

X = leaf(q : quiz,r : run,s : seen,nil) —> ;

X = leaf(t : tickle,u : ugly,v : venus,nil) —> ;

X = leaf(w : wax,x : xray,y : yes,z : zoom) —>

You use neither depth-first nor breadth-first search strategies for finding a word in this b-tree. You use a non-backtracking search strategy instead. To locate a word, the first letter of the word (the key) is compared to the value contained in a node. If the key is less than the node's key value, the left-hand branch is searched. If the key is greater than or equal to the node's key value,the right-hand branch is searched. This search strategy always finds the shortest path to the data and it never backtracks, as both breadth-first and depth-first searches do.

The predicate *find*, below, initiates the search by locating the root node and passing that structure to a predicate that will follow the path through the tree to the leaf.

```
find(X,Term) :-
    recorded(node,Root,__),
    btree(Root,X,Term).
```

The *btree* predicate determines which path to follow by recursively comparing the key you are looking for to the key at the current node. If the key is less than the key at the current node, it follows the left-hand branch. Otherwise, it follows the right-hand branch. When the end of a branch is reached, the leaf that contains the word has been found. The word can be in one of the four positions within that leaf.

The *btree* predicate is defined like this:

```
btree(node(Nkey,Left,__), Key, Term) :-
    Key @< Nkey,
    node__or__leaf(Left,Node__or__leaf),
    btree(Node__or__leaf, Key, Term).
btree(node(Nkey,__,Right), Key, Term) :-
    node__or__leaf(Right,Node__or__leaf),
    btree(Node__or__leaf,Key, Term).
btree(leaf(Key:Term,__,__,__), Key, Term).
btree(leaf(__, Key:Term, __,__), Key, Term).
btree(leaf(__,__, Key:Term,__), Key, Term).
btree(leaf(__,__,__, Key:Term), Key, Term).

node__or__leaf(Ref,Node) :-
    recorded(node,Node,Ref), !.
node__or__leaf(Ref,Leaf) :-
    recorded(leaf,Leaf,Ref).
```

To locate the word that begins with the letter *r*, you would execute the *find* program as follows:

```
?- find(r,X).
```

The *find* predicate first locates the root node, which has the key *n*, and passes the root node to the *btree* predicate. *Btree* compares the letter *r* with the key *n*. Because *r* is greater than *n*, *btree* next looks at the node on the right-hand side of the root node. This node contains the key *t*. The letter *r* is less than *t*, so *btree* follows the branch on the left-hand side. This branch leads to the node *q*. When *btree* compares *r* to *q*, it follows the right-hand branch and locates the correct *leaf*. The term is found at the second position within the structure:

```
leaf(q:quiz,r:run,s:seen,null
           ↑
```

Then the *find* predicate succeeds with the variable *X* instantiated to *run*.

A balanced tree is desirable for a number of reasons. First, it enables faster retrieval of information. The non-backtracking search strategy does not waste time following a path that cannot lead to the correct leaf. Second, it keeps data sorted.

To retrieve all the words in alphabetical order, you can call the *find* predicate like this:

```
?- find(X,Y).
X = a
Y = apple -> ;

X = b
Y = boy -> ;

X = c
Y = cart -> ;




.
.
.
```

Or you can include *find* in a loop, like this:

```
find_alpha :-
    find(X,Y),
    write(X), tab(1),
    write(Y), nl,
    fail.
find_alpha.
```

Summary

Much of Prolog's power and flexibility derive from its database. Prolog's power can be increased by applying both new and existing techniques to database design and database management.

The virtual database allows you to build large Prolog databases on small computers. The size of a virtual database compares favorably to databases built on the larger computers. In addition, the virtual database model requires no extensions to the Prolog language.

Worlds are another way to increase the database size that a Prolog system can handle. Worlds allow you to partition your program's database. Because each world is a separate database, you can build applications made up of many large pieces. However, the program must define how to partition the database into these separate entities. Therefore, worlds require some extensions to the language.

Hash tables and trees can increase the speed with which Prolog locates a term in the database. Using the existing set of Prolog predicates, you can build your own alternative access methods for specific applications. There are no clear guidelines for determining which storage and access method is best for a particular type of application. However, it is generally true that if you are writing a sophisticated system requiring large amounts of database information, you should use more sophisticated storage and access methods, such as balanced trees provide. If you are writing a simple system with few database requirements, then you can use the less sophisticated methods, such as Prolog's sequential method or hash tables.

4

A Relational Database in Prolog

Relational database management systems store data in tables, or "relations." Chapter 1 showed such a table to store information about the distance from the sun to the planets in the solar system and how the relational table is similar to Prolog facts. This chapter illustrates how to create a database to catalog the recordings in a record collection.

Relational database management systems are also characterized by the operations that they can perform on tables. The operations are derived from a branch of mathematics known as relational algebra, and they are similar to the operations that can be performed on sets. For example, a relational database management system can find the union or the intersection of tables, or a subset of a table based on relationships such as equality, inequality, greater than, less than, and so on. This chapter explores the similarities between Prolog queries and relational database queries.

Components of a Relational Database Management System

A relational database management system is built from four basic components: a front end, a data dictionary, a query facility, and the database manager. Figure 4-1 shows how these components fit together. This chapter shows how it is possible to build each of these components in Prolog and layer them on top of the Prolog Database.

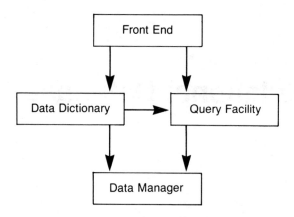

Figure 4-1: Components of a Relational Database Management System

The Front End

The front end accepts input from the user. It performs the initial parsing of the user's input to determine whether the user has entered a valid query or command. It then passes the input either to the data dictionary to define new tables, or to the query facility to access information stored in the database.

The front end also returns information to the user. Most important, it returns the results of queries. In addition, it reports errors that may occur when the program is trying to execute a command or query.

There are many different models for the front end of a relational database system:

- Query-by-example lets the user enter the kinds of answers that are desired. The system follows these examples to determine what information to retrieve from the database.

- Graphical query systems display tables pictorially. The user forms queries by pointing to the information that the system should return. More than one table can be involved in a query by drawing connections between the tables.

- Menu-driven query facilities display lists, or menus, of the names of tables and columns that are currently defined. The user forms queries by choosing from the various menus.

These systems can be very simple for a user to learn. In addition, they make it difficult for the user to form an incorrect query even if the query does not generate the information that the user intended. As a result, a user's success rate is very high.

- Yet another model, the Structured Query Language (SQL), is probably the most common type of relational database language. SQL defines a set of English-like commands that allow the user to communicate with the database. These commands can create or alter tables in the data dictionary and they can add or return information from the database in the form of tables.

Because SQL is the language most commonly found in relational database management systems, the examples in this chapter contrast SQL queries to Prolog queries. For a complete description of the SQL language, you should refer to *A Guide to DB2*, by C.J. Date (Addison-Wesley, 1984).

The front end of an SQL system would need to convert an SQL statement to a form that the system can recognize. Some techniques for language processing are discussed in chapter 6. This chapter assumes that the SQL statement has already been converted to a form that Prolog can recognize.

The Data Dictionary

The data dictionary defines the terminology with which the user can formulate queries. It does so by maintaining a catalog of the names of tables and the columns that are defined for those tables. Information cannot be added to the database unless it conforms to one of the table definitions.

Given Prolog's flexible handling of data, it may seem unnecessary to have a data dictionary at all. Prolog allows you to create terms at any time to hold any type of information. It does not restrict the kinds of information you can enter. This is precisely why a data dictionary is needed — to maintain order within the database. The data dictionary can make sure that the user enters the correct number of arguments so that similar information is stored in the same way (agreement among rows). The data dictionary can also contain data type information to make sure that the arguments always contain similar types of information (agreement among columns).

The Query Facility

The query facility adds information to or returns information from the database. A query is formed in terms of the data dictionary. That is, the user refers to tables and columns by their data dictionary names. The query facility translates the data dictionary representation of the query into an executable Prolog question.

The result of any query is another table, although it may be only a part of a table or a combination of more than one table. SQL distinguishes between "logical" and "physical" tables. A physical table is the form in which the information is stored in the database; a logical table is a table that is the result of a query. Logical tables do not exist in the database and they do not affect how the information is stored internally.

Internally, the information is stored as Prolog structures. At one time, a structure can be used as a fact and stored in the database. At another, it can be used as an executable goal and return information from the database. A structure can be converted to a list, which makes it possible to look for specific arguments (with the *member* predicate) or add arguments to the structure (with the *append* predicate). Later, the list can be converted back to a structure.

Therefore, the routines in this chapter will accept queries that refer to tables and columns by their data dictionary names. They will convert that information into a valid Prolog query. Additional arguments to the routines will determine whether certain arguments are instantiated or whether additional tests must be performed.

The Data Manager

Prolog's built-in database provides mechanisms for storing and accessing terms. A relational database management system can take advantage of the Prolog internal database. That is, tables can be stored in the form of Prolog structures. Access to these tables is provided by Prolog's built-in mechanisms for storing and retrieving information.

Prolog provides sequential storage and access methods into the database. You do not need to code special data handling primitives. In addition, alternate storage and access methods can be employed, as described in chapter 3. Using these techniques, information can be stored in worlds and indexed by hash tables or b-trees, giving the relational database even more powerful storage and retrieval methods.

Designing a Database

When writing a program to catalog the recordings in a record collection, you might want to store the following information about each recording:

- The title of the recording.
- The name of the band.
- The record label under which the record was published.
- The titles of the songs on the record.
- The date the recording was published.
- The names of the members of the band.
- The instruments that each performer plays.

The objects that are being stored fall into two categories: recordings and performers. Initially, you could create one table for each of these categories, as shown in figure 4-2.

RECORDING

Title	Band	Publisher	Date	Songs

PERFORMER

Name	Band	Instruments

Figure 4-2: Initial Design of the Recording Database

This first attempt at organization is logical because all related information is gathered together. However, this organization can be improved. An optimum organization not only should group objects logically for the user, but should also allow the system to update and delete information efficiently.

Normalization is the method that is used to rearrange the information in the database so that each object is defined once, and only once. Five ''normal forms'' provide guidelines that you can apply to your database to determine whether it has an optimum organization. C.J. Date provides a thorough explanation of the normal forms in his book *An Introduction to Database Systems*, third edition (Addison-Wesley, 1982). Only the first normal form will be dealt with here.

Consider the RECORDING relation. For each recording, there are attributes that occur once and attributes that occur more than once. For example, there can be only one record publisher for any record but there can be many songs on that record. The current definition of the RECORDING table is not efficient. To update one song requires that all songs be updated; to retrieve one song is to retrieve all songs.

A relation is in first normal form (1NF) when all of its attributes are simple, atomic objects. Thus, a list of songs cannot appear in a relation if it is to be in first normal form. To make this information conform to first normal form, the RECORDING table needs to be divided into two tables, as shown in figure 4-3. One contains the title, band name, publisher, and date; the other contains the title of the recording and the titles of the songs. For each record, there is only one instance in the RECORDING table, but there are many instances (one for each song) in the new RECORDING__SONG table.

RECORDING

Title	Band	Publisher

RECORDING__SONG

Title	Song

Figure 4-3: Recording Information in First Normal Form

First normal form is preferred because it allows you to find an individual song on a recording and it allows you to add, change, or delete one song without rewriting all songs. There is a trade-off for these advantages. When you separate the songs from the RECORDING relation, you duplicate the record name in each instance of a song. As a result, the information is not as compact as if the songs were contained in a list. In this case, the duplication does not make a difference to the application. In another case, it may make a difference. You must judge whether the benefits of one method outweigh the disadvantages.

The PERFORMER relation can be put in first normal form, too. A performer may play with many bands and a performer may play many instruments. Therefore, a different arrangement of the performer information may be more desirable, as shown in figure 4-4.

PERFORMER__BAND		PERFORMER__INSTRUMENT	
Name	Band	Name	Instrument

Figure 4-4: Performer Information in First Normal Form

Although information is broken out into more tables, no information is lost. Instead, it is connected by shared attributes of the relations. Knowing the title, you can get to all of the songs on a specific recording; knowing the name of a band, you can get to the individual performers in that band; and so on. Figure 4-5 shows how the tables in the database are connected. A column that connects one table with another is called a "foreign key."

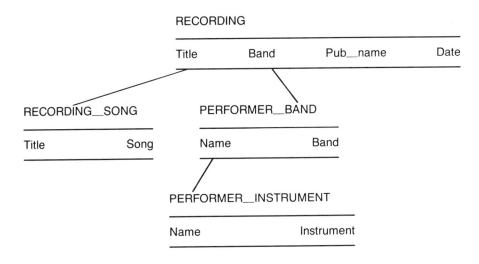

Figure 4-5: Final Organization of the Recording Database

A relational database management system may require each table to have a "primary key." A primary key is a column, or group of columns, that makes each row of the table unique. Prolog does not require terms in the database to be unique. It is possible to have a Prolog term that is identical to another term. Each is treated as a unique object. Although this flexibility makes Prolog an excellent programming language, it can become a problem when Prolog is used as a database management language. Prolog has no built-in mechanism for maintaining the integrity of the database. Integrity constraints have to be imposed on the database by the application.

Consider what can happen when no primary keys are defined. Suppose there are two recordings with the same title. These recordings are published under different labels by different bands, and they have different songs. In the current database design, only the *title* column defines the relationship between the RECORDING table and the RECORDING__SONG table. When the *title* column is not unique, the RECORDING__SONG table contains erroneous information because the songs from both recordings appear to be part of the same recording.

The Data Dictionary

The data dictionary maintains information about each of the tables in the database. Each entry in the data dictionary is a template of the table being defined, giving the name of the table and the names of the columns of the table. In SQL, this information is added to the data dictionary with the CREATE TABLE command. In Prolog, table definitions can be written as a collection of structures. For example:

```
table(recording(title,band,pub__name,date)).
table(performer__band(name,band)).
table(performer__instrument(name,instrument)).
table(recording__song(title,song)).
```

In SQL systems, the data dictionary also contains data typing information. For instance, it can define the data types of objects, whether an object can be null, and what range of values are valid for a numeric object. The Prolog language is not as type sensitive as SQL. However, a Prolog-based system can be made more type sensitive by adding data typing information to the data dictionary.

You can add this information to the table definition, as in:

```
table(performer__instrument(name:atom, instrument:atom)).
```

Or, you can split the data type information from the table definition, as in:

table(performer__instrument(name,instrument)).

    .

    .

    .

type(name(atom,notnull)).
type(instrument(atom,null)).

In either case, you would then need to write predicates to check that the data type of an object conforms to the type specification in the data dictionary whenever a new row is added to a table.

The Database

At this point, you know what attributes will appear together. The title, band name, publisher, and date of publication are attributes of a recording; the titles of the songs are additional attributes of a recording stored in a separate table. The name and band affiliation are attributes of a performer; the instruments played are additional attributes of a performer stored in a separate table.

Now that you know how to structure the information, you can store information in the tables. In Prolog, each of the table names is a functor, and each column is an argument to the functor. Here is some information about two recordings as it would be stored in the Prolog database:

```
recording('River Bottom','Country Gentlemen','Sugar Hill',1978).
recording('Blue Ridge Cabin Home','Foggy Mountain Boys', 'Rounder',1981).

performer__band('Charlie Waller','Country Gentlemen').
performer__band('Bill Yates','Country Gentlemen').
performer__band('Rick Allred','Country Gentlemen').
performer__band('Kent Dowell','Country Gentlemen').
performer__band('Ed Ferris','Country Gentlemen').

performer__band('Lester Flatt','Foggy Mountain Boys').
performer__band('Earl Scruggs','Foggy Mountain Boys').
performer__band('Paul Warren','Foggy Mountain Boys').
performer__band('Curly Sechler','Foggy Mountain Boys').
performer__band('Buck Graves','Foggy Mountain Boys').
performer__band('Jake Tullock','Foggy Mountain Boys').
```

performer__instrument('Charlie Waller',guitar).
performer__instrument('Bill Yates',vocals).
performer__instrument('Rick Allred',mandolin).
performer__instrument('Rick Allred',dobro).
performer__instrument('Kent Dowell',guitar).
performer__instrument('Ed Ferris',bass).

performer__instrument('Lester Flatt',guitar).
performer__instrument('Earl Scruggs',banjo).
performer__instrument('Paul Warren',fiddle).
performer__instrument('Curly Sechler',mandolin).
performer__instrument('Buck Graves',dobro).
performer__instrument('Jake Tullock',bass).

recording__song('River Bottom','River Bottom').
recording__song('River Bottom','Riverboat Fantasy').
recording__song('River Bottom','Coal, Black Coal').
recording__song('River Bottom','Electricity').
recording__song('River Bottom','Things in Life').

recording__song('Blue Ridge Cabin Home','Blue Ridge Cabin Home').
recording__song('Blue Ridge Cabin Home','Some Old Day').
recording__song('Blue Ridge Cabin Home','Six White Horses').
recording__song('Blue Ridge Cabin Home','On My Mind').
recording__song('Blue Ridge Cabin Home','Shuckin the Corn').
recording__song('Blue Ridge Cabin Home','No Mother in This World').

In SQL, information is added to a table with the INSERT command. This command has the following general form:

INSERT
INTO table-name
VALUES (column1, column2, ...)

If you want to follow the SQL model more closely, you can write an *insert* predicate like the one that follows:

```
insert(Table,Args,Term) :-
    Term  = .. [Table|Args],
    assertz(Term).
```

This predicate takes a table name and a list of arguments; it returns a Prolog structure created from this information. The *assertz* predicate adds the term to the database. For example, to add a song to the ''River Bottom'' record, you would use *insert* in this way:

```
?- insert(recording__song,['River Bottom','Some Old Day'],Term).
```

Insert uses a predicate called *univ* (= ..) to construct the appropriate term. This predicate will be discussed in more detail in the next section.

Transforming SQL Queries into Prolog Questions

Information is retrieved in an SQL system with the SELECT statement, which has the general form:

```
SELECT column(s)
FROM table(s)
WHERE predicate ;
```

The SELECT portion of the query states which columns are part of the answer. An output routine uses this information when printing the table. The FROM portion of the query states which tables are involved in the query. The WHERE portion is optional. It states any additional tests that need to be performed.

This general form can be used to ask three basic types of query:

- Queries that return all rows of all columns of one or more tables.

- Queries that return only some columns.

- Queries that return only some rows.

To construct Prolog questions from their data dictionary representation, you can use three evaluable predicates, *functor*, *arg*, and *univ*:

- *functor(Structure, Name, Arity)* locates the correct table and creates a valid Prolog question to access that table.

  Given a structure, the *functor* predicate returns that structure's name and arity. Given a name and arity, the predicate returns a structure with that name and the proper number of distinct variables as arguments. A structure in which all arguments are distinct variables is called a ''general structure'' because it can unify with any structure having the same name and number of arguments.

- *arg(Position, Structure, Value)* accesses specific arguments in a structure.

  Given the position of an argument within a structure, the *arg* predicate returns the value of the argument at that position. Given a general structure and an argument value, the predicate instantiates the argument within the structure to the specified value. The *arg* predicate differs from the *arg0* predicate of the previous chapter in that arguments are numbered upward from 1 rather then 0.

- *Structure* =.. *List* allows you to handle a term as either a list or a structure when one form is more convenient than the other.

  Some operations are more easily performed on lists than on structures and vice versa. The =.. predicate, called *univ*, converts a structure to a list or a list to a structure, in which the functor is the head of the list and the arguments are the tail.

Returning All Instances of All Columns

This first example returns all of the information contained in the PERFORMER__BAND table. The result is a table like the one shown in figure 4-6.

PERFORMER__BAND

Performer	Band
Charlie Waller	Country Gentlemen
Bill Yates	Country Gentlemen
Rick Allred	Country Gentlemen
•	•
•	•
•	•

Figure 4-6: A Table Showing All Instances of All Columns

In SQL, the query is written:

SELECT *
FROM PERFORMER__BAND;

The equivalent Prolog question is written as:

?- performer__band(X,Y).

To generate this query given only the name of a table, you can use a predicate like the one defined below:

```
from(Functor, Table, Query) :-
    table(Table),
    functor(Table, Functor, ArgC),
    functor(Query, Functor, ArgC).
```

The predicate uses the data dictionary to locate the first table definition whose functor matches the *Functor* argument. The first call to the *functor* predicate tests that the correct table definition is found and then returns the structure's number of arguments. The second call to *functor* creates a duplicate structure having uninstantiated variables as arguments. When you call *from* like this:

?- from(performer__band,Table,Query).

the *Table* variable becomes instantiated to the structure defined in the data dictionary, *performer__band(name, band),* and the *Query* variable becomes instantiated to the Prolog question *performer__band(X, Y).* The query can return all rows of the *performer__band* table when used as a goal in a fail loop.

Returning Only Some Instances

The next example returns those performers who play guitar. The shaded area of the table in figure 4-7 shows those parts of the table that are not returned by the query. In effect, by specifying *guitar*, the query masks out those rows that do not contain *guitar* in the instrument column.

PERFORMER__INSTRUMENT

Performer	Instrument
Charlie Waller	guitar
Bill Yates	vocals
Rick Allred	mandolin
Ken Dowell	guitar
Ed Ferris	bass
Lester Flatt	guitar
•	•
•	•
•	•

Figure 4-7: A Table Showing Some Instances of All Columns

In SQL, the query would be written:

```
SELECT *
FROM PERFORMER__INSTRUMENT
WHERE INSTRUMENT = guitar;
```

In Prolog, it would be written:

```
?- performer__instrument(X,guitar).
```

Generating this Prolog query is only slightly more difficult than generating the query in the previous section. After creating the general structure, you must instantiate a particular argument and leave the rest of the arguments as variables.

The general structure can be created with the *from* predicate:

from(Functor,Table,Struct)

Next, the correct position is found within the general structure to hold the WHERE value. In this example, you need to find the position of the *instrument* argument. This information is held in the data dictionary entry:

table(performer__band(name,instrument))

The table definition is then passed to a predicate that will count arguments until it has found the desired one. In the following predicate, called *nth__arg*, the first argument (*Arg*) is the name of the argument that needs to be instantiated. The second argument (*Table*) is the structure that contains the table definition. The third argument (*N*) is a variable to which *nth__arg* returns the argument number.

```
nth__arg(Arg,Table,N) :-
    Table = .. Z,
    ctr__set(0,0),
    nth__member(Arg,Z),
    ctr__is(0,N).
```

The first goal of *nth__arg* converts the *performer__band* table definition to a list with *univ* so that a variation of *member* called *nth__member* can count the elements of the list. The *nth__member* predicate simply increments a counter until it has located the desired argument.

```
nth__member(X, [X|__]).
nth__member(X, [__|Y]) :- ctr__inc(0,__), nth__member(X,Y).
```

You may like this version of *nth__arg* better:

```
nth__arg(Arg,Table,N) :-
    functor(Table,__,M),
    nth__arg(Arg,Table,N,1,M).
```

```
nth__arg(Arg,Table,M,M,M) :- !, arg(M,Table,Arg).
nth__arg(Arg,Table,I,I,M) :- arg(I,Table,Arg).
nth__arg(Arg,Table,N,I,M) :-
    I1 is I + 1,
    nth__arg(Arg,Table,N,I1,M).
```

Once the position of the *instrument* argument is known, *arg* can instantiate the same argument of the general structure to *guitar*:

```
arg(N,S,Val)
```

All of these steps are performed by the following predicate, called *where*. It takes the name of the table, the argument that is being instantiated, and the value of that argument. It returns the Prolog question to the fourth argument.

```
where(Functor,Arg,Val,Query) :-
    from(Functor,Table,Query),
    nth__arg(Arg,Table,N),
    arg(N,Query,Val).
```

When you call *where* like this:

```
?- where(performer__instrument,instrument,guitar,Query).
```

the *Query* argument is instantiated to *performer__band(X,guitar)*. This goal can be used within a fail loop to return all the performers who play the guitar.

Returning Only Some Columns

The next example returns the title and band columns from the recording table. By naming only certain columns of the table, the query masks out any other columns that the table may contain. The shaded area in figure 4-8 shows those columns that are not returned by the query.

RECORDING

Title	Band	Pub__name	Date
River Bottom	Country Gentlemen	Sugar Hill	1978
Blue Ridge Cabin Home	Foggy Mountain Boys	Rounder	1981

Figure 4-8: A Table Showing Some Columns

In SQL, this query is written:

SELECT TITLE, BAND
FROM RECORDING;

It is equivalent to the Prolog question:

?- recording(Title,Band,__,__).

The method used to generate the query is the same as the method used above. However, an output routine prints only the columns named in the query.

The top-level predicate in this example is called *select*, as it handles the information given on the SELECT line of a query. Given a list of argument names and a table name, *select* generates the query and prints the resulting table.

```
select(Argvals, Functor) :-
    from(Functor, Table, Query),
    get_nums(Argvals,Table,Argnums),
    get_instance(Query, Argnums).
```

In order to print only the desired columns, *select* converts a list of argument names to a list of their corresponding positions within the table. For example, the *title* and *band* columns from the *recording* table would be specified as the list:

[title,band]

These arguments are in the first and second positions within the table. Therefore, they are converted to the list:

[1,2]

A predicate called *get_nums* generates the list of argument numbers from the list of argument names. It calls itself recursively to find the argument number for each argument in the list.

```
get_nums([],__,[]).
get_nums([H|T],Table,[N|Argnums]) :-
    nth_arg(H,Table,N),
    get_nums(T,Table,Argnums).
```

The *get__instance* routine uses the query and the argument number list to execute the query and determine which columns to print. The columns are placed in a list and passed to the output routine.

```
get__instance(Query,Argnums) :-
    call(Query),
    get__columns(Query,Argnums,List),
    output(List),
    fail.
get__instance(__,__).

get__columns(Query,[],[]).
get__columns(Query,[H|T],[Val|List]) :-
    arg(H,Query,Val),
    get__columns(Query,T,List).
```

The *output* routine recursively prints the arguments in the list. The output routine described here does not align columns and it does not print headings. However, it would not take much work to make the routine do these things. How you would extend it depends upon the facilities provided with your Prolog system. For example, to make the columns line up, you may have to pad each column or you may be able to move the cursor to an arbitrary column position on the screen.

```
output([]) :- nl.
output([H|T]) :-
    write(H),
    tab(4),
    output(T).
```

When you call *select* with the list *[title, band]* and the table name *recording*, it returns the following table:

```
?- select([title,band],recording).
```

River Bottom   Country Gentlemen
Blue Ridge Cabin Home   Foggy Mountain Boys

SQL Predicates

The version of *where* described earlier used unification to check for equality. It could check only that an argument was equal to a value. The WHERE portion of a query performs other tests as well to determine what information to return.

- Comparison predicates test for inequality, greater than or less than relationships, as well as equality.
- The BETWEEN predicate determines whether an argument falls within a given range of values.
- The IN predicate determines if an argument is in a set of values.
- Conjunctions check whether more than one condition is true; disjunctions check whether one or another condition is true.

In order to apply any of these tests to a query, the *where* predicate must be rewritten. The new version of *where* uses *from* to generate the general form of the query. It uses *get_nums* to return the list of argument numbers involved in the test. Then, it calls a predicate called *do*, supplying the argument number, operator, value involved in the test, and the query.

```
where(Functor,(Arg, Op, Val),Query) :-
    from(Functor,Table,Query),
    nth_arg(Arg,Table,Argnum),
    do((Argnum, Op, Val), Query).
```

The *do* predicate executes the query and extracts the argument value from the structure that is returned by *call*. It then performs the specified test on the actual argument value. *Univ* strips off the head of the structure and passes the arguments to *output* as a list. These steps are placed in a fail loop so that all instances in the database can be tested and printed.

```
do((Arg,Op,Val), Query) :-
    call(Query),
    arg(Arg,Query,X),
    test(X, Op, Val),
    Query =.. [_|L],
    output(L),
    fail.
do(_,_).
```

Just what test is performed depends on the predicate that is named in the *Op* argument. A *test* predicate can perform each of the tests allowed in an SQL query, as described below.

Comparison Predicates

A comparison operation can use any of the predicates listed in table 4-1. There are two types of comparison predicates in Prolog. The first performs arithmetic comparisons (for numeric data); the second performs textual comparisons (for non-numeric data). Table 4-1 also shows the SQL operators that perform the same functions.

Table 4-1: Comparison Predicates

Comparison	Arithmetic	Textual	SQL Operator
Equal to	=:=	==	=
Not equal to	=\=	\==	¬=
Less than	<	@<	<
Less than or equal to	=<	@=<	<= ¬>
Greater than	>	@>	>
Greater than or equal to	>=	@>=	>= ¬<

The *test* predicate performs the comparison specified by the operator argument.

```
test(X,Op,Val) :-
     Goal = .. [Op,X,Val],
     call(Goal).
```

With *test* defined in this way, an SQL query can request a table of all the recordings made after 1978:

```
SELECT *
FROM RECORDING
WHERE DATE > 1978;
```

In Prolog, this query would be written:

?- where(recording,(date, > ,1978),X).

The query produces the table:

Blue Ridge Cabin Home   Foggy Mountain Boys   Rounder 1981

The BETWEEN Predicate

The BETWEEN predicate makes it possible to specify a range of values as part of the WHERE statement. A row is included in the table if a certain value falls between two values. For example, the following SQL command returns the names of recordings published between the years 1977 and 1980:

```
SELECT *
FROM RECORDING
WHERE DATE BETWEEN 1977 AND 1980;
```

A *between* predicate in Prolog can test whether a value is within a given range. A column is between a high and a low value if it is greater than or equal to the low value and less than or equal to the high value:

```
between(Col,Low,High) :-
    Col > = Low,
    Col = < High.
```

Now you can issue a query to return the recordings published between 1977 and 1981:

?- where(recording,(date,between,(1977,1981)),X).

The result of this query is the table:

River Bottom   Country Gentlemen   Sugar Hill   1978

The IN Predicate

The IN predicate allows a list of values to be given as part of the WHERE statement. A row is included in a table if a certain column matches a value in the list. For example, the following SQL query requests the name of the band with which Lester Flatt and Earl Scruggs play:

```
SELECT *
FROM PERFORMER__BAND
WHERE NAME IN ['Lester Flatt', 'Earl Scruggs'];
```

The *in* predicate simply checks that the argument value is a member of the list.

```
in(X,L) :- member(X,L), !.
```

Where can now find the name of the bands with which Lester Flatt and Earl Scruggs play:

```
?- where(performer__band,(name,in,['Lester Flatt','Earl Scruggs']),X)
```

This query returns the table:

Lester Flatt	Foggy Mountain Boys
Earl Scruggs	Foggy Mountain Boys

Conjunctions and Disjunctions

A conjunction is a set of test conditions separated by the key word AND. All the conditions must succeed for the column to be included in the table. In the following example, SQL checks that the name column is equal to "Charlie Waller" and the instrument column is equal to "guitar." This query returns a table with only one column.

```
SELECT *
FROM PERFORMER__INSTRUMENT
WHERE NAME  = 'Charlie Waller'
AND INSTRUMENT  = guitar;
```

A disjunction is a set of test conditions separated by the key word OR. Only one of the conditions must succeed for the column to be included in the table. In the next example, SQL checks that either the name column is equal to "Earl Scruggs" or the instrument column is equal to "guitar." This query returns a table with many columns.

```
SELECT *
FROM PERFORMER__INSTRUMENT
WHERE NAME  =  'Earl Scruggs'
OR INSTRUMENT  =  guitar;
```

Both AND and OR can be handled in Prolog with a modified version of *where* that takes two *(Argument, Operator, Value)* variables separated by either *and* or *or*.

```
where(Functor, (Arg1, Op1, Val1), Op, (Arg2,Op2,Val2), Query) :-
    from(Functor,Table,Query),
    nth__arg(Arg1,Table,Argnum1),
    nth__arg(Arg2,Table,Argnum2),
    do( (Argnum1,Op1,Val1),Op,(Argnum2,Op2,Val2), Query).
```

A new version of *do* is also required. The first *do* clause succeeds if the operator argument is *and*. It executes the query and locates the two arguments being tested. It then calls *test* to test each condition. Because the two calls to *test* are separated by a comma (Prolog's conjunction operator), both tests must succeed for the instance to be included in the table.

```
do( (Arg1,Op1,Val1), and, (Arg2,Op2,Val2), Query) :-
    call(Query),
    arg(Arg1,Query,X1),
    arg(Arg2,Query,X2),
    test(X1,Op1,Val1), test(X2,Op2,Val2),
    Query =.. [__|L],
    output(L),
    fail.
```

The second *do* clause succeeds if the operator is *or*. It also calls the query and locates the two arguments involved in the test. However, the two calls to *test* are separated by a semicolon (Prolog's disjunction operator). Therefore, only one of the tests must succeed for the instance to be included in the table.

```
do( (Arg1,Op1,Val1), or, (Arg2,Op2,Val2), Query) :-
    call(Query),
    arg(Arg1,Query,X1),
    arg(Arg2,Query,X2),
    ( test(X1,Op1,Val1) ; test(X2,Op2,Val2) ),
```

```
Query = .. [__|L],
output(L),
fail.
```

A third *do* clause simply succeeds. It is executed when no more instances can be found in the database.

```
do(__,__,__,__).
```

Where can now be called with a conjunction of goals:

```
?- where(performer__instrument,(name, = =, 'Charlie Waller'),
      and, (instrument, = =, guitar),X).
```

In this example, *where* returns the table:

Charlie Waller   guitar

Where can also be called with a disjunction of goals:

```
?- where(performer__instrument,(name, = =,'Earl Scruggs'), or,
      (instrument, = =,guitar),X).
```

It returns the table:

Charlie Waller   guitar
Kent Dowell   guitar
Lester Flatt   guitar
Earl Scruggs   banjo

Arithmetic Operations

SQL allows arithmetic operations to be performed on the information in the database. For instance, all values in a column can be multiplied by some number or two columns can be multiplied together. Arithmetic operations are placed on the SELECT line of the query, as in:

```
SELECT value arith-op value
FROM table
```

Table 4-2 shows the arithmetic operators supplied by both Prolog and SQL.

Table 4-2: Arithmetic Operators

Operation	Operator (Prolog and SQL)
Addition	+
Subtraction	−
Multiplication	*
Division	/

Other arithmetic operations are available in SQL. These are provided with the built-in functions SUM, COUNT, MIN, MAX, and AVG. You must write predicates to handle these operations in Prolog. This chapter will discuss the SUM and COUNT predicates.

Arithmetic operations return information that does not exist in the database. They derive new information from the information that is already stored in the database. Whenever they are used, the query produces a column of information for which there is no predefined column name in the data dictionary. SQL systems provide a way for the user to name the new column as part of the query. Otherwise, the information is placed in a column with no heading.

None of the information currently in the recording database is suitable for arithmetic operations. For the following examples, it will be necessary to add a new table to the database. Another table can be added to the database to store revenue information for each recording.

    table(revenues(title,copies,unit__price)).

You can then insert information into the table:

    insert(revenues,['River Bottom',1000,7],__).
    insert(revenues,['Blue Ridge Cabin Home',1500,7],__).

This information can be manipulated in a number of ways using arithmetic operations.

Performing Calculations

The total revenues of each recording can be calculated by multiplying the number of copies sold by the unit price. In SQL, the query to perform this operation would be written like this:

```
SELECT *, COPIES * UNIT_PRICE
FROM REVENUES;
```

In Prolog, you can write a predicate to do the arithmetic given a list of argument numbers, an arithmetic operator, and a Prolog query. The *calculate* predicate executes the query with *call*. It then locates the two arguments involved in the calculation using the *arg* predicate, performs the arithmetic operation on the two arguments, and outputs the result.

```
calculate((Arg1,*,Arg2),Query) :-
    call(Query),
    arg(Arg1,Query,X1),
    arg(Arg2,Query,X2),
    Ans is X1 * X2,
    output([X1,X2,Ans]),
    fail.
calculate(__,__).
```

Notice that the multiplication operator is explicitly given in the head of this clause. This is because Prolog cannot handle variable operators, as in:

```
Ans is X1 Op X2
```

Therefore, each arithmetic operator needs its own clause and *calculate* should be written like this:

```
calculate((Arg1,Op,Arg2),Query) :-
    call(Query),
    arg(Arg1,Query,X1),
    arg(Arg2,Query,X2),
    do_arith((X1,Op,X2)),Ans),
    output([X1,X2,Ans]),
    fail.
calculate(__,__).
```

```
do_arith((X1, + ,X2),Ans) :- Ans is X1 + X2.
do_arith((X1,-,X2),Ans) :- Ans is X1 — X2.
do_arith((X1,*,X2),Ans) :- Ans is X1 * X2.
do_arith((X1,/,X2),Ans) :- Ans is X1 / X2.
```

Returning the total revenues with the *calculate* predicate involves first generating the query with *from*, converting the argument names to their corresponding argument numbers, and passing the argument numbers, arithmetic operator, and the query to *calculate*. The *arithmetic* predicate handles these operations:

```
arithmetic((Arg1,Op,Arg2),Functor) :-
     from(Functor,Table,Query),
     nth_arg(Arg1,Table,Argnum1),
     nth_arg(Arg2,Table,Argnum2),
     calculate((Argnum1,Op,Argnum2),Query).
```

When you call *arithmetic* in this way:

```
?- arithmetic((copies,*,unit_price),revenues).
```

the predicate prints out the following:

```
1000    7    7000
1500    7    10500
```

The COUNT Built-in Function

The COUNT function determines how many instances of a column are present in a table. For example, the following SQL query counts the number of songs appearing on the "River Bottom" recording:

```
SELECT COUNT(SONG)
FROM RECORDING_SONG
WHERE TITLE = 'River Bottom';
```

In Prolog, you can write a predicate to increment a database counter each time a goal succeeds. The *count* predicate, defined below, uses *from* to generate a query and *ctr_set* to initialize a counter. The *counter* predicate calls the query and increments the counter each time the query succeeds. When *counter* completes, the number can be returned from the database with the *ctr_is* predicate.

```
count(Functor,Arg1,(Arg2,Op,Val),Count) :-
    from(Functor,Table,Query),
    nth_arg(Arg2,Table,Num),
    ctr_set(0,0), !,
    counter((Num,Op,Val),Query),
    ctr_is(0,Count).

counter((Num,Op,Val),Query) :-
    call(Query),
    arg(Num,Query,X),
    test(X,Op,Val),
    ctr_inc(0,_),
    fail.
counter(_,_).
```

When called with the following arguments, the predicate returns with *X* instantiated to the number 6.

```
?- count(recording_song,song,(title, = = ,'River Bottom'),X).

X = 6
```

The SUM Built-in Function

The SUM function calculates the sum of all the values contained in a column. For example, the total number of copies sold for all recordings can be calculated with the following SQL query:

```
SELECT SUM(COPIES)
FROM REVENUES;
```

In Prolog, you must write a predicate to store the running total in the database. Initially, *select_sum* erases the key to make sure that no previous sums are still present in the database. Then, it uses *from* and *nth_arg* to form the Prolog query and determine which column to sum.

```
select__sum(Functor,Arg,Sum) :-
    eraseall(sum),
    from(Functor,Table,Query),
    nth__arg(Arg,Table,N),
    do__sum(Query,N),
    recorded(sum,Sum,__).
```

The *do__sum* predicate executes the query, locates the argument to be added to the sum, calls a predicate to perform the actual sum operation, then fails in order to execute the query again.

```
do__sum(Query,N) :-
    call(Query),
    arg(N,Query,X),
    sum(X),
    fail.
do__sum(__,__).
```

Two clauses handle the sum operation. The first clause retrieves the current sum from the database, adds the next value to the sum, and replaces the old sum with the new. The second clause handles the case when no sums have been stored in the database yet. This clause executes the first time through the fail loop.

```
sum(Sum) :-
    recorded(sum,X,Ref),
    X1 is X + Sum
    replace(Ref,X1),
    !.
sum(Sum) :-
    recorda(sum,Sum,__).
```

Select__sum returns the total number of recordings sold when called with the following arguments:

```
select__sum(revenues,copies,X).
```

```
X = 2500
```

Using Lists to Collect Results

Some SQL operations can be implemented by collecting results in a list. Two operations that fall into this category are the DISTINCT and ORDER BY built-in functions.

The DISTINCT Built-in Function

DISTINCT returns only one occurrence of a repeating entry in a table. For example, when returning the titles of the recordings by accessing the *recording__song* table, DISTINCT can be used so that only one instance of each recording name is returned.

```
SELECT DISTINCT TITLE
FROM RECORDING__SONG;
```

Of course there are more efficient ways to return this information. (The *recording* table does not contain duplicate title entries.) However, the users of a database system are not always familiar with the details of a database design. They may not know how to return the information in the most efficient manner.

The query to collect the record titles from the *recording__song* table would generate a list of titles, adding a title to that list only if it is not already a member of the list. The list of distinct values is placed in the database. With the query generated by *from* and the argument number for the distinct argument returned by *nth__arg*, the *distinct* predicate calls the query and then checks whether it contains a distinct argument value.

```
select__distinct(Arg,Functor,List) :-
    eraseall(distinct),
    from(Functor,Table,Query),
    nth__arg(Arg,Table,N),
    distinct(N,Query),
    recorded(distinct,List,__).

distinct(N,Query) :-
    call(Query),
    is__distinct(N,Query),
    fail.
distinct(__,__).
```

Three *is_distinct* clauses handle whether or not to add a value to the list. The first clause succeeds when the value is a member of the list. It then finds the next instance of the query in the database. If the value is not a member, the second *is_distinct* clause succeeds, which adds the value to the list and replaces the old list with the new one. The third *is_distinct* clause succeeds when there is no *distinct* list in the database. It executes the first time through the fail loop and adds the first instance to the list.

```
is_distinct(N,Query) :-
    arg(N,Query,X),
    recorded(distinct,List,_),
    member(X,List),
    !.
is_distinct(N,Query) :-
    arg(N,Query,X),
    recorded(distinct,List,Ref),
    append(List,[X],NewList),
    replace(Ref,NewList),
    !.
is_distinct(N,Query) :-
    arg(N,Query,X),
    recorda(distinct,[X],_).
```

Select_distinct can be called with the following arguments to return the list of titles contained in the *recording_song* table:

```
?- select_distinct(title,recording_song,List).
```

List = ['River Bottom','Blue Ridge Cabin Home'].

The ORDER BY Built-in Function

Sometimes data is not stored in the order in which the user wants. Prolog, for instance, stores information in the order in which it was entered. At one time, the user may want to sort the information by one column; at another time, by a different column. The ORDER BY built-in function collects the results of a query in a list and sorts that list.

This SQL query sorts a list of performer names in alphabetic order:

```
SELECT NAME
FROM PERFORMER_BAND
ORDER BY NAME;
```

A predicate to sort a list of values can be implemented using the same procedure as *select_distinct*, with only a few differences. The *order_by* predicate does not have to remove duplicate values and it must sort the list.

Like *select_distinct*, *order_by* keeps the list in the database. The query is generated by *from* and the argument on which the list is sorted is found with the *nth_arg* predicate. *Collect_all* calls the query and locates the argument to be added to the list. *Add_to* retrieves the list from the database and adds the new value to the list. It does not check for duplicates. After the value is added to the list, *collect_all* fails in order to find the next row of the table. After all the values have been found, *order_by* sorts the final list and returns the sorted list to the *NewList* argument.

```
order_by(Arg,Functor,NewList) :-
      eraseall(orderby),
      from(Functor,Table,Query),
      nth_arg(Arg,Table,N),
      collect_all(N,Query),
      recorded(orderby,List,_),
      sort(List,NewList).

collect_all(N,Query) :-
      call(Query),
      arg(N,Query,X),
      add_to(X,List),
      fail.
collect_all(_,_).

add_to(X,List) :-
      recorded(orderby,List,Ref),
      append(List,[X],NewList),
      replace(Ref,NewList),
      !.
add_to(X,List) :-
      recorda(orderby,NewList,_).
```

Many Prolog implementations provide a built-in *sort* predicate. If your Prolog system does not supply this predicate, here are two sorting algorithms that you can use — the bubble sort and the insert sort:

```
bubble(L1,L2) :-
    append(U,[A,B|V],L1),
    B @< A,
    append(U,[B,A|V],M),
    bubble(M,L2).
bubble(L1,L1).

insort([H|T],S) :- insort(T,L), insert(H,L,S).
insort([],[]).

insert(X,[H|T],[H|L]) :- H @< X, !, insert(X,T,L).
insert(X,L,[X|L]).
```

Now, when called with the arguments:

```
?- order__by(title,recording__song,X).
```

order__by instantiates *X* to the list:

```
[Bill Yates,Buck Graves,Charlie Waller,Curly Sechler,
Earl Scruggs,Ed Ferris,Jake Tullock,Kent Dowell,Lester
Flatt,Paul Warren,Rick Allred]
```

The *between* and *order__by* predicates defined here are of limited use because they handle only single columns of information. You may find the alternative method for collecting results described in the next subsection more useful.

An Alternative Method for Collecting Results

A group of evaluable predicates — *setof*, *bagof*, and *findall* — can be used to implement the DISTINCT and ORDER BY functions. These predicates collect the results of a query in a Prolog list. They differ in whether they accept what are called "existential quantifiers," whether they remove duplicate members from the list, and whether they sort the resulting list. These predicates were originated by D.H.D. Warren; R.A. O'Keefe is credited with further refining them.

- *setof(Vars, Goal, List)*, given one or more variables, generates a list of those variables occurring as arguments to the *Goal*. The list is sorted and duplicates are removed.

- *bagof(Vars, Goal, List)*, given one or more variables, generates a list of those variables occurring as arguments to the *Goal*. The list is not sorted and duplicates are not removed.

- *findall(Vars, Goal, List)*, given one or more variables, generates the list of those variables occurring as arguments to the *Goal*. All variables not mentioned in the *Vars* argument are treated as if they were existentially quantified. The list is not sorted and it contains duplicates.

When using the *setof* and *bagof* predicates, any argument to the *Goal* that is not included in the *Vars* argument may be existentially quantified. Existential quantification has the effect of instantiating the variable to all possible values at the same time. A few examples should clarify how existential quantifiers effect the result of the *setof* and *bagof* predicates.

In the following examples, *X* is mentioned in the *Vars* argument; *Y* is not. Therefore, *Y* may be existentially quantified. In the first example, it is not. Therefore, *setof* returns a separate list of *X* values for each occurrence of *Y*.

```
?- setof(X,recording__song(X,Y),L).

X = A
Y = 'A Hundred Years from Now'
L = ['Blue Ridge Cabin Home'] —> ;

X = A
Y = 'Blue Ridge Cabin Home'
L = ['Blue Ridge Cabin Home'] —> ;

X = A
Y = 'Coal, Black Coal'
L = ['River Bottom'] —> ;
      .
      .
      .
```

If *Y* is existentially quantified, as in the next example, *setof* returns one list of *X* values for all occurrences of *Y*.

?- setof(X,Y^recording__song(X,Y),L).

X = A
Y = B
L = ['Blue Ridge Cabin Home', 'River Bottom'] —> ;

no

The key words in these two examples are "for each" and "for all." Without the existential quantifier, the *setof* predicate returns one list for each Y value. With the existential quantifier, the *setof* predicate returns one list for all Y values.

Now consider the SQL query:

SELECT *
FROM PERFORMER__BAND
ORDER BY BAND;

This query asks for a table of performers and bands, sorted in band name order. *Setof* can return the same result:

?- setof((X,Y), performer__band(X,Y), L).

L = [('Country Gentlemen', 'Bill Yates'), ('Country Gentlemen', 'Charlie Waller'), ('Country Gentlemen', 'Ed Ferris'), ('Country Gentlemen', 'Kent Dowell'), ('Country Gentlemen', 'Rick Allred'), ('Foggy Mountain Boys', 'Buck Graves'), ('Foggy Mountain Boys', 'Curley Sechler'), ('Foggy Mountain Boys', 'Earl Scruggs'), ('Foggy Mountain Boys', 'Jake Tullock'), ('Foggy Mountain Boys', 'Lester Flatt'), ('Foggy Mountain Boys', 'Paul Warren')]

The results may also be sorted by *name*. In SQL, such a query is written:

SELECT *
FROM PERFORMER__BAND
ORDER BY NAME;

In Prolog, the query is written:

?- setof((Y,X), performer__band(X,Y),L).

L = [('Bill Yates', 'Country Gentlemen'),('Buck Graves', 'Foggy Mountain Boys'), ('Charlie Waller', 'Country Gentlemen'), ('Curley Sechler', 'Foggy Mountain Boys'), ('Earl Scruggs', 'Foggy Mountain Boys'), ('Ed Ferris', 'Country Gentlemen'), ('Jake Tullock', 'Foggy Mountain Boys'), ('Kent Dowell', 'Country Gentlemen'), ('Lester Flatt', 'Foggy Mountain Boys'), ('Paul Warren', 'Foggy Mountain Boys'), ('Rick Allred', 'Country Gentlemen')]

A special *output* clause must be written to break these lists into rows and columns. For example, knowing that each row has the form *(X, Y)*, you can write the output routine to recognize this form:

```
output([(X,Y)|T]) :-
    write(X), tab(4),
    write(Y), nl,
    output(T).
```

Setof and *output* can be used to produce a table like this:

?- setof((X,Y),performer__band(X,Y),L), output(L).

Bill Yates	Country Gentlemen
Buck Graves	Foggy Mountain Boys
Charlie Waller	Country Gentlemen
Curly Sechler	Foggy Mountain Boys
Earl Scruggs	Foggy Mountain Boys
Ed Ferris	Country Gentlemen
Jake Tullock	Foggy Mountain Boys
Kent Dowell	Country Gentlemen
Lester Flatt	Foggy Mountain Boys
Paul Warren	Foggy Mountain Boys
Rick Allred	Country Gentlemen

Accessing More Than One Table (Joins)

So far, the queries described in this chapter have accessed only one table at a time. In SQL, it is possible to combine information from more than one table. Queries that access more than one table are called "joins." For example, returning the title, band, and songs of the recordings in the database requires joining both the RECORDING and the RECORDING_SONG tables, as shown in figure 4-9. The join is effected through the *title* column because both tables share the information contained in those columns.

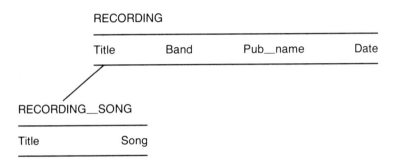

Figure 4-9: Joining Two Tables

SQL does not require that the columns effecting a join have the same name, as in this example. In fact, all columns have a unique name. In SQL, the full name of any column consists of the table name followed by a period followed by the column name. The full column name is not needed in queries involving only one table. The system can safely assume that the columns have the same table name prefix. However, when tables are joined, the column names may become ambiguous, as is the *title* column in this example. The system cannot tell which *title* column you are referring to unless you supply the table name prefix. Therefore, a SELECT statement that joins two tables must give the full column names.

SQL can join tables in two way: it can perform a "natural" join or an "outer" join. A natural join constructs a table of those rows in which a value in the joined column appears in both tables. The natural join is like the intersection of two sets. An element is included in the intersection if it occurs in both sets. An outer join contains those rows in which a value in the joined column appears in either table. The outer join is like the union of two sets. An element is in a union if it is found in one or the other sets. In SQL, constructing an outer join involves creating a table and inserting the results of a number of queries into that table. These operations are beyond the scope of this chapter.

A conjunction of goals in Prolog will correctly find the natural join of two tables. For example, the natural join of the *recording* and the *recording__song* tables would be requested with the SQL query:

```
SELECT RECORDING.TITLE, RECORDING.BAND,
    RECORDING__SONG.SONG
FROM RECORDING, RECORDING__SONG
WHERE RECORDING.TITLE = RECORDING__SONG.TITLE;
```

It would result in the table shown in figure 4-10. Notice that the new recording does not appear in the table because there are no corresponding songs in the *recording__song* table.

TITLE	BAND	SONG
River Bottom	Country Gentlemen	River Bottom
River Bottom	Country Gentlemen	Riverboat Fantasy
River Bottom	Country Gentlemen	Coal, Black Coal
River Bottom	Country Gentlemen	Electricity
River Bottom	Country Gentlemen	Things in Life
Blue Ridge Cabin Home	Foggy Mountain Boys	Blue Ridge Cabin Home
Blue Ridge Cabin Home	Foggy Mountain Boys	Some Old Day
Blue Ridge Cabin Home	Foggy Mountain Boys	Six White Horses
Blue Ridge Cabin Home	Foggy Mountain Boys	Shuckin' the Corn
Blue Ridge Cabin Home	Foggy Mountain Boys	On My Mind

Figure 4-10: A Natural Join of Recordings and Recording__songs

The *n__join* predicate defined below generates the conjunction of goals required for a natural join. This predicate accepts full column names, where the table name is separated from the column name by the colon. The full name is treated as a single argument, but the name can be separated into its two values when needed. Given two *functor:column* pairs, *n__join* uses *from* to return the general structure for the two queries. It uses *get__nums* to find the argument numbers for the columns that must match in the two queries, and it then tries to unify those columns. If the unification succeeds, then the information from the tables is included in the join. The third argument is a conjunction of the two goals.

```
n_join(Func1:Col1, Func2:Col2, (Q1 , Q2)) :-
    from(Func1,Table1,Q1),
    from(Func2,Table2,Q2),
    get_nums(Table1,[Col1],__,N1),
    get_nums(Table2,[Col2],__,N2),
    unify(Q1,Q2,N1,N2), !.

unify(Q1,Q2,[N1|__],[N2|__]) :-
    arg(N1,Q1,U),
    arg(N2,Q2,U).
```

A join does not have to be based only on equality. It can be based on any of the conditional predicates, such as greater than, less than, not equal, and so on. Therefore, basing the join operation on unification is not general enough to handle all possible conditions. A different version of *n_join* must be written to accept any of the conditional operators. The operator is passed to a predicate called *do_join* which performs the specified test. Like the second version of *where*, *do_join* uses the *test* predicate to perform the comparison operation.

```
n_join(Func1:Col1, Op, Func2:Col2) :-
    from(Func1,Table1,Q1),
    from(Func2,Table2,Q2),
    get_nums(Table1,[Col1],__,Arg1),
    get_nums(Table2,[Col2],__,Arg2),
    do_join((Q1,Op,Q2),Arg1,Arg2), !.

do_join((Q1,Op,Q2),[Arg1],[Arg2]) :-
    call(Q1), call(Q2),
    arg(Arg1,Q1,X),
    arg(Arg2,Q2,Y),
    test(X,Op,Y),
    format(Q1,Q2,L),
    output(L),
    fail.
do_join(__,__,__).
```

```
format(Q1,Q2,L) :-
    Q1 =.. [F1|T1],
    Q2 =.. [F2|T2],
    append(T1,T2,L).
```

Now *n_join* can handle other kinds of join conditions. For example, you can add sales information showing the number of recordings sold by region:

```
table(sales(region,copies)).
```

```
sales(east,110000).
sales(west,15000).
sales(central,9500).
```

When you join this table with the *revenues* table with a query such as this:

```
?- n_join(revenues:copies, <, sales:copies).
```

n_join prints the table:

River Bottom	10000	7	east	110000
River Bottom	10000	7	west	15000

Other Data Dictionary Operations

A flexible database system should allow the user to redefine a table. This involves two problems: updating the data dictionary so that the table description contains the new definition and updating the existing instances so that they conform to the new definition. It should also allow the user to remove a table that is no longer needed.

Changing a Table Definition

In SQL, columns can be added to a table but not removed. When a new column is added to a table, the value *null* is placed in that column for each existing instance in the table. The ALTER TABLE command is provided by SQL to add a new column to a table. It has the general form:

```
ALTER TABLE table-name
    ADD column-description;
```

The column description can contain data type information to be added to the data dictionary. However, for the purposes of these examples, no data type information will be included.

Thus, a column named *salesman* is added to the *sales* table with the SQL command:

```
ALTER TABLE SALES
      ADD SALESMAN;
```

To add the column to the Prolog data dictionary, you can write a predicate like *alter__table*:

```
alter__table(Name,Field) :-
      from(Name,X,S),
      new__struct(X,[Field],NewS),
      retract(table(X)),
      assertz(table(NewS),
      alter__instances(S).
```

First, *alter__table* finds the current table definition, using the *from* predicate. It saves the general structure in the variable *S*. Next, it constructs a new table definition containing the new column. This is done with a predicate called *new__struct*, defined like this:

```
new__struct(S,Val,NewS) :-
      S  = .. List,
      append(List,Val,NewList),
      NewS  = .. NewList.
```

Here, *univ* creates a list from the structure, appends the new column name to the end of the list, and creates a new structure again with *univ*. The old table definition is retracted and the new structure is asserted into the database.

Next, the new column must be added to the existing instances in the database, supplying the value of *null* in each instance. Given the general structure that was created earlier, you can write a predicate like *alter__instances* to update the database:

```
alter__instances(S) :-
    call(S),
    new__struct(S,null,NewS),
    retract(S),
    assertz(NewS),
    fail.
alter__instances(__).
```

To add the salesman column to the database, you can call *alter__table* like this:

```
?- alter__table(sales,salesman).
```

The *salesman* column is added to the table definition and the value *null* is added to each instance in the database. For example, you can check that the column has been added with the *select* query:

```
?- select([region,copies,salesman],sales).
```

east	110000	null
west	155000	null
central	95000	null

Removing a Table

Removing a table involves removing its definition from the data dictionary and all instances of the table from the database. In SQL, this is done with the DROP TABLE command. In Prolog, this is done by finding the table definition and the general structure with *from*. The table definition can be used as an argument to *retract*; the general structure as an argument to *eraseall*.

```
drop__table(Functor) :-
    from(Functor,X,S),
    retract(table(X)),
    eraseall(S).
```

Other checking may be needed before removing a table. For example, it may be necessary to check that there are no dependencies between the table being removed and the other information in the database. This sort of dependency information should be stored just like the table definitions. Another step is then required during the *drop—table* operation which checks that dependencies do not exist.

Accepting SQL Queries Directly

If you decide to build an SQL language processor, you will want to reduce the query to a canonical form. A canonical form is the most general form in which a statement in a language can be expressed. When you have determined the form that is most suitable for your application, you will need to rewrite the predicates in this chapter to accept this form.

Some techniques for language processing in Prolog are described in chapter 7. These techniques can be used for parsing SQL statements and converting them to a canonical form.

Summary

Relational database management systems are characterized by the way that they represent data and by the operations that can be performed on the data. Relational database applications can be built with Prolog. Prolog's database and its method for accessing the database closely resemble the relational model. This chapter examined the components of a relational database management system and how SQL operations can be performed in Prolog.

The data dictionary stores information about relational tables. To manage a data dictionary, the system must be able to:

- Create a new table definition.
- Change a definition and the information already contained in the table. In SQL, this operation is resticted to adding a new column; columns cannot be removed.
- Delete a table definition and the information store in the table.

This chapter showed how these data dictionary operations could be handled in Prolog.

Queries to retrieve information from the database can be written as Prolog questions. SQL provides the SELECT statement as a way to request information from the database. The SELECT statement determines which columns, tables, and rows are retrieved. This chapter showed how the different options in the SELECT statement can be handled in Prolog.

5

Techniques for Building Expert Systems

Expert systems try to emulate human expertise. As a result, an expert system does not behave like other kinds of programs. In other programs, the user learns a set of commands or actions to make the system perform in a certain way. The system is task oriented and the user initiates the tasks that the system performs. Expert systems usually behave more as consultants do. They ask questions to elicit information from the user; they answer questions the user may have during the course of the consultation. In this way, the user and the expert system enter into a dialogue.

A different approach to programming and design is required to develop this sort of system. Rather than build a set of tasks that a system can perform, you build a body of knowledge from which the system can draw many conclusions. You supply the system with this knowledge and with methods for problem solving.

Prolog is an ideal language for building expert systems because it is descriptive rather than prescriptive. Prolog allows you to define a program in terms of facts and rules. The language can derive solutions to questions based on those facts and rules. This chapter describes two simple programs that illustrate some of the techniques for building expert systems in Prolog.

In order to build an effective expert system in Prolog, you must understand how we humans store knowledge and how we apply that knowledge to solve everyday problems. This is one of the focuses of artificial intelligence research and cognitive science. Research in these areas has revealed the following facts:

- Experts have the ability to acquire knowledge over time and there is no limit to the amount of knowlege that the expert can acquire. Thus, expert systems should also have the ability to acquire and accept knowledge, even after the initial application is built.

- Experts can predict or project other things to be true based on the knowledge that they possess. Expert systems must therefore go beyond the function of the computer programs in the past, which could simply calculate unknown values from known values using well-defined formulas.

- Experts can put knowledge together in different ways. For example, information about the temperature, wind direction, and barometric pressure can be used to forecast the weather or to determine what clothes to wear. The expert system should represent knowledge so that it, too, can be used in more than one way.

- Experts are not always 100 percent certain that they have come to the correct conclusion. Expert systems use confidence factors to indicate how certain they are that a result is correct.

- Experts apply rules of thumb, or "heuristics," in order to arrive at a solution quickly. Expert systems need to use heuristics rather than general knowledge in order to keep the size of the system within reasonable bounds.

- Experts can explain how they arrived at a conclusion; some expert systems also have an explanation facility to describe the reasons for their conclusions.

Each of these characteristics can be produced by the Prolog language, its built-in database, and its method for solving problems.

Components of an Expert System

To varying degrees, expert systems are made up of the components shown in figure 5-1.

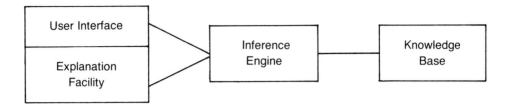

Figure 5-1: Components of an Expert System

The Knowledge Base

The knowlege base holds the description of the knowledge. There are many methods for describing knowledge and they all mirror the different ways that we approach knowledge and solutions to problems.

Semantic networks describe relationships between objects. The simplest relationships are *isa* relationships, as in "A dog is a pet," or "A tree is a plant." These kinds of relationships can be translated directly into Prolog facts, such as:

```
isa(dog,pet).
isa(tree,plant).
```

Production rules describe knowledge as "if-then" rules. Much of our knowledge can be expressed in this form. For example, we know that "If it is Saturday, then we can sleep late." This kind of information is easily described in Prolog, too. For example:

```
sleep(late) :- today(saturday).
```

Frames are useful for the kinds of problems that require chunks of information to be collected before a solution is found. For example, choosing a restaurant involves deciding what type of food to eat, how much money to spend, how far to travel, and so forth. Because Prolog allows you to build arbitrary data structures, you can express this kind of information quite easily. For example, a frame for describing a specific restaurant might be written like this:

```
restaurant([name:eat_n_run,
            type:fast_food,
            price:inexpensive,
            location:local]).
```

Taxonomies can describe chunks of information, as in frames, and they can describe how information is related, as in semantic networks. For example, one frame can describe the characteristics of cats and another frame can describe the characteristics of a particular type of cat. You can then define the relationship between these two frames, as in:

```
cat([family:felidae,
     genus:domesticus]).

tabby([coat:striped]).

isa(tabby,cat).
```

The *cat* frame describes a cat as a member of the family *felidae* and of the genus *domesticus*. The *tabby* frame says only that a tabby has a striped coat, but the *isa* relationship states that the *tabby* is a *cat*. This implies that all of the characteristics of *cat* are also characteristics of *tabby*. In this example, the *isa* relationship describes what is known as "inheritance," which makes a taxonomy more powerful than either frames or semantic networks alone.

Inference Engine

Information in a knowledge base is static until some outside force analyzes the semantic network, sets the production rules into action, or begins to fill in and analyze the slots of a frame. These jobs are performed by what is called an "inference engine."

Inference engines mimic the kinds of thinking that we employ when we try to solve a problem. That is, they can start with a conclusion and try to find evidence to support that conclusion or they can start with the evidence that is available and try to determine what conclusions the evidence supports. In expert systems, these two methods are called "backward chaining" and "forward chaining." Backward chaining, which tries to prove a goal by proving its subgoals, is like Prolog's own solution strategy. One example in this chapter shows how Prolog can solve a problem using backward-chaining techniques.

Other inference techniques can also be written in Prolog. A second example in this chapter uses unification to find a solution.

Consultation and Explanation Facilities

Expert systems gather information from the user by asking questions, much as a consultant does. Therefore, this part of the system is often called the "consultation facility." In addition, users can ask questions about how the system has arrived at a particular conclusion or why the system has asked a particular question. This part of the system is called the "explanation facility."

An example of a simple expert system with both a consultation and an explanation facility is included in this chapter.

Defining Knowledge as Rules

We know that if the temperature is 30 degrees Fahrenheit, then the weather is cold. A seemingly infinite amount of knowledge can be expressed by an *if* followed by some condition, followed by a *then* and some conclusion. In logic, the *if* portion of the statement is called the "antecedent;" it states what condition is being proved. The *then* portion is called the "conclusion." In Prolog, the *if* portion is called the "body;" the *then* portion is called the "head." For example, the relationship between the temperature and the weather can be described in Prolog by the rule:

```
weather(cold) :-
     temp(X),
     X =< 32.
```

When used to build expert systems, if-then rules are called "production rules" and a system that is based on such rules is called a "production system."

Production Rules

It is natural to conceptualize a problem, or its solution, in terms of production rules. For instance, Patrick Henry Winston presents a grocery bagging problem in terms of production rules in his book *Artificial Intelligence*, second edition (Addison-Wesley, 1984). Here is his example. Robbie the Robot is a grocery bagger. Given knowledge about the items sold in the grocery store, he can bag an order with a certain amount of expertise:

- Large items are bagged first so that they are on the bottom of the bags.
- Frozen items must be put in a freezer bag before being bagged with the other items.
- Small items are bagged last.
- A bag cannot contain too many items (six is Robbie's maximum) or the bag will be too heavy.

These rules for bagging groceries can be written in Prolog. The supply of brown bags and freezer bags are stored in the Prolog database as facts. Each bag must be unique so that Robbie does not get them confused. Therefore, the *bag* facts assign numbers to the brown bags. For the demonstration program, only one freezer bag is required. You can store any number of brown bags and one freezer bag in the database in this way:

```
bag(1).
bag(2).
    .
    .
    .

bag(freezer).
```

Robbie must also know some of the characteristics of each item sold in the grocery store. These characteristics are the name of the item, what kind of container it is sold in, whether it is small, medium, or large, and whether it is frozen or unfrozen. The grocery store's inventory is therefore stored in the database as a collection of facts. Other characteristics, such as price, are not included here because they are not relevant to the bagging operation.

```
item(bread,bag,medium,notfrozen).
item(jelly,jar,small,notfrozen).
item(granola,box,large,notfrozen).
item(icecream,carton,medium,frozen).
item(pepsi__tm,bottle,large,notfrozen).
item(chips,bag,medium,notfrozen).
```

Any subset of these items constitutes an order. Initially, no items in an order are bagged. Therefore, an order is entered into the knowledge base as a collection of *unbagged* items:

unbagged(chips).
unbagged(jelly).
unbagged(bread).
unbagged(icecream).
unbagged(granola).

All of this knowledge is handled adequately by Prolog structures. Though this information is required for the grocery bagging operation, it is also generally useful for other purposes and can be accessed easily with Prolog questions. For example, a user could determine what items the store carries by asking the question:

?- item(X,_,_,_).

X = bread —> ;
X = jelly —> ;
X = granola —> ;
X = icecream —> ;
X = pepsi_tm —> ;
X = chips

Much of the power of an expert system comes from the general knowledge that it possesses. This information should not be kept solely for solving the specific problem. Many expert systems allow the user to ask general questions to retrieve this kind of information, as in a database system.

In addition to this general information, production rules describe Robbie's knowledge about bagging an order. Each rule defines the heuristic for solving one step of the bagging problem.

Step 1: Checking the Order

It is possible to make Robbie a more "intelligent" grocery bagger. For example, you could make Robbie check an order to see that if it contains chips it also contains Pepsi, reasoning that the customer must have something to drink with the chips because they are salty. Therefore, step 1 states:

If an order contains chips and
the order does not contain Pepsi
Then add Pepsi to the order.

In Prolog, step 1 is written as the rule:

```
check_order :-
     unbagged(chips),
     not(unbagged(pepsi_tm)),
     write('Adding Pepsi (TM) to order.') , nl,
     assertz(unbagged(pepsi_tm)), !.
check_order.
```

The order is expressed as the collection of *unbagged* facts. Therefore, chips are included in the order if the goal *unbagged(chips)* can be satisfied; Pepsi is not included in the order if the goal *not(unbagged(pepsi_tm))* can be satisfied. When these two goals succeed, Pepsi is added to the order by asserting the fact *unbagged(pepsi_tm)*.

The second *check_order* clause handles the case in which the order either does not contain potato chips or it contains both potato chips and Pepsi.

Step 2: Bagging Large Items

Robbie knows to bag the large items first, so that they do not crush the smaller items. Bottles are bagged before the other large items. They are always placed in an empty bag. Furthermore, if a bag contains more than six items, a new bag is started. Thus, step 2 is made up of three rules:

If there is a large bottle
Then put the item in an empty bag.

If there is a large item and
    there is a bag with less than 6 items
Then put the item in the bag.

If there is a large item and
    there is an empty bag
Then put the item in the bag.

In Prolog, you can describe these rules with three clauses. The first checks whether the item being bagged is a bottle. If so, it puts the bottle in an empty bag. The *empty* predicate searches through the collection of bags for one in which no items have been bagged.

```
bag__large__items(Item) :-
    item(Item,bottle,large,__),
    empty(Bag), !,
    bag(Bag,Item).

empty(Bag) :-
    bag(Bag), not(bagged(Bag,__)), !.
```

The second clause handles any large item that is not a bottle. This clause calls the predicate *n__items* to find a bag containing fewer than six items. *N__items* returns that bag's number and *bag__large__items* passes the bag number and the item to a predicate called *bag* to place the item in the bag.

```
bag__large__items(Item) :-
    item(Item,__,large,__),
    n__items(Bag), !,
    bag(Bag,Item).
```

The *n__items* predicate uses the counter predicates defined in chapter 2 to find out how many items are packed in a bag. *Ctr__set* initializes the counter to 0. The database is searched for the first bag number. This bag is passed to the *count* predicate, which counts the items in the bag using *ctr__inc* in a fail loop. *Ctr__is* returns the final number and *n__items* checks that the number is less than six. If so, then that bag number is returned to *bag__large__items*. If not, then the next bag is checked.

```
n__items(Bag) :-
    ctr__set(0,0),
    bag(Bag),
    count(Bag),
    ctr__is(0,N),
    N < 6, !.

count(Bag) :-
    ctr__inc(0,__),
    bagged(Bag,__),
    fail.
count(Bag).
```

The last *bag_large_items* clause handles the case in which there is no bag with more than zero items and fewer than six items. This clause packs the item in an empty bag.

```
bag_large_item(Item) :-
      item(Item,_,large),
      empty(Bag),
      bag(Bag,Item).
```

Step 3: Bagging Medium Items

When bagging medium items, Robbie knows to look for items that are frozen. There is only one frozen item in the inventory and it is a medium item. If the grocery store began to carry large or small frozen items, the *bag_large_items* and *bag_small_items* clauses would each need an extra clause to handle frozen items, as does rule 3, which states:

> **If** an item is a medium item and
>   it is frozen
> **Then** put the item in a freezer bag and
>   put the item in a brown bag.

> **If** there is a medium item and
>   there is a bag with less than 6 items
> **Then** put the item in the bag.

> **If** there is a medium item and
>   there is an empty bag
> **Then** put the item in the bag.

Frozen items must be packed twice — first in a freezer bag and then in a brown bag. Therefore, the clause to handle the frozen items contains a *fail*. The *fail* causes Robbie to backtrack over *bag_medium_items* and bag the frozen item twice. The second clause packs an item in a bag with from one to six items and the third clause packs the item in an empty bag.

```
bag_medium_items(Item) :-
      item(Item,_,medium,frozen),
      not(bagged(frozen,Item)),
      bag(freezer,Item),
      fail.
```

```
bag__medium__items(Item) :-
    item(Item,__,medium,__),
    n__items(Bag),
    bag(Bag,Item), !.
bag__medium__items(Item) :-
    item(Item,__,medium,__),
    empty(Bag),
    bag(Bag,Item).
```

Step 4: Bagging Small Items

Robbie bags small items last, being sure not to put a small jar in a bag with a large bottle. Step 4 states that:

If there is a small item and
    there is a bag that has no bottle
    and that bag contains less than 6 items
Then place the item in the bag.

If there is a small item and
    there is an empty bag
Then place the item in the bag.

The first clause must search for a bag that does not contain a bottle. It first checks that the item is a small item. Then it locates a bag. This bag is passed to the predicate called *isnot__bottle*, which looks through the bag for a bottle. If one is found, then *isnot__bottle* uses a cut/fail. The *cut* makes sure that *isnot__bottle* is bypassed during backtracking; the *fail* causes *isnot__bottle* to fail. The cut/fail combination causes *bag__small__items* to then look for another bag, which is checked by *isnot__bottle*.

When *isnot__bottle* finds a bag that does not contain a bottle, it must then make sure there are fewer than six items in the bag. When a bag that passes both tests is found, the item is packed in that bag.

```
bag__small__items(Item) :-
    item(Item,__,small,__),
    bag(Bag),
    isnot__bottle(Bag),
    n__items(Bag),
    bag(Bag,Item), !.
```

```
isnot__bottle(Bag) :-
    bagged(Bag,Item),
    item(Item,bottle,__,__),
    !, fail.
isnot__bottle(Bag).
```

The second *bag__small__items* clause handles the case in which every bag contains either a bottle or more than six items. It packs the item in an empty bag.

```
bag__small__items(Item) :-
    item(Item,__,small,__),
    empty(Bag),
    bag(Bag,Item), !.
```

Reporting the Outcome

After all the items are bagged, Robbie displays the results. The *list__items* predicate goes through the database to find the items contained in each bag.

```
list__items :-
    bag(Bag), nl,
    write('Bag': Bag), nl,
    list__rest(Bag),
    fail.
list__items.

list__rest(Bag) :-
    bagged(Bag,Item),
    tab(4), write(Item), nl.
list__rest(__).
```

The Bagging Operation

The inventory of the store and the rules for bagging an order are static information. This information does not change during the course of the program or from one execution of the program to another.

Robbie also stores dynamic information that changes during the course of the program. The dynamic information describes what items are unbagged and what items are bagged. As an item is placed in a bag, Robbie removes its *unbagged* entry and makes a corresponding *bagged* entry in the database. In this way, facts about the state of an item change as the program progresses. Dynamic information is controlled by asserting and retracting facts in the database with the clause:

```
bag(freezer,Item) :-
    assertz(bagged(freezer,Item)), !.
bag(Bag,Item) :-
    assertz(bagged(Bag,Item)),
    retract((unbagged(Item))), !.
```

Each time an item is bagged, a new *bagged* entry is made in the database. The entry states the number of the bag and the name of the item placed in the bag. The item's *unbagged* entry is then retracted from the database. Frozen items are bagged twice; its *unbagged* entry is not retracted until it has been put in a brown bag. In this way, the current state of the order is updated each time an item is placed in a bag. At any time, the user could look at the *bagged* entries and see how much of the order is currently in bags or look at the *unbagged* entries and see how much of the order remains to be bagged.

Often, the area of the knowledge base that changes at run time is called the "blackboard" because information is added and erased as the program progresses.

Backward and Forward Chaining

At this point, Robbie possesses knowledge about the grocery store inventory, knowledge about bagging groceries, and a method for placing an item in a bag. What remains is a plan for executing the program. It is the purpose of an inference engine to control the program's execution path. Because this program is written in Prolog, Robbie can take advantage of Prolog's solution strategies to do most of the work. All that is required is a top-level predicate to control the order in which the rules are executed. The program can allow Prolog to control the order in which individual clauses within those rules are executed.

The top-level predicate called *robbie* sets the rules into action in the proper order. That is, Robbie first checks the order, bags the items from largest to smallest, then prints the result.

```
robbie :-
      check__order, fail.
robbie :-
      unbagged(Item),
      bag__large__items(Item), fail.
robbie :-
      unbagged(Item),
      bag__medium__items(Item), fail.
robbie :-
      unbagged(Item),
      bag__small__items(Item), fail.
robbie :- list__items.
```

Prolog's strategy for proving a goal is to prove all of the subgoals for that goal. If a subgoal is defined in terms of other subgoals, then all of those subgoals must also be proven. Take a look at two of the clauses from the *bag__large__items* rule to illustrate how Prolog proves whether a goal is true.

```
[1]   bag__large__items(Item) :-
[2]        item(Item,__,large,__),
[3]        n__items(Bag), !,
[4]        bag(Bag,Item).
[1]   bag__large__item(Item) :-
[5]        item(Item,__,large),
[6]        empty(Bag),
[7]        bag(Bag,Item).

[3]   n__items(Bag) :-
[8]        ctr__set(0,0),
[9]        bag(Bag),
[10]       count(Bag),
[11]       ctr__is(0,N),
[12]       N < 6, !.

[10]  count(Bag) :-
[13]       ctr__inc(0,__),
[14]       bagged(Bag,__),
[15]       fail.
[10]  count(Bag) :-
[16]       true.
```

  [6] empty(Bag) :-
  [17]   bag(Bag), not(bagged(Bag,__)), !.

In the program listing, each of the goals and subgoals is assigned a number. In figure 5-2, these clause numbers are drawn as an ''and-or'' tree. Each node in the tree corresponds to a clause from above. The goals are connected by links that are either ''and'' links or ''or'' links. All subgoals in an ''and'' link must succeed for the calling goal to succeed. Only one goal of an ''or'' link must succeed for the calling goal to succeed. The dark line in the figure shows the execution path through the goals in the tree.

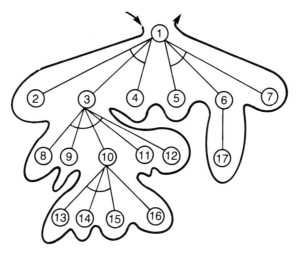

Figure 5-2: Prolog Clauses as an And-Or Tree

The technique Prolog uses to solve a goal is similar to backward chaining because the solution moves backward through the chain of subgoals toward the goal. For example, goal 13 must succeed before goal 8 can succeed; goal 8 must succeed before goal 3 can succeed; goal 3 must succeed before goal 1 can succeed; and so on. Backward chaining is goal-directed; the system chooses a goal and tries to prove the subgoals that support it. Therefore, the system always knows what goal it is trying to prove.

A forward-chaining system works in the opposite direction. It looks at the subgoals it knows it can prove and then determines which goals are proven by those subgoals. Forward-chaining systems are data-directed rather than goal-directed because forward chaining is more sensitive to the information that is currently known to the system. As a result, a forward-chaining system's ''train of thought'' is not as easy to follow because the system seems to jump around the solution space to find the right answer.

Both backward-chaining and forward-chaining systems need a way to choose which goal to execute when more than one goal applies. Prolog chooses goals in sequential order and forward-chaining systems can use this method, too. If a solution space is very large, however, sequential search may not be the most efficient method for either type of system. Other search techniques can be applied, such as is used by the next expert system example in this chapter.

With the top-level goal now written, you can run the grocery bagging program and it displays the results of the bagging job:

    ?- robbie.

    Adding Pepsi (TM) to order.

    Bag : 1
        granola
        pepsi_tm

    Bag : 2
        chips
        bread
        icecream
        jelly

    Bag : freezer
        icecream

Defining Knowledge with Frames

We solve many types of problems by gathering information in chunks. As more information becomes available to us, we classify it so that related information is stored together. The solution is found when enough information is available. Frame-based systems model this process.

Frames

A frame holds a chunk of related information. It is divided into ''slots'' and each slot holds one piece of the chunk. Slots are filled in by the system as information is gathered. Some slots can be filled in with information from the user or from a database. Other slots can be derived from information that has already been entered into other slots.

Consider a simple frame-based system that gives advice on financial investments. In order to give advice, this ''CFO Advisor'' needs to know:

1. Whether interest rates will rise, fall, or remain unchanged during a twelve-month period.
2. Whether revenues will go up or down during that same period of time.
3. Whether expenses will be greater than or less than budget.
4. How much risk the user is willing to take.

Given these values, the system can recommend the term of an investment and one of four investment types.

A frame in the knowledge base has slots for interest, revenues, expenses, risk, term, and investment, as shown in figure 5-3. Those slots that the system fills in from derived information are marked with an asterisk. The other slots must be filled in by the user.

```
      interest    : _____
      revenues    : _____
      expenses    : _____
      risk        : _____
   *  term        : _____
   *  investment  : _____
```

Figure 5-3: A Frame

In Prolog, the frame can be defined as a structure containing a list of slots. Each slot has a name and a value separated by a colon. Prolog treats a *Name:Value* pair as a single argument but the different parts of the argument can be accessed as needed.

```
cfo_frame([ interest:Interest,
     revenues:Revenues,
     expenses:Expenses,
     risk:Risk,
     term:Term,
     investment:Investment ]).
```

Frames do not necessarily hold only factual information, as in the *cfo_frame* structure. Information called "procedural attachments" may be defined for use by the procedures within the program. For instance, procedural attachments can define a question or a list of valid values that can appear in that slot. The system uses this additional information to ask an appropriate question when it needs to fill in the slot or to check that the user has supplied the correct type of information for a particular slot.

Figure 5-4 shows the CFO frame with procedural attachments. One attachment is a question to ask when the system requires a value for a slot. The other is a list of valid values for that slot. When the system needs to fill in the *interest* slot, it will ask the question, "What do you expect interest rates to do within the next year?" When the user enters the answer, it will check that the answer is one of the valid values (+ , – , or *unchanged*).

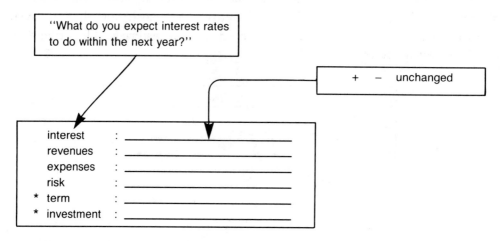

Figure 5-4: A Frame with Procedural Attachments

The following *valdef* structures hold the procedural attachments to define the valid values that a slot can hold. For example, the definition of *expenses* states that there are two valid values for this slot. A plus sign means that expenses are expected to exceed budget by more than 10 percent; a minus sign means that expenses are expected to be under budget by more than 10 percent.

```
valdef(expenses,'Exceed budget (by more than 10%)', +).
valdef(expenses,'Under budget (by more than 10%)', –).
valdef(expenses,'Unchanged', =).
```

```
valdef(revenues,'Exceed expected (by more than 10%)', + ).
valdef(revenues,'Shortfall (by more than 10%)', – ).
valdef(revenues,'Unchanged', = ).

valdef(interest,'Up',up).
valdef(interest,'Unchanged',unchanged).
valdef(interest,'Down',down).

valdef(risk,'Low',low).
valdef(risk,'Low-Medium',low – medium).
valdef(risk,'Medium-High',medium – high).
valdef(risk,'High',high).

valdef(investment,
       'U.S. Government & Treasury Securities',
       usgov).
valdef(investment,
       'Offshore Banks or Eurodollars',
       offshore).
valdef(investment,
       'Unrated Corporate Bonds or CDs of Savings & Loan',
       unrated).
valdef(investment,
       'Obligations of large Banks or Corporations',
       obligs).

valdef(term,'Short (1–3 mos.)',short).
valdef(term,'Medium (3–6 mos.)',medium).
valdef(term,'Long (6–12 mos.)',long).
```

Question structures hold the questions that are associated with each slot in the frame.

```
question(interest,
       'What do you expect interest rates to do within the next year? ').
question(expenses,
       'How much might your expenditures diverge from expectations? ').
question(revenues,
       'How much might your revenues diverge from expectations? ').
```

```
question(risk,
    'What is your tolerance for risk? ').
```

In the CFO Advisor, the term of an investment is derived from the values supplied for *interest*, *revenues*, and *expenses*. Each of the following rules defines a term of investment that corresponds to a particular combination of interest, revenues, and expenses. The rules are written as frames that have been completely filled in. For example, the recommended investment term is *short* if *interest* is *down*, if *revenues* are − , and if *expenses* are either + or = .

```
rule(term:short,[interest:[down],revenues:[ − ],expenses:[ + , = ]]).
rule(term:medium,[interest:[down],revenues:[ − ],expenses:[ − ]]).
rule(term:medium,[interest:[down],revenues:[ = ],expenses:[ + ]]).
rule(term:long,[interest:[down],revenues:[ = ],expenses:[ − , = ]]).
rule(term:long,[interest:[down],revenues:[ + ],expenses:[ + , = , − ]]).
rule(term:short,[interest:[up],revenues:[ + , = , − ],expenses:[ + , = , − ]]).
rule(term:short,[interest:[unchanged],revenues:[ − ],expenses:[ − , + , = ]]).
rule(term:medium,[interest:[unchanged],revenues:[ = ],expenses:[ = , − ]]).
rule(term:short,[interest:[unchanged],revenues:[ = ],expenses:[ + ]]).
rule(term:long,[interest:[unchanged],revenues:[ + ],expenses:[ = , − ]]).
rule(term:medium,[interest:[unchanged],revenues:[ + ],expenses:[ + ]]).
```

An *investment* is determined by the values of the *risk* and *term* slots. Thus, if the *risk* is *low* and the *term* is either *medium* or *long*, then the recommended investment is *usgov*, or 'U.S. Government & Treasury Securities.' These rules are also written as fully-qualified frames:

```
rule(investment:usgov,[risk:[low],term:[medium,long]]).
rule(investment:obligs,[risk:[low],term:[short]]).
rule(investment:obligs,[risk:[low-medium],term:[medium,long]]).
rule(investment:offshore,[risk:[low-medium],term:[short]]).
rule(investment:offshore,[risk:[medium-high],term:[short,medium,long]]).
rule(investment:unrated,[risk:[high],term:[short,medium,long]]).
```

Frames can hold many different kinds of information, as shown by the CFO Advisor. The *cfo_frame* defines the current set of conditions that are being analyzed. The *valdef* and *question* structures define procedural attachments for the frame. Finally, rules for determining which investment to recommend are also represented by frames.

Consulting the User

The CFO Advisor has a more expert-system-like user interface compared to the grocery bagger. The user interface controls how information is gathered from the user and how the results are returned to the user.

In the grocery bagging system, each item changed from an *unbagged* to a *bagged* state as the program worked through the bagging problem. The CFO system uses static and dynamic information differently. The definition of a frame, its procedural attachments, and heuristics constitute the system's static information. These things remain the same throughout the course of the program and from one execution of the program to another. However, each time the program is run, the user fills in what can be thought of as a fresh copy of the frame. This constitutes the system's dynamic information. Frame-based systems differentiate between a ''definition'' of a frame and an ''instance'' of that frame. Every instance has the same number and type of slots. All procedural attachments and heuristics apply equally to all instances. However, each instance has different values for its slots.

When it is invoked, therefore, the first thing CFO must do is retrieve a copy of the *cfo_frame* from the database:

    cfo_frame([Interest,Revenues,Expenses,Risk,Term,Investment])

After it retrieves the frame, CFO asks the questions associated with the *interest*, *revenues*, *expenses*, and *risk* slots and checks the user's answers against the valid values for those slots. These steps are part of a recursive loop (*bind_all*) performed on the list of slots that require a user's input.

    bind_all([ ],_).
    bind_all([S:V|Slots],I):-
        first_unbound_slot([S:V|Slots], I, Index),
        user_choose_value([S:V|Slots], Index),
        bind_all(Slots,Index).

The *first_unbound_slot* predicate recursively searches the list for those elements that are not yet filled in. The predicate succeeds if the *Val* argument is a variable. Otherwise, it skips over instantiated variables and tests whether the next element is a variable.

```
first_unbound_slot([Slot:Val|Slots]) :-
    var(Val), !.
first_unbound_slot([__|Slots]) :-
    first_unbound_slot(Slots).
```

When an unbound element is found, *bind_all* passes the list to a predicate called *user_choose_value*. It asks the question associated with the unbound slot and calls *get_ans* to fill in the slot with the user's answer.

```
user_choose_value([Slot:Val|Slots]) :-
    question(Slot,Q),
    write(Q),
    get_ans(Slot,Val,Q),
    !.
```

Get_ans reads the user's answer and checks that it is valid. If not, *get_ans* prints a message showing the valid values defined for the slot. It then asks the question again and allows the user to reenter the answer.

```
get_ans(Slot,Ans,Q) :-
    read(Ans),
    valdef(Slot,__,Ans), !.
get_ans(Slot,Ans,Q) :-
    write('Valid values for slot':Slot), nl,
    get_ans_aux(Slot,Q),
    get_ans(Slot,Ans,Q).

get_ans_aux(Slot,Q) :-
    valdef(Slot,Prompt,Def),
    tab(4), write(Prompt:Def), nl, fail.
get_ans_aux(Slot,Q) :-
    nl, write(Q).
```

Pruning the Solution Space

In any problem beyond the most trivial, you have to make certain decisions about how to prune the solution space. As the number of variables and the number of valid values that those variables can take on increase, the number of possible combinations grows so quickly that you soon have an unmanageable solution space. This phenomenon is called the "combinatorial explosion." The increase is not incremental. Rather, all possible values for all possible variables are combined.

In the case of the CFO problem, there are three possible values for *interest*, *expenses*, and *revenues*, four for *risk*, three for *term*, and four for *investment*. The size of this solution space is calculated by taking the product, as follows:

$$3 \times 3 \times 3 \times 4 \times 3 \times 4 = 1296$$

Luckily, of the 1,296 possible combinations, only 108 are valid. The rules for the CFO Advisor's inference engine remove all but those 108 solutions. Furthermore, the 108 possible solutions can be written with only seventeen rules. They define the valid combinations of values that the frame may hold. Finding a solution then requires only that the current instance of the frame match one of the patterns defined in a rule.

The inference engine's method for finding the correct rule is neither backward nor forward chaining. Applying the rules to an instance of the frame is as simple as unification. Because a rule can define a list of values for a slot, any one of which makes the rule valid, then the engine cannot rely completely on Prolog's unification scheme. It calls a predicate called *unify* to check that the value in a slot is a member of the list of values in the rule.

```
apply__rules(Trole:Tval,Froles) :-
      rule(Trole:Tval, FRole__list),
      unify(Froles,FRole__list).

unify([],[]).
unify([H:Val|T],[H1:Val1|T1]) :-
      member(Val,Val1),
      unify(T,T1).
```

CFO first applies its rules to determine the value of *term*. Then it applies the rules to determine the *investment*. This is done by adding two *apply__rules* goals to the main *cfo* predicate.

```
cfo :-
      cfo__frame([Interest,Revenues,Expenses,Risk,Term,Investment]),
      bind__all([Interest,Revenues,Expenses,Risk],1),
      apply__rules(Term,[Interest,Revenues,Expenses]),
      apply__rules(Investment,[Risk,Term]).
```

Explaining the Results of a Consultation

Given the filled-in frame, you can write an explanation of the answer that the system derived. Explanation facilities are usually more complex than the facility described here. For example, while eliciting information, many systems allow the user to ask "Why?" The system then presents an explanation of the goal that it is trying to prove with the current line of questioning. When an answer has been found, the user can ask "How?" The system then walks the line of reasoning back through the chain of goals that it proved in order to arrive at the solution. However, constructing a more comprehensive explanation facility is not much more complex than is described here. That is, you define all the pieces of the explanation and the ways in which the system can put the pieces together.

Explanation text is another procedural attachment to a slot. If the pieces of the explanation text are carefully constructed, they can be put together into one coherent statement.

```
explain(interest : down,
        'Because you expect interest rates to head down, you
        would normally want to invest long term, thereby locking
        in current high rates.').
explain(interest : up,
        'Because you expect interest rates to head up, you would
        normally want to invest short term, thereby allowing you
        to reinvest later at higher rates.').
explain(interest : unchanged,
        'Because you are expecting interest rates to remain
        unchanged, they do not influence the term of your
        investment.').

explain(revenues : - ,
        'As your revenues may be lower than anticipated, ').
explain(revenues : + ,
        'As your revenues should be higher than anticipated, ').
explain(revenues : = ,
        'As your revenues are not expected to diverge much
        from budget, ').

explain(expenses : - ,
        'and your expenses may be lower than anticipated, ').
```

explain(expenses : + ,
     'and your expenses should be higher than anticipated, ').
explain(expenses : = ,
     'and your expenses are not expected to deviate much
     from budget, ').

explain(term : short,
     'staying short term is advisable.
     Because the recommended term is short').
explain(term : medium,
     'play it safe and invest medium term.
     As the recommended term is medium').
explain(term : long,
     'long term is a good strategy.
     Because the recommended term is long').

explain(risk : low,
     'and you prefer a low risk,
     a good investment vehicle for you ').
explain(risk : low – medium,
     'and you prefer a low to medium risk,
     a good investment vehicle for you ').
explain(risk : medium – high,
     'and you prefer a medium to high risk,
     a good investment vehicle for you ').
explain(risk : high,
     'and you prefer a high risk,
     a good investment vehicle for you ').

explain(investment : usgov,
     'is (virtually no risk) U.S. Government and Treasury
     securities.').
explain(investment : obligs,
     'is low risk obligations of large banks or large
     corporations.').
explain(investment : offshore,
     'is offshore banks or Eurodollars. (Low risk short term;
     and medium risk for longer terms.)').
explain(investment : unrated,
     'is high risk, high yield unrated corporate bonds or CDs
     issued by a Savings & Loan institution.').

An explanation is built by retrieving the appropriate pieces of text. Then the pieces of text are passed to a predicate that prints them in the proper order.

```
get_explain([Interest,Revenues,Expenses,Risk, Term,Investment]) :-
    nl,
    explain(_,Interest,I_Exp),
    explain(_,Revenues,Revs_Exp),
    explain(_,Expenses,Exp_Exp),
    explain(_,Risk,Risk_Exp),
    explain(_,Term,T_Exp),
    explain(_,Investment,Inv_Exp),
    show_explanation([I_Exp,Revs_Exp,Exp_Exp,T_Exp,
        Risk_Exp,Inv_Exp]).

show_explanation([]).
show_explanation([H|T]) :-
    write(H), nl,
    show_explanation(T).
```

With a minimal explanation facility in hand, the CFO program can give advice in this way:

```
?- cfo.
What do you expect interest rates to do within the next year? up.
How much might your actual revenues diverge from expectations? up.

Valid values for slot : revenues
    Exceed expected (by more than 10%) :  +
    Shortfall (by more than 10%) :  -

How much might your actual revenues diverge from expectations?  + .
How much might your actual expenditures diverge from expectations?  + .
What is your tolerance for risk? low.

Because you expect interest rates to head up, you would
normally want to invest short term, thereby allowing you
to reinvest later at higher rates.
As your revenues should be higher than anticipated,
and your expenses should be higher than anticipated,
staying short term is advisable.
```

Because the recommended term is short
and you prefer a low risk,
a good investment vehicle for you
is low risk obligations of large banks or large
corporations.

Dealing with Uncertainty

In real life, experts cannot always form conclusions with absolute certainty. Expert systems would mislead their users if they were not aware of the uncertainty of some of their findings, too. For example, you would act differently if a system stated with a confidence factor of $+1$ that there is a leak in the cooling system of a nuclear power plant as opposed to its saying with a confidence factor of $-.5$ that that same condition exists. In the first case, you would want to begin evacuation, in the second, you would want to perform some tests on the cooling system before becoming alarmed. In order to be used responsibly, expert systems must be able to communicate a confidence factor so that the user can judge the system's findings.

There are three basic approaches to confidence factors, each with a slightly different meaning:

- The confidence factor can designate the relative strength of a conclusion, ranked as a number between 0 and 1 or between -1 and 1. This approach will be called "standard;" it is the method employed by the Mycin system.

- Some researchers feel it is more natural to express confidence using quantifiers such as "some" and "most" rather than numbers. This approach is based on "fuzzy logic." Like the standard method, the confidence factor calculated with fuzzy logic expresses the relative strength of a conclusion. Internally, however, these quantifiers can be mapped to numbers, manipulated by the system, and then translated back to quantifiers to report the result.

- A confidence factor can define the statistical probability that a certain conclusion is correct. This approach is based on Bayesian probability. Like the standard method, this method expresses the confidence factor as a number between 0 and 1 or between -1 and 1. However, the number indicates a percentage of accuracy rather than a relative strength.

Confidence factors can occur in two places. First, they can be applied to the information that the system needs in order to form a conclusion. Second, they can be applied to the conclusions. The expert system must combine the confidence factors at different stages during the execution of a goal. These are the steps it must follow:

1. Determine the confidence factors of the antecedents (subgoals) and combine them.
2. Determine the confidence factor of the conclusion and combine it with the combined confidence factor of the antecedents.
3. Determine whether this conclusion occurs more than once and combine the confidence factors of the conclusions.

This section will examine confidence factors within the context of the rule to determine how many car lengths drivers should keep between themselves and the car in front.

Combining the Confidence Factors of the Antecedents

A well-known rule of thumb states that drivers should keep one car length behind the car in front of them for every 10 miles per hour that the car is traveling. In Prolog, the rule can be written:

```
car__lengths(Lengths) :-
    speed(X),
    Lengths is X / 10.
```

However, if a car's brakes are not good or if the speedometer is not accurate, the result of this rule is not reliable. In an expert system, a user can apply a confidence factor to an antecedent (or subgoal) to indicate the degree of confidence in the information being supplied. For example, to indicate speed, the condition of the car's brakes, and the degree of confidence in the accuracy of the information, these facts could be supplied:

```
speed(63/0.9).
brakes(good/0.8).
```

Both of these facts must be considered when applying the *car__lengths* rule. How do you calculate the confidence factor of a conclusion based on these two subgoals? Depending upon the method for inexact reasoning, they are combined in one of the ways shown in table 5-1.

Table 5-1: Calculating the Confidence Factor of Antecedents

Method	Formula
Standard	Confidence factor of the conclusion is the minimum confidence factor of the antecedents.
Fuzzy	Confidence factor of the conclusion is the minimum confidence factor of the antecedents.
Bayesian	Confidence factor of the conclusion is the product of the confidence factors of the antecedents.

In Prolog, the confidence factor for the *car__lengths* rule would be calculated as follows using standard or fuzzy logic:

```
car__lengths(Lengths,CF) :-
    speed(X/Cfx),
    brakes(good/Cfy),
    Lengths is X / 10,
    min(Cfx,Cfy,CF).

min(X,Y,X) :- X < Y.
min(X,Y,Y) :- Y < X.
min(X,X,X).
```

Using Bayesian probability, the confidence factor is calculated in this way:

```
car__lengths(Lengths,CF) :-
    speed(X/Cfx),
    brakes(good/Cfy),
    Lengths is X / 10,
    CF is Cfx * Cfy.
```

Calculating the Confidence Factor of a Conclusion

You can also assign a confidence factor to a conclusion as part of the definition of the rule. This confidence factor indicates how confident you are of the conclusion if the user is completely confident in the antecedents. For example, the head of the *car_lengths* rule can specify a confidence factor for the result (the *Lengths* argument) in this way:

```
car_lengths(Lengths/0.8,CF) :-
    .
    .
    .
```

When a conclusion defines a confidence factor, it must combine that number with the combined confidence factor of the antecedents, using one of the formulas in table 5-2.

Table 5-2: Calculating the Confidence Factor of a Conclusion

Method	Formula
Standard	Confidence factor of the conclusion is the product of the confidence factor of the rule and the combined confidence factor of the antecedents.
Fuzzy	Confidence factor of the conclusion is the confidence factor assigned to the rule.
Bayesian	Confidence factor of the conclusion is the product of the confidence factor of the rule and the combined confidence factor of the antecedents.

Using the standard method, the system would first take the minimum confidence factor of the antecedents and then multiply it times the confidence factor of the rule, as in:

```
car_lengths(Lengths/0.8,CF) :-
    speed(X/Cfx),
    brakes(good/Cfy),
    Lengths is X / 10,
    min(Cfx,Cfy,ACF),
    CF is 0.8 * ACF.
```

Using Bayesian probability, the system would first take the product of the antecedents and then multiply it times the confidence factor for the rule, as in:

```
car__lengths(Lengths/0.8,CF) :-
    speed(X/Cfx),
    brakes(good/Cfy),
    Lengths is X / 10,
    ACF is Cfx * Cfy,
    CF is 0.8 * ACF.
```

For fuzzy logic, the confidence factor of the conclusion is the confidence factor assigned to the rule. The system ignores the confidence factor of the antecedents:

```
car__lengths(Lengths/0.8,0.8) :-
    speed(X/__),
    brakes(good/__),
    Lengths is X / 10.
```

Combining the Confidence Factors of Multiple Conclusions

More than one rule can draw the same conclusion and the same rule can draw the same conclusion more than once. The confidence factors of the conclusions should be combined to give an overall confidence factor. Multiple conclusions would not occur when calculating the number of car lengths to keep between one car and the car in front, but they do occur in more sophisticated systems.

To deal with multiple conclusions, the expert system should record in the database the confidence factor of each conclusion. Then, whenever the system draws that conclusion again, the new confidence factor can be combined with the old confidence factor. For example, the *check__cf* predicate looks in the database for the confidence factor of some *Goal*. If one if found, the old confidence factor is combined with the new and the result is placed in the database. If a confidence factor is not already stored in the database, then it is simply recorded.

```
check__cf(Goal,CF) :-
    recorded(Goal,X,__),
    combine(CF,X,NewCf),
    replace(cf,NewCf).
```

```
check__cf(Goal,CF) :-
    recorda(Goal,CF,__).
```

The confidence factors of conclusions are combined with the formulas shown in table 5-3, depending on the method you use.

Table 5-3: Calculating the Overall Confidence Factor

Method	Formula
Standard	Overall confidence factor is the maximum confidence factor for the conclusion.
Fuzzy	Overall confidence factor is the maximum confidence factor for the conclusion.
Bayesian	Overall confidence factor is (1 – Old Confidence Factor) * New Confidence Factor + Old Confidence Factor.

These formulas define the *combine* predicate that was called in *check__cf* earlier. For both standard and fuzzy logic, the *combine* predicate would determine the maximum of the two confidence factors:

```
combine(CF,X,NewCf) :-
    max(CF,X,NewCf).

    max(X,Y,X) :- X > Y.
    max(X,Y,Y) :- Y > X.
    max(X,X,X).
```

For Bayesian probability, *combine* would be written like this:

```
combine(CF,X,NewCf) :-
    NewCf is (1 — CF) * X + CF.
```

Finally, in systems that allow negative confidence factors, multiple conclusions may produce both positive and negative results. In this case, the formulas in table 5-4 are applied.

Table 5-4: Combining Positive and Negative Confidence Factors

Method	Formula
Standard	Overall confidence factor is the sum of the positive and negative confidence factors.
Fuzzy	Overall confidence factor is the confidence factor having the largest absolute value.
Bayesian	Overall confidence factor is the sum of the positive and negative confidence factors.

To handle this case using fuzzy logic, you would add two clauses to the beginning of the *combine* predicate. These clauses check to see if either confidence factor is negative and then return the confidence factor with the larger absolute value:

```
combine(Cf1,Cf2,Cf1) :-
    ( Cf1 < 0 ; Cf2 < 0 ),
    abs(Cf1,Abs1),
    abs(Cf2,Abs2),
    max(Abs1,Abs2,Abs1).
combine(Cf1,Cf2,Cf2) :-
    ( Cf1 < 0 ; Cf2 < 0 ),
    abs(Cf1,Abs1),
    abs(Cf2,Abs2),
    max(Abs1,Abs2,Abs2).
```

For standard and Bayesian probability, you would add the following clause to the beginning of the *combine* predicate:

```
combine(Cf1,Cf2,CF) :-
    ( Cf1 < 0 ; Cf2 < 0 ),
    CF is Cf1 + Cf2
```

The *lengths* predicate can be executed within a fail loop to collect all instances of the conclusion and to combine their confidence factors, like this:

```
find_lengths :-
    lengths(X/CF),
    check_cf(lengths,CF),
    fail.
find_lengths.
```

Determining Which Method To Use

Standard and fuzzy logic favor the strongest rule and the weakest conclusion. That is, within the antecedents, they pick the strongest rule; within the conclusions, they pick the weakest conclusion, as illustrated in figure 5-5. In your expert system, if negative information tends to override positive information, then standard or fuzzy logic methods are more appropriate.

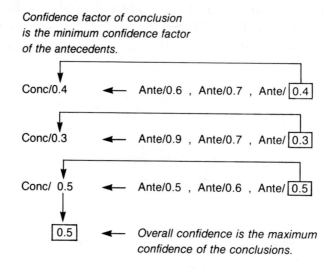

Figure 5-5: Picking the Strongest/Weakest Conclusion with Standard and Fuzzy Logic

With Bayesian probability, confidence factors accumulate, as shown in figure 5-6. The Bayesian method is more appropriate when negative information tends only to moderate positive information.

Confidence factor of conclusion is the
product of the confidence factors
of the antecedents.

Conc/ 0.168 ← Ante/0.6, Ante/0.7, Ante/0.4

Conc/ 0.15 ← Ante/0.5, Ante/0.6, Ante/0.5

0.293 ← (1 — 0.168) * 0.15 + 0.168

Conc/ 0.189 ← Ante/0.9, Ante/0.7, Ante/0.3

0.426 ← overall confidence factor is
(1 — 0.293) * 0.189 + 0.293.

Figure 5-6: Accumulating Confidence Factors with Bayesian Probability

It is not clear that the result of any of these methods is a practical application of the theories upon which they are based. For example, the confidence factor resulting from Bayesian probability methods cannot be considered an accurate statistical measure. However, it has been shown with the Mycin project
that although the actual numbers may not be accurate, the ranking of conclusions based on these numbers is accurate. That is, if a number of conclusions
can be drawn, each having a different confidence factor, then the conclusion
with the highest confidence factor is the best conclusion, the conclusion with the
lowest is the worst, and the others fall between in the order of their confidence
factors. Therefore, confidence factors are most practical as a way to rank conclusions rather than as an exact measure.

Summary

Conventional applications deal with complete information. They solve problems
by applying algorithms to known values. Their solutions are absolute. Many
problems are not so clear cut. We often deal with information that is incomplete. We solve problems using rules of thumb, which are not as easily translated into algorithms, and we produce solutions about which we are not abso-
lutely certain.

Expert systems attempt to represent knowledge in terms that are similar to those of human experts:

- Production systems describe knowledge in terms of if-then rules.
- Frames represent chunks of data, procedural attachments to each of the slots in the frame, and heuristics for deriving information.
- Semantic networks describe both objects and their relationships to other objects.
- Taxonomies organize chunks of information into hierarchies, allowing the system to use the semantic richness of frames while being able to describe the relationships between those frames as in a semantic network.

The inference engine attempts to mimic our methods for solving problems:

- Backward-chaining systems begin with a conclusion and try to prove the subgoals that support that conclusion. They tend to narrow down the possible paths that the system can take as information becomes known. Backward chaining lends itself to diagnosis.
- Forward-chaining systems begin with a set of proven subgoals and then propose those conclusions that can be proven by the subgoals. They tend to produce alternatives based on the paths that could possibly be taken by the system. Forward chaining lends itself to planning.
- Often, simple problems can be solved using unification. Unification is appropriate to use when a fixed number of variables can occur in a limited number of combinations.

The expert system developer must choose the knowledge representation scheme and inference technique that best suits the application and then choose the implementation techniques that are most appropriate.

Prolog is well suited for writing rule-based systems and for finding solutions using backward-chaining, as shown in the first expert system example in this chapter. The second example showed how Prolog can be used for writing frame-based systems and for finding solutions using unification. Finally, three methods for calculating confidence factors were discussed.

It is more common, however, to write expert systems with the aid of an expert system shell. An expert system shell simplifies the job of developing an expert system. The shell determines how information is stored internally, it determines what inference techniques are used, and it provides methods for calculating confidence factors. An expert system shell is the subject of the next chapter.

6

An Expert System Shell

Most expert systems have a knowledge base in which to store their expertise, an inference engine to determine what rules to apply and when, a user interface to determine both how information is obtained from the user and how it is given back to the user, and methods for dealing with uncertainty. Because they share these components, it is possible to create general-purpose "shells" with which to build expert systems. Chapter 5 discussed some of the different models for expert systems development. Few expert system shells support all possible techniques. When building or buying a shell, you should be aware of the features you will need and make sure they are provided by the shell.

This chapter describes how to build a rule-based expert system shell similar to M1^{TM} which was developed at Teknowledge, Inc. Though the sample shell described in this chapter does not have all of the features of M1, it does provide many similar features.

The expert system shell shown here defines a language for describing knowledge. This rule language allows you to express knowledge as production rules, as the objects manipulated by the rules, and as a top-level goal defining the objective of the expert system. The shell translates these rules into Prolog clauses.

The shell provides an inference engine to supervise the execution of the rules. It uses backward chaining to satisfy the top-level goal. The engine also determines how and when information is requested from the user. When it needs information in order to satisy the goal, the engine first checks to see if the necessary information is already stored in the database. If not, it asks the user to supply the information.

Prolog Programming

The rule language allows you to apply confidence factors to a conclusion. The engine allows the user to apply confidence factors to the antecedents. Confidence factors are combined by the engine using Bayesian probability (see chapter 5).

Expert system shells provide a convenient framework upon which to build an expert system. To develop a system with a shell, you load the knowledge base with specific information required by the system, rules for forming conclusions, and questions for the consultation. The shell handles how the rules are applied, how confidence factors are combined, and the other internal workings of the system. In this way, expert system shells allow you to concentrate on what the system needs to know rather than on how the system will handle that information internally. For this reason, when using an expert system shell, you often do not need to know the underlying programming language.

Defining a Rule Language

A rule language allows the expert system developer to describe the contents of the expert system's knowledge base. The rule language for the shell discussed here accepts only three types of statements. The first is the definition of the rules for drawing conclusions. The second is the definition of the objects manipulated by those rules. The third is the definition of the top-level goal, which states the objective of the expert system.

Rule Statements

Rule statements define the conditions that need to be proven in order for a solution to be true. The conditions that need to be proven are called the antecedents; the solution that is supported by the antecedents is called the conclusion.

The antecedents give the name of one or more objects and specific values for each object. Antecedents look like Prolog goals in that they have a name followed by some number of arguments enclosed in parentheses. When more than one antecedent is needed to form a conclusion, they can be separated by a comma (for conjunction) or a semicolon (for disjunction). The antecedents are separated from the conclusion by the $->$ symbol.

The conclusion gives the name of an object and a value for that object. The conclusion has the effect of instantiating the object to that value when each of the antecedents is proven true.

For example, the following rule states that if an object called *power* has the value *no*, then the *problem* is "Plug in the machine and try again."

```
power(no)
— > problem('Plug in the machine and try again.').
```

More than one conclusion can be based on the same set of antecedents. Multiple conclusions are separated by commas. For example, the following rule states that if there is power to the computer, if the cursor does not appear, and if the brightness knob is turned up, then one of two problems may be the cause. Either the monitor connection is loose or the picture tube has gone bad.

```
power(yes),
cursor(no),
brightness(yes)
— > problem('The monitor connection may be loose.'),
problem('The picture tube may be bad.').
```

The rule language also allows the expert system developer to assign a confidence factor to a conclusion. Confidence factors are added to the conclusion as a backslash followed by a number between 0 and 1, where 0 indicates complete uncertainty and 1 indicates complete certainty. When no confidence factor is given, then the system assumes a confidence factor of 1. The confidence factor that is assigned to a conclusion is the highest confidence that the conclusion can ever have. For example, the following confidence factors can be applied to the previous rule, as follows:

```
power(yes),
cursor(no),
brightness(yes)
— > problem('The monitor connection may be loose.')/0.9,
    problem('The picture tube may be bad.')/0.1.
```

This rule states that given the conditions *power(yes), cursor(no),* and *brightness(yes)*, the conclusion that 'The monitor may be loose' will be correct 90 percent of the time; the conclusion that 'The picture tube may be bad' will be correct 10 percent of the time.

Some shells support negative confidence factors. Negative confidence factors can indicate the confidence with which you can state that a condition is false in a given situation. Refer to chapter 5 for methods of combining negative confidence factors.

Question Statements

The rule language also allows the expert system developer to define the objects that are manipulated by the rules. Each object must have a name, a list of values that it can have, and a question for the system to ask if its value is not known. All this information is defined in a question statement.

For example, the previous rules refer to the objects named *power*, *cursor*, and *brightness*. These objects can be defined in this way:

```
question(power, [yes,no]) =
'Is the computer plugged in?'.

question(cursor, [yes,no]) =
'Does the cursor appear in the top right corner of the screen?'.

question(brightness, [yes,no]) =
'Is the brightness knob turned up?'.
```

The Top-level Goal

Every expert system developed with this shell requires one and only one "top-level goal." This goal defines the objective of the system. In all the examples so far, the conclusion is an answer to a *problem*. The top-level goal for these rules is defined as:

```
goal = problem.
```

Translating the Rule Language into Prolog

A rule compiler translates statements in the rule language into Prolog. The rule compiler assumes that the rules have been placed in a text file. It reads each rule contained in the file and produces one of three types of clauses, corresponding to the three types of statement. This is how the rule compiler is written.

The *rule_compile* predicate opens the file that contains the rules. Within a repeat/fail loop, it reads a rule and translates it into Prolog. When the end of file is reached, it closes the file and performs some bookkeeping operations on the database. In this way, *rule__compile* controls the overall actions of the program.

```
rule__compile(File) :-
    open(H, File, r),
    repeat,
    read(H,X),
    rule__compile__p(X),
    close(H),
    !,
    rule__compile__epilog.
```

The *rule__compile__p* predicate defines how each type of rule is translated into Prolog. The first clause detects the *end__of__file* marker and terminates the repeat/fail loop.

```
rule__compile__p(end__of__file).
```

The second clause translates *question* definitions, adding the resulting clauses to the database and recording the name of the predicate under a key called *rule__compiled*.

```
rule__compile__p(question(Name, Legalvals) = Question) :-
    NameTerm =.. [Name,X,CF],
    assertz((NameTerm :- question(Question,Legalvals,X,CF))),
    recordz(rule__compiled, Name, __),
    !, fail.
```

In this way, a term of the form *question(Name, Legalvals) = Question* is translated into the clause:

```
Name(X,CF) :- question(Question,Legalvals,X,CF).
```

Translation of the top-level goal is handled by the following *rule__compile__p* clause:

```
rule__compile__p(Goal = Obj) :-
    GoalTerm =.. [Goal,X,CF],
```

```
      ObjTerm  = .. [Obj,X,CF],
      assertz((GoalTerm :- ObjTerm)),
      recordz(rule__compiled, Goal, __),
      !, fail.
```

The previous clause translates a top-level goal into the following:

```
goal(X,CF) :- Goal(X,CF).
```

Rule statements are more difficult to compile, as they have both antecedents and conclusions. Antecedents make up the body of the clause. They are
translated into goals to find the value for a question. If the rule consists of more
than one antecedent, additional goals are added to keep track of the current
value of the confidence factor.

Conclusions are translated into the head of a clause, where the conclusion's
name is the functor and its value is an argument to the functor. Additional
translations are made for conclusions having a confidence factor. The confidence
factor of the conclusion is added to the head of the clause and a goal is added to
the body to multiply the confidence factor of the antecedents by the confidence
factor of the conclusion.

The name of each clause is recorded under the *rule__compiled* key after it
has been asserted into the database.

```
      rule__compile__p((Antecedents— >Conclusions)) :-
          xlat__ante(Antecedents, P__Ante, CF),
          xlat__conc(Conclusions, P__Ante, CF),
          !, fail.
      xlat__ante((A1,A2), (P__A1,P__A2), CF) :- !,
          xlat__one__ante(A1, P__A1, Out),
          xlat__rest__ante(A2, P__A2, Out, CF).
      xlat__ante(A, P__A, CF) :-
          xlat__one__ante(A, P__A, CF).

      xlat__rest__ante((A1,A2), (P__A1,Temp2 is In*Temp1,P__A2), In, Out) :- !,
          xlat__one__ante(A1, P__A1, Temp1),
          xlat__rest__ante(A2, P__A2, Temp2, Out).
      xlat__rest__ante(A, (P__A,Out is In*Temp), In, Out) :-
          xlat__one__ante(A, P__A, Temp).
```

```
xlat__one__ante((A1;A2), (P__A1;P__A2), Out) :- !,
    xlat__ante(A1, P__A1, Out),
    xlat__ante(A2, P__A2, Out).
xlat__one__ante(Term, find(Atom,Val,Out), Out) :-
    Term =.. [Atom, Val].


xlat__conc((C1,C2), P__A, Out) :-
    xlat__one__conc(C1, P__A, Out),
    xlat__conc(C2, P__A, Out).
xlat__conc(C, P__A, Out) :-
    xlat__one__conc(C, P__A, Out).


xlat__one__conc(Term/CF, P__A, Out) :- !,
    Term =.. [H,Val],
    RealTerm =.. [H,Val,Out1],
    assertz((RealTerm :- P__A, Out1 is Out*CF)),
    recordatom(H).
xlat__one__conc(Term, P__A, Out) :-
    Term =.. [H,Val],
    RealTerm =.. [H,Val,Out],
    assertz((RealTerm:-P__A)),
    recordatom(H).


recordatom(Atom) :- recorded(rule__consulted, Atom, __), !.
recordatom(Atom) :- recordz(rule__consulted, Atom, __).
```

The *rule__compile__epilog* predicate completes the translation process by generating a *findaux* clause for each of the objects defined in the system and it writes the Prolog code to a file named RULES.OUT.

```
rule__compile__epilog :-
    create(H, 'rules.out'),
    dup(H, 1),
    output__goalpreds,
    listing(findaux/3),
    close(H),
    open(H1, con, w),
    dup(H1, 1).
```

```
output_goalpreds :-
    recorded(rule_consulted, Atom, _),
    Goal  = .. [Atom,Value,CF],
    assertz((findaux(Atom,Value,CF):-Goal)),
    listing(Atom/2),
    nl,
    fail.
output_goalpreds.
```

The result of the rule compiler is a collection of Prolog clauses that can be executed by the inference engine.

Finding the Solution to a Problem

The inference engine controls the overall execution of the expert system. In particular, the engine controls the order in which clauses are executed, beginning with the top-level goal and working through the solution tree in depth-first order. It controls what information is requested from the user, asking questions if values for an object are not already known. It also controls the calculation of confidence factors, using Bayesian probability.

The *go* predicate attempts to satisfy the top-level goal. The top-level goal depends on one or more antecedents. By calling the top-level goal, the engine starts to search the solution space. When the top-level goal has been satisfied, *go* writes out the answer and the confidence factor for the answer. The *go* predicate is written as a fail loop so that all solutions can be found.

```
go :-
    find(goal, Value, Conf),
    nl, write(value  =  Value), nl,
    write(confidence  =  Conf), nl,
    fail.
go.
```

Within *go*, the *find* predicate performs most of the work in finding the solution. First, the predicate checks to see if a value for the object is known. If so, it returns the value and the confidence factor for the object.

```
find(Atom, Value, CF) :-
    recorded(Atom,__,__),
    !,
    recorded(Atom, found(Value,CF), __).
```

If a value is not known, the second *find* clause is executed. It uses *findaux* to ask the question associated with the object and it uses *add_evidence* to add the value to the database. This *find* clause executes within a fail loop so that all possible values for the object are generated.

```
find(Atom, Value, CF) :-
    findaux(Atom, V, CFTemp),
    add_evidence(Atom, V, CFTemp),
    fail.
```

After this *find* clause breaks out of the fail loop, the next *find* clause retrieves the object's value from the database, if one was recorded.

```
find(Atom, Value, CF) :-
    recorded(Atom,__,__),
    !,
    recorded(Atom, found(Value,CF), __).
```

The last *find* clause handles the case in which no value can be found; the value is *unknown* and it has a confidence factor of 1.0.

```
find(Atom, unknown, 1.0) :-
    recordz(Atom, found(unknown,1.0), __).
```

Now take a closer look at the way goals are executed by the second *find* clause. Remember that for each rule, the rule compiler generated a *findaux* clause to invoke the rule, for example:

```
findaux(goal,A,B) :-
    goal(A,B).
findaux(problem,A,B) :-
    problem(A,B).
findaux(power,A,B) :-
    power(A,B).
```

The clauses that *findaux* invokes can be the top-level goal called *goal*, the *problem* goal which is the conclusion that the system is looking for, or a goal associated with an antecedent, such as the *power* goal. It is interesting to see how each type of goal is executed by *find* and *findaux*.

Executing the Top-level Goal

The rule compiler translated the top-level goal into the following clause:

```
goal(A,B) :- problem(A,B).
```

Therefore, when *findaux* invokes *goal*, it simply invokes the *problem* predicate.

Finding the Conclusion

The *problem* predicate is a series of clauses defining the solution to the problem and its confidence factor, depending on the value of the clause's antecedents. For example, the first *problem* clause is defined as:

```
problem('Plug in the machine and try again.',A) :-
      find(power,no,A).
```

This clause invokes *find* to determine if the value of *power* is *no*. At this point in the program, the *find* predicate is involved in a recursive loop.

Finding the Antecedents

If a value for *power* is not recorded in the database, the second *find* clause succeeds. This time, *findaux* invokes the *power* predicate, which is defined as follows:

```
power(A,B) :-
      question('Is the computer plugged in?',[yes,no],A,B).
```

Questions are asked and answers are read by the predicate called *question*. When it reads an answer, *question* checks that the answer is a good answer, where a good answer is a member of the list of valid values or the value *unknown*.

The user can enter more than one answer to a question. The system must check each answer. When it knows that all answers are good, it returns them to the head of the clause with *allanswers*.

```
question(Question, Legalvals, X, CF) :-
    write(Question),
    tab(1),
    read(Y),
    goodanswer(Y, Legalvals), !,
    allanswers(Y, X, CF).
question(Question, Legalvals, X, CF) :-
    write('All values must be in '),
    write(Legalvals),
    nl,
    question(Question, Legalvals, X, CF).

goodanswer((A,B), Legalvals) :- !,
    goodanswer(A, Legalvals),
    goodanswer(B, Legalvals).
goodanswer(Y/__, Legalvals) :- !,
    goodanswer(Y, Legalvals).
goodanswer(Y, Legalvals) :-
    (
        member(Y, Legalvals)
    ;
        Y = unknown
    ),
    !.

allanswers((A,B), X, CF) :- !,
    (
        allanswers(A, X, CF)
    ;
        allanswers(B, X, CF)
    ).
allanswers(X/CF, X, CF) :- !.
allanswers(X, X, 1.0).
```

Calculating Confidence Factors

As the inference engine collects answers, it calculates confidence factors using the formulas for Bayesian probability. Confidence factors are calculated in this way:

- As it collects answers, the inference engine multiplies the confidence factors of each of the antecedents. If the user does not supply a confidence factor to an antecedent, then the system assumes a confidence factor of 1.

- The combined confidence factor of the antecedents is then multiplied by the confidence factor of the conclusion.

- If the confidence factor of some goal is A, then it is possible to say that $1 - A$ amount of confidence remains. When a new confidence factor that must go into A is found, the overall confidence factor is calculated with the formula:

  $$A + NewCF * (1.0 - A)$$

  The inference engine applies this formula when more than one clause determines the value of an object.

In the following rule, two conclusions can be drawn from the same set of antecedents. Ninety percent of the time, the *problem* is 'The monitor connection is loose'; 10 percent of the time, the *problem* is 'The picture tube has burned out'. The confidence factors associated with these rules indicate the probability of the cause of the problem. No matter what the confidence factor of the antecedents may be, the confidence factor for the conclusions will never be higher than these values.

```
power(on),
cursor(no),
brightness(yes)
—> problem('The monitor connection may be loose.')/0.9,
    problem('the picture tube may be bad.')/0.1.
```

To calculate the overall confidence factor for these conclusions, the system must find the confidence of *power* and *cursor* by asking the questions "Is the computer plugged in?" and "Does the cursor appear at the top right corner of the screen?" The confidence factors of these two objects are multiplied together.

Then, the confidence factor for *brightness* is found. This is multiplied by the previous confidence factor.

The *problem* clause generated by the rule compiler illustrates how the product of the confidence factors for the antecedents is calculated. That is, *B* and *C* are the confidence factors of *power* and *cursor*; *D* is their product. *F* is the product of *D* and the confidence factor of *brightness*. *F* is then multiplied by 0.9 to give the confidence of the conclusion 'The monitor may be loose.' It is multiplied by 0.1 to give the confidence of the conclusion 'The picture tube may be bad.'

```
problem('The monitor connection may be loose.',A) :-
    find(power,yes,B),
    find(cursor,no,C),
    D is B * C,
    find(brightness,yes,E),
    F is D * E,
    A is F * 0.5.
problem('The picture tube may be bad.',A) :-
    find(power,yes,B),
    find(cursor,no,C),
    D is B * C,
    find(brightness,yes,E),
    F is D * E,
    A is F * 0.5.
```

Within the second *find* clause, *add_evidence* combines the confidence factors when more than one set of antecedents prove the same conclusion.

```
add_evidence(Atom, Value, CFNew) :-
    recorded(Atom, found(Value,CFOld), Ref), !,
    CFMerge is CFOld + CFNew * (1.0 - CFOld),
    replace(Ref, found(Value,CFMerge)).
```

A second *add_evidence* clause adds the value to the database when only one set of antecedents exists for a conclusion:

```
add_evidence(Atom, Value, CFNew) :-
    recordz(Atom, found(Value,CFNew), _).
```

Using the Shell

The rule language, the rule compiler, and the inference engine are all that is necessary for building an expert system. The first expert system developed here will be small and simple in order to demonstrate the basic features of the shell. It will diagnose problems that someone may have when trying to boot up a personal computer. The "PC Expert" walks the user through a set of questions to try to determine the cause of the problem. It tries to locate the problem by asking questions such as "Is the computer plugged in?" or "Does the light at drive C come on?" It then suggests what the cause of the problem may be, such as "Your boot disk may be corrupted," or it suggests a solution, such as "Turn up the brightness knob and try again." The solution space looks like the decision tree in figure 6-1.

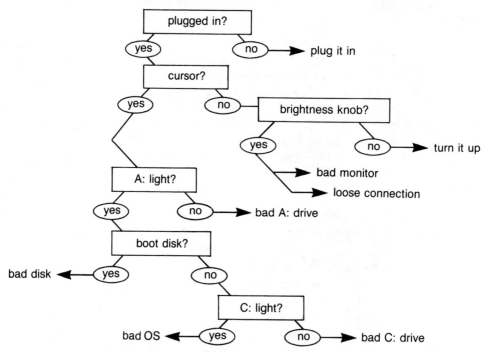

Figure 6-1: Decision Tree for PC Expert

Rules for PC Expert

You can define the entire decision tree for the PC Expert with only seven rules. In the PC Expert, the objects named *power, cursor, brightness, a_drive, a_boot,* and *c_drive* define the antecedents. In any rule, these objects have one of the values *yes* or *no*. The object named *problem* forms the conclusion. When the values of the antecedents are matched to a rule, the *problem* becomes instantiated. For example, if the object named *power* has the value *no*, then *problem* becomes instantiated to 'Plug in the machine and try again.'

```
% Rule 1
power(no)
— > problem('Plug in the machine and try again.').

% Rule 2
power(yes),
cursor(no),
brightness(no)
— > problem('Turn up the brightness knob and try again.').

% Rule 3
power(yes),
cursor(no),
brightness(yes)
— > problem('The monitor connection may be loose.')/0.9,
    problem('The picture tube may be bad.')/0.1.

% Rule 4
power(yes),
cursor(yes),
a__drive(no)
— > problem('You have a problem with your A drive.')/0.8.

% Rule 5
power(yes),
cursor(yes),
a__drive(yes),
a__boot(yes)
— > problem('Your boot disk may be corrupted.').

% Rule 6
power(yes),
cursor(yes),
a__drive(yes),
a__boot(no),
```

```
   c__drive(no)
  —> problem('You have a problem with your C drive.').
```

```
% Rule 7
power(yes),
cursor(yes),
a__drive(yes),
a__boot(no),
c__drive(yes)
—> problem('The bootup procedures are not installed on your C drive.')/0.7.
```

For each of the objects that form the antecedents, you must also define a *question*. The *question* consists of the name of the object, a list of valid values for the object, and the wording of a question to ask when no value is known. Each of the objects in the PC Expert can have one of two values, either *yes* or *no*.

```
question(power, [yes,no])  =
'Is the computer plugged in?'.
```

```
question(cursor, [yes,no])  =
'Does the cursor appear in the top right corner of the screen?'.
```

```
question(brightness, [yes,no])  =
'Is the brightness knob turned up?'.
```

```
question(a__drive, [yes,no])  =
'After waiting a few moments, does the light at disk drive A come on?'.
```

```
question(a__boot, [yes,no])  =
'Is a boot disk in drive A?'.
```

```
question(c__drive, [yes,no])  =
'Does the light at disk drive C come on?'.
```

A top-level goal states the object for which the system must find an answer. In this example, the system must try to find the cause of the user's problem. You would write the top-level goal as:

```
goal  = problem.
```

The rules cannot be executed until they are translated into Prolog by the rule compiler.

Compiling the Rules

If you place the rules for the PC Expert in a file named DIAGNOSE.RUL, you can translate the rules into Prolog by calling *rule_compile* like this:

```
?- rule_compile('diagnose.rul').
```

The top-level *goal* determines the value and confidence factors for the *problem*. It is translated into the following clause:

```
goal(A,B) :-
    problem(A,B).
```

Each *problem* clause is defined as one or more *find* goals to locate the value of an object, such as *power* or *brightness*, and to calculate the confidence factor for the answer.

```
problem('Plug in the machine and try again.',A) :-
    find(power,no,A).
problem('Turn up the brightness knob and try again.',A) :-
    find(power,yes,B),
    find(cursor,no,C),
    D is B * C,
    find(brightness,no,E),
    A is D * E.
problem('The monitor connection may be loose.',A) :-
    find(power,yes,B),
    find(cursor,no,C),
    D is B * C,
    find(brightness,yes,E),
    F is D * E,
    A is F * 0.9.
problem('The picture tube may be bad.',A) :-
    find(power,yes,B),
    find(cursor,no,C),
    D is B * C,
    find(brightness,yes,E),
```

```
        F is D * E,
        A is F * 0.1.
    problem('You have a problem with your A drive.',A) :-
        find(power,yes,B),
        find(cursor,yes,C),
        D is B * C,
        find(a_drive,no,E),
        F is D * E,
        A is F * 0.8.
    problem('Your boot disk may be corrupted.',A) :-
        find(power,yes,B),
        find(cursor,yes,C),
        D is B * C,
        find(a_drive,yes,E),
        F is D * E,
        find(a_boot,yes,G),
        A is F * G.
    problem('You have a problem with your C drive.',A) :-
        find(power,yes,B),
        find(cursor,yes,C),
        D is B * C,
        find(a_drive,yes,E),
        F is D * E,
        find(a_boot,no,G),
        H is F * G,
        find(c_drive,no,I),
        A is H * I.
    problem('The bootup procedures are not installed on your C drive.',A) :-
        find(power,yes,B),
        find(cursor,yes,C),
        D is B * C,
        find(a_drive,yes,E),
        F is D * E,
        find(a_boot,no,G),
        H is F * G,
        find(c_drive,yes,I),
        J is H * I,
        A is J * 0.7.
```

The *question* statements are translated into predicates with the same name as the object being defined and with two arguments. The first argument is the value that is given to the object; the second is its confidence factor. The body of each clause contains a call to a predicate named *question*, which finds the value of the object.

```
power(A,B) :-
      question('Is the computer plugged in?',[yes,no],A,B).

cursor(A,B):-
      question('Does the cursor appear in the top right corner of the screen?',
      [yes,no],A,B).

brightness(A,B) :-
      question('Is the brightness knob turned up?', [yes,no],
      A,B).

a__drive(A,B) :-
      question('After waiting a few moments, does the light at
      disk drive A come on?',[yes,no],A,B).

a__boot(A,B) :-
      question('Is a boot disk in drive A?',[yes,no],A,B).

c__drive(A,B):-
      question('Does the light at disk drive C come on?',
      [yes,no], A,B).
```

Finally, a *findaux* clause is defined for each object. *Findaux* is used to invoke the goals.

```
findaux(goal,A,B) :-
      goal(A,B).
findaux(problem,A,B) :-
      problem(A,B).
findaux(power,A,B) :-
      power(A,B).
findaux(cursor,A,B) :-
      cursor(A,B).
```

```
findaux(brightness,A,B) :-
    brightness(A,B).
findaux(a_drive,A,B) :-
    a_drive(A,B).
findaux(a_boot,A,B) :-
    a_boot(A,B).
findaux(c_drive,A,B) :-
    c_drive(A,B).
```

Running the Expert System

The expert system is invoked with the predicate *go*. As the system asks questions, the user supplies the following types of answers:

- A single value, such as *yes* or *no*. Single values have a confidence factor of 1.

- A confidence factor applied to a single value. Confidence factors are applied by adding a backslash and the floating-point number, as in *yes/0.8*.

- Multiple values, with or without confidence factors. These values are separated by commas. The system treats multiple answers as separate consultations. The first argument of an answer is paired with the first arguments of the other answers; second arguments are paired with second arguments; and so on. The system returns the answers for all possible values that have been supplied.

- The value *unknown*. All *unknown* values are given a confidence factor of 1.0.

The user must end all answers with a period and a carriage return and, if the user enters an invalid answer, the system displays a message listing the valid values for the object.

To run the PC Expert, the user invokes the *go* predicate, like this:

```
?- go.
Is the computer plugged in? yes.

Does the cursor appear in the top right corner of the screen? yes.

After waiting a few moments, does the light at disk drive A come on? maybe.
All values must be in [yes,no]
After waiting a few moments, does the light at disk drive A come on? yes/0.5.
```

Is a boot disk in drive A? yes/0.2.

value = Your boot disk may be corrupted.
confidence = 0.5

After the expert system has run once, the database contains values for the top-level goal and for each of the antecedents that support the conclusion. If the user wants to run the system again, the database must be reinitialized so that these values no longer exist. This can be done with the *reinit* predicate, which removes any information that is stored about each of the terms under the *rule_compiled* key.

```
reinit :-
      recorded(rule_compiled,X,_),
      eraseall(X),
      fail.
reinit.
```

Before running the PC Expert again, the user must remove the previous answers from the database with the *reinit* predicate. For example:

```
?- reinit, go.
Is the computer plugged in? yes.
```

Does the cursor appear in the top right corner of the screen? no.

Is the brightness knob turned up? yes.

value = The monitor connection may be loose.
confidence = 0.9

value = The picture tube may be bad.
confidence = 0.1

A Rock-climbing Expert

Expert system shells are general-purpose and can be used to solve many different kinds of problems. In the previous example, you saw the PC Expert diagnose problems with computers. Here is a second example that solves a different kind of problem. The rock-climbing expert determines where a rock climber should place the next chock. For those of you who are not rock climbers, here is a brief introduction to rock climbing and some definitions of terms.

A ''chock'' is a metal wedge that a climber inserts into a rock crevice. The climber's rope runs through a loop on the chock, called a ''carabiner.'' Chocks are very important because they determine how far the climber will fall if he or she should lose the footing or grip.

Only one person climbs at a time. The first person places the chocks along the face of the rock. The other person, the ''belayer,'' gives out the rope to the climber. The belayer must prevent any more rope to be given out if the climber falls.

The first person up has the most difficult job; it is this person who could be hurt if the chock is misplaced. The factors that go into deciding whether to place a chock are as follows:

- How serious would the fall be from this position?

- How strenuous is it to maintain the current stance? For example, if the climber can barely maintain the current stance, then it would not be advisable to add another chock. The strenuousness of the current stance depends on the rock angle, the type of hand hold the position offers, and so on.

- How secure will the chock be in this position? This depends on the cracks that are available for the chock and on the availability of a suitable chock.

- How hard will the next move be? That is, the climber probably wants to place a chock just before beginning a particularly difficult move.

The decision to place a chock has many more considerations than the PC Expert needed to find a solution to the problem. Although the rock-climbing expert has many more rules, the methods for defining the system are the same. You define the rules for forming conclusions, you define the objects manipulated by those rules, and you define the top-level goal for the system. All of the necessary rules, objects, and goals for the rock-climbing expert are given in the following program listing:

```
goal = place.

serious(not__serious),
move(easy)
        —> place('Do not place chock here').
```

serious(not_serious),
stance(not_strenuous),
placement(shakey),
move(moderate)
      — > place('Do not place chock here')/0.9.

serious(not_serious),
stance(not_strenuous),
placement(shakey),
move(desperate)
      — > place('Do not place chock here')/0.6.

serious(not_serious),
stance(not_strenuous),
placement(good),
move(moderate)
      — > place('Do not place chock here')/0.8.

serious(not_serious),
stance(not_strenuous),
placement(good),
move(desperate)
      — > place('Do not place chock here')/0.51.

serious(not_serious),
stance(not_strenuous),
placement(bomber),
move(moderate)
      — > place('Do not place chock here')/0.7.

serious(not_serious),
stance(not_strenuous),
placement(bomber),
move(desperate)
      — > place('Place chock here')/0.6.

serious(not_serious),
stance(strenuous),
placement(shakey),
move(moderate)
      — > place('Do not place chock here')/0.95.

```
serious(not__serious),
stance(strenuous),
placement(shakey),
move(desperate)
      — > place('Do not place chock here')/0.8.

serious(not__serious),
stance(strenuous),
placement(good),
move(moderate)
      — > place('Do not place chock here')/0.9.

serious(not__serious),
stance(strenuous),
placement(good),
move(desperate)
      — > place('Do not place chock here')/0.7.

serious(not__serious),
stance(strenuous),
placement(bomber),
move(moderate)
      — > place('Do not place chock here')/0.85.

serious(not__serious),
stance(strenuous),
placement(bomber),
move(desperate)
      — > place('Do not place chock here')/0.65.

serious(not__serious),
stance(desperate),
placement(shakey),
move(moderate)
      — > place('Do not place chock here').
serious(not__serious),
stance(desperate),
placement(shakey),
move(desperate)
      — > place('Do not place chock here')/0.9.
```

serious(not_serious),
stance(desperate),
placement(good),
move(moderate)
    —> place('Do not place chock here').

serious(not_serious),
stance(desperate),
placement(good),
move(desperate)
    —> place('Do not place chock here')/0.8.

serious(not_serious),
stance(desperate),
placement(bomber),
move(moderate)
    —> place('Do not place chock here')/0.9.

serious(not_serious),
stance(desperate),
placement(bomber),
move(desperate)
    —> place('Do not place chock here')/0.7.

serious(serious),
stance(not_strenuous),
placement(shakey),
move(easy)
    —> place('Do not place chock here')/0.6.
serious(serious),
stance(not_strenuous),
placement(shakey),
move(moderate)
    —> place('Place chock here')/0.75.
serious(serious),
stance(not_strenuous),
placement(shakey),
move(desperate)
    —> place('Place chock here')/0.95.

```
serious(serious),
stance(not__strenuous),
placement(good),
move(easy)
        — > place('Place chock here')/0.7.
serious(serious),
stance(not__strenuous),
placement(good),
move(moderate)
        — > place('Place chock here').
serious(serious),
stance(not__strenuous),
placement(good),
move(desperate)
        — > place('Place chock here').
serious(serious),
stance(not__strenuous),
placement(bomber),
move(easy)
        — > place('Place chock here')/0.9.
serious(serious),
stance(not__strenuous),
placement(bomber),
move(moderate)
        — > place('Place chock here').
serious(serious),
stance(not__strenuous),
placement(bomber),
move(desperate)
        — > place('Place chock here').

serious(serious),
stance(strenuous),
placement(shakey),
move(easy)
        — > place('Do not place chock here').
serious(serious),
stance(strenuous),
placement(shakey),
move(moderate)
        — > place('Do not place chock here')/0.6.
```

serious(serious),
stance(strenuous),
placement(shakey),
move(desperate)
    — > place('Place chock here')/0.7.

serious(serious),
stance(strenuous),
placement(good),
move(easy)
    — > place('Do not place chock here')/0.9.
serious(serious),
stance(strenuous),
placement(good),
move(moderate)
    — > place('Place chock here')/0.75.
serious(serious),
stance(strenuous),
placement(good),
move(desperate)
    — > place('Place chock here')/0.95.

serious(serious),
stance(strenuous),
placement(bomber),
move(easy)
    — > place('Do not place chock here')/0.8.
serious(serious),
stance(strenuous),
placement(bomber),
move(moderate)
    — > place('Place chock here')/0.8.
serious(serious),
stance(strenuous),
placement(bomber),
move(desperate)
    — > place('Place chock here').

serious(serious),
stance(desperate),
placement(shakey),

```
move(easy)
      —> place('Do not place chock here')/0.8.
serious(serious),
stance(desperate),
placement(shakey),
move(moderate)
      —> place('Place chock here')/0.7.
serious(serious),
stance(desperate),
placement(shakey),
move(desperate)
      —> place('Place chock here')/0.9.

serious(serious),
stance(desperate),
placement(good),
move(easy)
      —> place('Do not place chock here')/0.75.
serious(serious),
stance(desperate),
placement(good),
move(moderate)
      —> place('Place chock here')/0.6.
serious(serious),
stance(desperate),
placement(good),
move(desperate)
      —> place('Place chock here')/0.8.

serious(serious),
stance(desperate),
placement(bomber),
move(easy)
      —> place('Do not place chock here')/0.7.
serious(serious),
stance(desperate),
placement(bomber),
move(moderate)
      —> place('Place chock here')/0.8.
serious(serious),
stance(desperate),
```

placement(bomber),
move(desperate)
    — > place('Place chock here')/0.9.

serious(screamer),
stance(not__strenuous),
placement(shakey),
move(easy)
    — > place('Place chock here')/0.75.
serious(screamer),
stance(not__strenuous),
placement(shakey),
move(moderate)
    — > place('Place chock here')/0.85.
serious(screamer),
stance(not__strenuous),
placement(shakey),
move(desperate)
    — > place('Place chock here')/0.95.

serious(screamer),
stance(not__strenuous),
placement(good),
move(easy)
    — > place('Place chock here').
serious(screamer),
stance(not__strenuous),
placement(good),
move(moderate)
    — > place('Place chock here').
serious(screamer),
stance(not__strenuous),
placement(good),
move(desperate)
    — > place('Place chock here').

serious(screamer),
stance(not__strenuous),
placement(bomber),
move(easy)
    — > place('Place chock here').

```
serious(screamer),
stance(not_strenuous),
placement(bomber),
move(moderate)
        —> place('Place chock here').
serious(screamer),
stance(not_strenuous),
placement(bomber),
move(desperate)
        —> place('Place chock here').

serious(screamer),
stance(strenuous),
placement(shakey),
move(easy)
        —> place('Do not place chock here')/0.7.
serious(screamer),
stance(strenuous),
placement(shakey),
move(moderate)
        —> place('Place chock here')/0.8.
serious(screamer),
stance(strenuous),
placement(shakey),
move(desperate)
        —> place('Place chock here')/0.95.

serious(screamer),
stance(strenuous),
placement(good),
move(easy)
        —> place('Place chock here')/0.85.
serious(screamer),
stance(strenuous),
placement(good),
move(moderate)
        —> place('Place chock here')/0.95.
serious(screamer),
stance(strenuous),
```

placement(good),
move(desperate)
     —> place('Place chock here').

serious(screamer),
stance(strenuous),
placement(bomber),
move(easy)
     —> place('Place chock here')/0.95.
serious(screamer),
stance(strenuous),
placement(bomber),
move(moderate)
     —> place('Place chock here').
serious(screamer),
stance(strenuous),
placement(bomber),
move(desperate)
     —> place('Place chock here').

serious(screamer),
stance(desperate),
placement(shakey),
move(easy)
     —> place('Do not place chock here')/0.7.
serious(screamer),
stance(desperate),
placement(shakey),
move(moderate)
     —> place('Place chock here')/0.5.
serious(screamer),
stance(desperate),
placement(shakey),
move(desperate)
     —> place('Place chock here')/0.6.

serious(screamer),
stance(desperate),
placement(good),
move(easy)
     —> place('Do not place chock here')/0.6.

```
serious(screamer),
stance(desperate),
placement(good),
move(moderate)
        — > place('Place chock here')/0.9.
serious(screamer),
stance(desperate),
placement(good),
move(desperate)
        — > place('Place chock here').

serious(screamer),
stance(desperate),
placement(bomber),
move(easy)
        — > place('Do not place chock here')/0.6.
serious(screamer),
stance(desperate),
placement(bomber),
move(moderate)
        — > place('Place chock here')/0.9.
serious(screamer),
stance(desperate),
placement(bomber),
move(desperate)
        — > place('Place chock here').

question(placement, [bomber,good,shakey) =
        'How good would the placement here be?
        (bomber, good, shakey) '.

question(move, [desperate,moderate,easy) =
        'How difficult is the next move?
        (desperate, moderate, easy) '.

cliff__angle(overhanging)
        — > stance(desperate).

( foot__holds(none) ; foot__holds(tiny) ),
hand__holds(fingernail)
        — > stance(desperate).
```

foot__holds(none),
(hand__holds(fingertip) ; hand__holds(knuckle)),
cliff__angle(vertical)
      — > stance(desperate).

(foot__holds(none) ; foot__holds(tiny)),
cliff__angle(vertical),
(hand__holds(buckets) ; hand__holds(knuckle)
      — > stance(strenuous).

(foot__holds(none) ; foot__holds(tiny)),
cliff__angle(low__angle),
(hand__holds(fingertip) ; hand__holds(knuckle))
      — > stance(strenuous).

cliff__angle(low__angle),
hand__holds(buckets)
      — > stance(not__strenuous).

foot__holds(good),
hand__holds(buckets)
      — > stance(not__strenuous).

foot__holds(good),
cliff__angle(vertical),
hand__holds(fingertip)
      — > stance(strenuous).

foot__holds(good),
cliff__angle(vertical),
hand__holds(knuckle)
      — > stance(strenuous).

foot__holds(large__ledge
      — > stance(not__strenuous).

question(foot__holds, [none, tiny, good, large__ledge]) =
    'What are your foot holds like?
    (none, tiny, good, large__ledge) '.

```
question(hand__holds, [fingernail, fingertip, knuckle,
buckets]) =
     'What kind of hand holds do you have?
     (fingernail, fingertip, knuckle, buckets) '.

question(cliff__angle, [overhanging, vertical, low__angle]) =
     'What is the approximate cliff angle?
     (overhanging, vertical, low__angle) '.

dist__belayer(0-10),
last__pro(0-5)
     — > serious(not__serious).

dist__belayer(0-10),
last__pro(5-10)
     — > serious(serious).

dist__belayer(0-10),
last__pro(10-150)
     — > serious(screamer).

dist__belayer(10-50),
last__pro(0-5),
( last__place(bomber) ; last__place(good))
     — > serious(not__serious).

dist__belayer(10-50),
last__pro(0-5),
last__place(shakey)
     — > serious(serious).

dist__belayer(10-50),
last__pro(5-10),
( last__place(bomber) ; last__place(good) )
     — > serious(screamer)/0.4.

dist__belayer(10-50),
last__pro(5-10),
( last__place(bomber) ; last__place(good) )
     — > serious(screamer)/0.6.
```

dist__belayer(10-50),
last__pro(5-10),
last__place(shakey)
     — > serious(screamer)/0.9.

dist__belayer(10-50),
last__pro(10-150),
(last__place(bomber) ; last__place(good))
     — > serious(screamer)/0.7.

dist__belayer(10-50),
last__pro(10-150),
(last__place(bomber) ; last__place(good))
     — > serious(serious)/0.6.

dist__belayer(10-50),
last__place(shakey)
     — > serious(screamer)/0.7.

dist__belayer(50-150),
last__pro(10-150),
last__place(bomber)
     — > serious(serious)/0.7.

dist__belayer(50-150),
last__pro(10-150),
last__place(bomber)
     — > serious(not__serious)/0.2.

dist__belayer(50-150),
last__pro(10-150),
last__place(good)
     — > serious(serious)/0.5.

dist__belayer(50-150),
last__pro(10-150),
last__place(good)
     — > serious(screamer)/0.2.

```
    dist__belayer(50-150),
    last__pro(10-150),
    last__place(good)
         —> serious(not__serious)/0.4.

    dist__belayer(50-150),
    (last__pro(0-5) ; last__pro(5-10)),
    (last__place(good) ; last__place(bomber) )
         —> serious(not__serious).

    dist__belayer(50-150),
    (last__pro(0-5) ; last__pro(5-10)),
    last__place(shakey)
         —> serious(serious)/0.5.

    dist__belayer(50-150),
    (last__pro(0-5) ; last__pro(5-10)),
    last__place(shakey)
         —> serious(screamer)/0.5.

question(last__pro, [0-5,5-10,10-150) =
         'How many feet since last protection?
         (0-5,5-10,10-150) '.

question(last__place, [bomber,good,shakey]) =
         'How good was the last placement?
         (bomber, good, shakey) '.

question(dist__belayer, [0-10,10-50,50-150]) =
         'How many feet are between you and the belayer?
         (0-10,10-50,50-150) '.
```

Knowledge Engineering

As more and more shells have become available, a new area of study has opened up called "knowledge engineering." Knowledge engineering is the study of a particular area of expertise and the translation of that knowledge into expert systems. Knowledge engineers serve as the intermediaries between the experts and the expert system.

The knowledge engineer spends time interviewing the expert, or experts, and gathering information about their area of expertise. Initially, there may be no order to the information gathered.

The knowledge engineer then determines what objects are manipulated while solving a particular problem and what rules the expert applies to these objects. Together, the knowledge engineer and the expert begin to organize the information.

The knowledge engineer can then use a shell to load the knowledge base with information. Using a shell makes this loading process run more quickly than coding the entire system by hand. Expert system shells allow the knowledge engineer to define objects and write rules in a higher-level language without being concerned with how to store things internally. After the objects and rules are properly defined, the knowledge engineer does not have to be concerned with the procedural aspects of the system, such as implementing inference techniques or calculating confidence factors.

Once a minimum amount of information is entered into the system, verification can begin. Typical problems are tested with the system to determine what additional knowledge is required. Heuristics for handling exceptions, and so on, are added.

Expert system development is an ongoing process. Furthermore, the goal cannot be to achieve 100 percent accuracy but rather to achieve the same success rate that an expert achieves.

Summary

Expert system development is often done with the help of an expert system shell. The shell defines how information is stored internally and how conclusions are drawn from that information. This chapter discussed the development of an expert system shell in Prolog and showed two systems built with the shell. The PC Expert and the Rock-climbing expert are handled adequately by the shell shown in this chapter. Many problems require no more sophistication than this shell provides.

When designing an expert system shell, you must decide what knowledge representation schemes to use. The shell discussed in this chapter allowed the expert system developer to describe knowledge in a rule language. The rule language is a very high-level language for describing production rules, for describing the objects manipulated by those rules, and for defining the objective of the system. Because many shells provide a high-level language such as the rule language, expert systems developers often do not need to know any other programming language.

When designing a shell, you must decide what inference techniques are best for the kinds of problems the shell must solve. The shell in this chapter used backward chaining to solve a top-level goal. You must determine which methods for calculating confidence factors are most appropriate for the kinds of expert systems being developed. The shell in this chapter supported Bayesian probability for calculating confidence factors.

Finally, you must decide how the expert systems will interact with the user. This shell allows the expert system to ask questions and return solutions to the user. However, it cannot answer questions such as "how" or "why." Again, the requirements of the expert systems that will be developed with the shell determine which features are most important.

The availability of expert system shells makes it possible for the expert system developer to concentrate on the problem at hand rather than on its solution. Knowledge engineering, the translation of knowledge into expert systems, is a growing area of study. The techniques knowledge engineers use for gathering and encoding expertise were discussed briefly in this chapter.

7

Techniques for Language Processing

L anguage processing has a wide range of applications for computer program-ming. Interpreters and compilers for programming languages must process statements in the language and convert them into the machine's internal language. Query languages for databases, such as SQL, must convert the user's query into a form that the database management system can recognize. Object-definition languages for expert system shells, natural language systems, command languages, even mathematical statements must be treated as distinct languages by computer systems.

No matter what the language, the same steps are applied to understand statements in any language. Compilers, interpreters, and command processors all must separate a jumble of letters into words, they must apply rules for recognizing valid statements in the language, and possess methods for deriving the meaning of those statements. These steps are called "tokenization," "syntax analysis," and "semantic analysis." When taken together, tokenization and syntax analysis are referred to as "parsing." Each stage has well-defined inputs and well-defined results, as shown in figure 7-1.

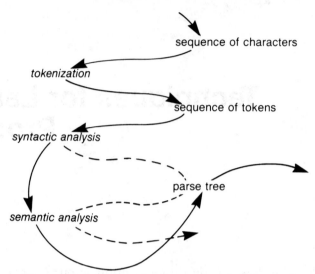

Figure 7-1: Stages in Language Processing

A "token" is the smallest meaningful object in the language, such as a word. Atoms, integers, operators, and variables are the tokens in Prolog. With these tokens, larger terms, such as structures and clauses, can be built.

When the user types a language statement at the keyboard, the computer reads this statement as a sequence, or list, of ASCII character codes. Tokenization is the process of finding the tokens in the list of characters. The tokenizer converts the list of characters into a list of tokens, which is then passed to the syntax and semantic analyzer.

The syntax of a language is its grammar rules. In English, for example, the grammar rules state that the subject of the sentence comes before the verb, which comes before an object or prepositional phrase. For example, grammar rules dictate that the word order is incorrect in the sentence, "Swim ducks pond in the." Other rules define how the verb tense and person must agree. During syntax analysis, these grammar rules are applied to the statement.

A sentence may be grammatically correct but still lack meaning. For example, the sentence "The fish drove 300 words per minute" is grammatically correct. However, fish cannot drive and the speed of a car (or a fish) is not measured in words per minute. The semantic rules for a language differentiate between meaningful statements and jibberish. During semantic analysis, these semantic rules are applied.

Often during syntax and semantic analysis, the language processor produces an intermediate representation of the statement. It groups the parts of the statement into a tree-like structure, or parse tree. One example in this chapter generates a parse tree that is directly executable as a Prolog goal. Most often, however, the parse tree is passed to another stage, called code generation.

The code generation phase is missing from this picture. It is the process by which a language statement is translated into a machine-executable form. Parsing and code generation are usually considered separately. Parsing deals with accepting language from the user; code generation deals with presenting language statements to the computer. Code generation is more specific to the computer being used because each type of hardware defines a different instruction set. Code generation goes beyond the scope of this chapter, but parsing will be discussed here, from the tokenization phase through Prolog's built-in parsing mechanisms. Prolog provides two built-in parsing mechanisms — one for operator-precedence grammars and one for definite clause grammars.

The Prolog reader can tokenize characters typed at the keyboard and it can check to see that the input is a valid Prolog term. That is, it recognizes the special tokens of the language, such as the characters [,], and !. The reader is a prefix Polish parser that can be altered with operator precedences. If a language can be expressed using prefix Polish notation and operator precedences, then you can process the language with the Prolog reader.

Prolog also provides a convenient notation for defining a language called "definite clause grammars" or DCGs. If your grammar is not expressible using operator precedences, but can be parsed using bottom-up methods, then you can process the language using DCGs.

Other parsing methods exist and they, too, can be implemented in Prolog. However, this chapter will concentrate on the methods that are built into the Prolog language.

Tokenization

Tokenization is the first stage in the process of understanding language. The computer must convert a sequence of characters into a sequence of tokens. The tokenizer defined here will convert a character string to a list of tokens. The character string is a quoted list and it is treated as the list of ASCII codes that make up the string. For example, the quoted string

"This is a string"

is the same as the following list of ASCII codes:

[116,104,105,115,32,105,115,32,97,32,115,116,114,105,110,103]

The quoted string

''2 + 3/5''

is the same as the list of ASCII codes:

[50,43,51,47,53]

Initially, the tokenizer will tokenize only arithmetic expressions. Later, it will take little effort to expand the program to handle words.

The tokens in an arithmetic expression consist of numbers and operators. A number begins with a digit, which is any ASCII code that falls between the codes for the numbers 0 and 9. The digit can be recognized by the following rule:

digit(C) :-
     C > = '0, C = < '9.

A number can end with a space (ASCII code 32) or with an arithmetic operator. Operators are the characters + , – , *, and /. They are treated as single-character tokens. These tokens can be recognized by the following facts:

token(' + , +).
token(' – , –).
token('*,*).
token('/,/).

The end of an expression is marked by the empty list.

The tokenizer is a recursive predicate that acts upon the head of the character list and passes the tail to the next iteration. Each iteration looks at the head of the list to determine whether it has encounterd a number, a token, a space, or the end of the list. The first argument to the tokenizer, therefore, is that part of the input list that has not yet been tokenized.

In its second argument, the tokenizer keeps a list of the tokens that it has found so far. Remember from the *append* predicate of chapter 2 that when a recursive predicate returns a value, it must have a variable argument that does not become instantiated until the last iteration of the loop. In the same way, the third argument to the tokenizer remains uninstantiated until the last token has been added to the list.

The first *tokenize* clause succeeds when the head of the list contains a digit. In this case, the tokenizer knows that it has encountered a number. It then passes the input list and the first digit of the number to *get_rest_num* to tokenize the rest of the number. When *get_rest_num* returns, *tokenize* appends the number to the token list and tokenizes the remainder of the input list.

```
tokenize([H|T],List,L) :-
    digit(H), !,
    get_rest_num(T,[H],Num,Rem),
    append(List,[Num],NewList),
    tokenize(Rem,NewList,L).
```

When an operator is found at the head of the list, the second *tokenize* clause succeeds. It appends the token to the token list and calls *tokenize* again with the remainder of the input list.

```
tokenize([H|T],List,L) :-
token(H,Token), !,
    append(List,[Token],NewList),
    tokenize(T,NewList,L).
```

Tokenize skips over spaces (ASCII character 32). Note that *tokenize* does not detect the first space that separates tokens; these are found by *get_rest_num*. *Tokenize* locates only extra spaces.

```
tokenize([32|T],List,L) :-
    !, tokenize(T,List,L).
```

The empty list marks the end of the character string. When the empty list is detected, tokenization is complete and the third argument becomes instantiated.

```
tokenize([],List,List).
```

Look more closely now at the way that the tokenizer handles numbers. When *tokenize* detects that it has encountered a digit, it passes the first digit and the rest of the list to *get_rest_num*. *Get_rest_num* collects the digits that make up a number and then converts those characters to a number. This is done by recursively checking the character at the beginning of the list. If the character is a digit, then the digit is appended to the second argument. *Get_rest_num* then calls itself with the remainder of the input list and the collection of digits continues.

```
get_rest_num([H|T],List,Num,X) :-
    digit(H), !,
    append(List,[H],Nlist),
    get_rest_num(T,Nlist,Num,X).
```

The digit may end with a space or it may end with a token (+ , − , *, or /). When it encounters either of these conditions, *get_rest_num* knows it has reached the end of the number. It then converts the list of digits to the number and returns the remaining list of characters. The list of ASCII characters is converted to a number by an evaluable predicate called *name*. This evaluable predicate converts lists to atoms and atoms to lists. Notice that the token is not removed from the list so that it can be handled by the *tokenize* predicate.

```
get_rest([32|T],List,Num,T) :-
    name(Num,List), !.
get_rest_num([H|T], List, Num, [H|T]) :-
    token(H,__),
    name(Num,List), !.
```

If *get_rest_num* encounters the empty list, then it knows that it has reached both the end of the number and the end of the input list. In this case, it converts the list of digits to the number, and returns the empty list to *tokenize*.

```
get_rest_num([],List,Num,[]) :-
    !, name(Num,List).
```

The rules for tokenizing a word are similar to those for tokenizing numbers. Words are comprised of a letter followed by an identifier, which is a letter, a digit, an underscore, or a dollar sign. Uppercase letters are converted to lowercase so that there is no confusion about whether the token is an atom or a variable. The tokenizer can check for letters and identifiers with the following rules:

```
letter(C,D) :-
    C > = 'A, C = < 'Z,
    D is C + 32.
letter(C,C) :-
    C > = 'a, C = < 'z.

identifier(C,D) :- digit(C,D).
identifier(C,D) :- letter(C,D).
identifier('_','_').
identifier('$','$').
```

The process of tokenizing words requires the addition of only one clause to the *tokenize* predicate. This clause checks to see if the first character of the word is a letter.

```
tokenize([H|T],List,L) :-
    letter(H,Letter), !,
    get_rest_word(T,[Letter],Word,Rem),
    append(List,[Word],NewList),
    tokenize(Rem,NewList,L).
```

The *get_rest_word* predicate, like *get_rest_num*, collects identifiers from the input stream until it reaches a space. Then, *name* converts the list to an atom. Notice that words are not separated by the arithmetic operators.

```
get_rest_word([H|T],List,Word,X) :-
    identifier(H,Id), !,
    append(List,[Id],Nlist),
    get_rest_word(T,Nlist,Word,X).
get_rest_word([32|T],List,Word,T) :-
    name(Word,List), !.
get_rest_word([],List,Word,[]) :-
    !, name(Word,List).
```

Now the tokenizer can convert lists of ASCII codes into words, digits, and arithmetic operators. For example:

```
?- tokenize(''5 + 2*4'',X,Y).

X  =  []
Y  =  [5, + ,2,*,4]

?- tokenize(''Once upon a time'',X,Y).

X  =  []
Y  =  [once,upon,a,time]
```

The Prolog Reader

Prolog's built-in reader accepts terms that are typed at the keyboard in response to the interpreter prompt, or terms that are consulted from a file. In addition, whenever a Prolog program invokes the *read* predicate, it is using the built-in reader. You can use the Prolog reader to build language processors when the input stream consists of valid Prolog terms. The reader tokenizes the input. It checks that the input is a valid Prolog term and it issues an error message if an error is found while trying to parse the term.

Prolog interpreters can be implemented with the Prolog reader. The interpreter example given here, called *interp*, will handle any Prolog goal except the *cut*. The first *interp* clause handles the unit clause, which has a body of *true*.

```
interp(true).
```

Separate clauses handle the conjunction and disjunction of goals, evaluable predicates, and clauses the user has stored in the database. For conjunctions and disjunctions, *interp* processes each portion of the term recursively, separating the recursive calls with either the comma or the semicolon.

```
interp((P,Q)) :-
      interp(P), interp(Q).
interp((P;Q)) :-
      interp(P) ; interp(Q).
```

Interp detects evaluable predicates by calling the evaluable predicate *system*. *System* checks to see if its argument is an evaluable predicate. However, the argument must be written as the predicate name followed by a backslash followed by the number of arguments. In order to supply the correct argument to *system*, *interp* has to call *functor* to return the name and number of arguments for the term. If the term is an evaluable predicate, then *interp* calls the goal.

```
interp(P) :-
    functor(P,F,N),
    system(F/N),
    !, call(P).
```

Clauses in the database must also be handled separately. *Interp* uses the *clause* predicate to return the body of the clause and it then calls itself recursively to interpret each goal in the body. Unit clauses are picked up during this recursive call.

```
interp(P) :-
    clause(P,Q),
    interp(Q).
```

Clauses having both a head and a tail are asserted into the database.

```
interp((P :- Q)) :-
    assertz((P :- Q)).
```

This interpreter can handle pure Prolog, without the *cut*, including terms using the standard operator definitions. Here are a few examples. The first example attempts to invoke a goal that is not an evaluable predicate or a clause that is stored in the database. The goal fails.

```
?- interp(hello).
```

no

The next example adds a definition for *hello* to the database. This succeeds.

```
?- interp((hello :- write(hello))).
```

yes

Now when the user tries to invoke *hello*, *interp* locates the clause in the database. It then interprets the body. Because *write* is an evaluable predicate, the *system* test succeeds and the goal *write(hello)* is called.

```
?- interp(hello).
hello
yes
```

When the syntax of the input language goes beyond pure Prolog, you can define additional operators to tell Prolog how to convert the input into Prolog terms.

Operator Definitions

Operator definitions allow you to alter the order in which an argument and its functor are written. Prolog defines a standard set of operators, listed in table 7-1.

Table 7-1: Operator Definitions

Operator	Associativity	Precedence Based on 1200	Precedence Based on 256
:- -->	xfx	1200	255
:- ?-	fx	1200	255
mode public	fy	1150	—
extrn visible module	fy	1150	—
;	xfy	1100	254
,	xfy	1000	253
case	fx	900	—
spy nospy	fy	900	252
not \ +	fy	900	60
-->	xfy	800	254
= is =.. \= == \==	xfx	700	40
@< @=< @> @>=	xfx	700	40
=\= <> =<>= =:=	xfx	700	40
+ - /\ \/	yfx	500	31
:	xfy	500	31
+ -	fx	500	31
* / >> << //	yfx	400	21
mod	xfx	300	11
^	xfy	200	8

An operator is defined with the built-in predicate called *op*, which defines the three characteristics of the operator. These characteristics are the operator's "precedence," its "associativity," and its name.

Precedence determines the order in which operators are evaluated in an expression. Operators with a higher precedence are evaluated before operators of a lower precedence. Precedence is defined as a number between 0 and 255 or between 1 and 1200. Implementations of the language differ in the range of numbers that are valid for an operator's precedence.

The associativity states how the operator combines with other expressions of the same precedence. In addition, the associativity determines whether the operators are evaluated from right to left or from left to right. Associativity is defined with the letters *x*, *f*, and *y*. The *f* stands for operator. The *x* stands for an operator with the same precedence and the *y* stands for an operator with the same or higher precedence. Wherever the *y* operator appears in the atom, that operator is evaluated first; the operator in the position of the *x* is evaluated last. When both positions have an *x*, the operator is nonassociative, meaning that two expressions with the same precedence cannot be combined.

The associativity also states whether the operator is a prefix, postfix, or infix operator. That is, when the *f* is placed before the operands, the operator is defined to be a prefix operator. When the *f* is placed between the operands, it is an infix operator. When the *f* is placed after the operands, it is a postfix operator.

Because they are so useful, it is easy to forget that operator definitions merely alter the syntax of Prolog terms for the *read*, *write*, and *writeq* predicates. Internally, statements that use operator definitions are treated exactly like other Prolog terms. Nonetheless, you can write entire language processors with operator definitions. For example, the EL database language is defined with operators (Deyi Li, *A Prolog Database System*, Research Studies Press Ltd., 1984). The next section will use operators for an object-definition language such as you might find in an expert system shell.

An Object-definition Language

Expert system developers do not normally write their expert systems in pure Prolog but rather in a more English-like language. Expert system shells written in Prolog can translate these statements directly into Prolog. Often, operator definitions are all that are required to handle this kind of language. The

Arity/Expert Development Package, for example, uses only operator definitions to process its concept classification and rule languages.

The object-definition language defined here requires only four operators: *define*, *isa*, *with*, and *and*. They are used to make statements having the following general form:

define name *isa* type [*with* characteristic [*and* characteristic]].

The *define* operator is a unary operator with a precedence of 1200. This is the same precedence and associativity as the neck symbol. The operator definition for *define* means that no other expression can appear to the left of this operator (the *x* is on the right) and the expression that is on the right of the operator must have a precedence lower than 1200.

```
:- op(1200,fx,define).
```

When the reader encounters a term that begins with the word *define*, it will expect to place the remainder of the term in parentheses as a single argument. This means that, in this language, you cannot say:

```
?- define this isa world with worries and define this isa world with cares.
```

The remaining operators are of slightly lower precedences, where *isa* is the higher and *and* is the lowest. All three have *xfy* associativity. That is, they are all evaluated from right to left. An expression on the left side of these operators must have a precedence lower than the operator; the precedence of the expression on the right may be the same or higher.

The *isa* operator is a binary operator that takes the name of the object and some description of the type and characteristics of the object. It is defined in this way:

```
:- op(1150,xfy,isa).
```

Characteristics are defined using the *with* operator. The *with* operator takes two arguments — the object type and the characteristics.

```
:- op(1100,xfy,with).
```

Finally, the *and* operator can separate two characteristics or two names.

:- op(1000,xfy,and).

Some people have difficulty deciding where to fit new operators into the operator precedence table. It may be helpful to visualize the operators on steps, as shown in figure 7-2. If you can determine the upper and lower limits within which to place the operators, then you can usually decide where the operators in the middle should fall. For example, the *define* operator is like the neck symbol. It is a prefix, unary operator that cannot combine with other expressions. Therefore, it can be placed at the same level as the neck. The lowest operator, *and*, is equivalent to the addition and subtraction operators. It can be placed at that level. The rest of the standard operators should fall below *and* so that they may be part of an *and* expression. The remaining operators are assigned precedences between the top and bottom.

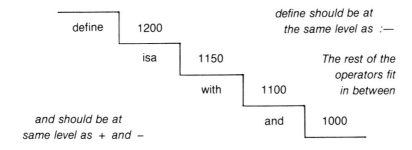

Figure 7-2: Visual Layout of Operator Procedences

Given the definitions above, the system can parse the following kinds of expressions:

?- define daisy isa dog.
?- define bird isa animal with song.
?- define dog isa animal with sound = woof.
?- define cow isa animal with milk and sound = moo.
?- define cat and dog isa pet.
?- define horse and cow isa pet with home = barn.

When read by Prolog, the expressions are translated into this form:

define(isa(daisy,dog)).
define(isa(bird,with(animal,song))).

```
define(isa(dog,with(animal, =(sound,woof))))).
define(isa(cow,with(animal,and(milk, =(sound,moo)))))).
define(isa(and(dog,cat),pet)).
define(isa(and(horse,cow),with(pet, =(home,barn))))).
```

The *display* predicate is now the only way to see these expressions in their prefix form. The *write* and *writeq* predicates will use the operator definitions to convert the structures to infix form.

The operator definitions allow the reader to check the syntax of expressions using these operators. However, the expressions are meaningless to Prolog. You must define the semantics of these expressions by building predicates to recognize and process them. Just as Prolog defines the actions to be take when an *is* or == predicate is encountered, you must define the actions to be taken when a *define* statement is encountered.

To define a new object, you may want to create database entries for the object. This gives *define* the semantics of adding an object to the database. When used as an argument to *define*, the *isa* expression also has a meaning in that it states the information to be stored. You may also want to give *isa* the semantics of returning an object's definition if it is not the argument to *define*. In order to give the operators meaning, therefore, you need to write predicates to recognize the expressions and to take the appropriate actions when they are encountered.

The operator definition describes *define* as taking one argument. The *define* predicate further specifies that this argument must be an *isa* expression. The *isa* expression is passed along to a predicate called *add*, which adds the object definition to the database. If the argument is not an *isa* expression, then it is semantically incorrect and an error message is issued.

```
define(isa(X,Y)) :- add(X,Y).
define(__) :-
        write('The argument must be an isa expression.'),
        nl.
```

You must also decide how to store these objects in the database. It is more logical to store the object name along with the *with* portion of the definition as opposed to the more general object type. That is, it is more desirable to say:

```
isa(bird,animal).
with(bird,song).
```

Rather than to say:

isa(bird,animal).
with(animal,song).

Although a bird is an animal, birds are the only animals with songs.

The *add* predicate must also be able to handle all the possible forms of *define* expression. For example, the expression may or may not have a *with* expression. The arguments to *add* are the name (or names) of the object and the type definition. The type definition may be a single word (as in *daisy isa dog*) or it may be a *with* expression. Regardless, *add* cannot add the object to the database until it knows which type of definition it is dealing with. To determine the form of expression and the correct object type, *add* passes the arguments to *new* and expects *new* to return the correct object type to the third argument.

add(X,Y) :- new(X,Y,Z), recordz(isa,isa(X,Z),__).

If the arguments to *new* contain a *with* expression, *new* adds the *with* expression to the database and returns the object type to *add*. If the arguments to *new* do not contain a *with* expression, the predicate simply returns the name of the object to *add*.

new(O,with(X,Y),X) :-
      recordz(with,with(O,Y),__).
new(X,Y,Y).

The previous definitions are stored in the database like this:

isa(daisy,dog).

isa(bird,animal).
with(bird,song).

isa(dog,animal).
with(dog, =(sound,woof).

isa(cow,animal).
with(cow,and(milk, =(sound,moo))).

isa(and(dog,cat),pet).

isa(and(horse,cow),pet).
with(and(horse,cow), =(home,barn)).

The next predicate will process *isa* statements as queries. *Isa* statements can take one of three forms. First, questions in which the object definition is a variable may be asked, as follows:

?- daisy isa X.
?- X isa Y.

In these cases, *isa* must succeed whether or not a *with* expression is defined for the object. Therefore, *isa* checks to see if the second argument is a variable. If so, it will succeed whether or not a *with* expression is found for the object.

```
isa(X,Y) :-
    var(Y),
    !,
    recorded(isa,isa(X,A),___),
    ( recorded(with,with(X,B),___), Y  =  with(A,B), ! ;
    Y = A ).
```

The user may also ask questions that request the system to find an object with certain characteristics, as in the following:

?- X isa pet with milk and sound = moo.
?- X isa pet with Y.

If the question specifies a *with* expression, then a *with* expression must be found for the object. Therefore, a *cut* is placed at the beginning of the second *isa* clause. It forces *isa* to fail if no *with* expression is found. However, if more than one matching object is desired, then the clause will backtrack to the *cut* in order to find the next occurrence.

```
isa(X,with(Y,Z)) :-
    !,
    recorded(isa,isa(X,Y),___),
    recorded(with,with(X,Z),___).
```

The third and last form of question does not specify a *with* expression. For example:

```
?- X isa dog.
?- X isa pet.
```

To handle this form of question, the system should simply look up the *isa* database entry for the object, ignoring whether there is a *with* expression for the object or not.

```
isa(X,Y) :-
        recorded(isa,isa(X,Y),__).
```

These three *isa* clauses can now handle questions like the following:

```
?- bird isa X.
X = animal with song.

?- dog isa animal with X.
X = sound = woof

?- X isa animal.
X = bird -> ;
X = dog -> ;
X = cow

?- X isa animal with Y and A = B.
X = cow
Y = milk
A = sound
B = moo
```

Notice how the operator definitions affect the way the results are written. When the answer contains an operator, as in the first and second examples, it is written in infix notation. In this way, operator definitions can be used by an output routine to make the answers to queries have a more English-like syntax, too.

Development of a parser using the Prolog reader and operator definitions is very fast. For this reason, it is a good method to choose whenever possible. However, it has its limitations. Only well-defined and strict grammars are suited to operator definitions. Operators cannot handle more complex grammars. For example, two operators cannot have the same name and associativity but have different precedences. This disallows the use of an operator in more than one context within the language. Many languages, especially natural languages, cannot be restricted in this way.

When you use the reader to parse statements, errors in the statement fail at the reader level. As a result, many errors cannot be caught by your program. Other parsing methods allow you to control when errors are caught and how they should be handled.

More complex grammars should be handled by other parsing techniques. One technique that is built into Prolog is the definite clause grammar, or DCG. Because DCGs do not take advantage of the reader, the input stream must be tokenized. Because DCGs do not have to produce Prolog code, as the reader does, the result of the parsing must be defined. For this reason, you can use DCGs to write compilers or interpreters for other programming languages and for natural languages.

Definite Clause Grammars

Definite clause grammars (DCGs) are an extension of the context-free grammar. Therefore, before discussing DCGs, something of context-free grammars must be covered. In a context-free grammar, each language element, from the largest to the smallest, must be defined separately.

Definitions are made up of "terminals" and "non-terminals." A non-terminal is defined in terms of other language elements. A terminal can be defined only in terms of itself. For example, a sentence can be made up of a *noun phrase* and a *verb phrase*. The *noun phrase* is a non-terminal because it is defined in terms of a *determiner* followed by a *noun*. The *determiner* is defined by the terminals *the*, *a*, and *an*, which cannot be defined further.

However, the most important quality of a context-free grammar is this: a grammar is context-free if each element is independent of the others — that is, no part of the grammar influences how another part of the grammar is parsed. In an arithmetic expression, all interdependencies can be handled by context-free grammars. However, the various parts of other language sentences can influence each other in subtle ways. For example, the tense, person, and in some cases the gender of the various parts of a natural language sentence must agree in order for the sentence to be grammatically correct.

One notation that is commonly used for writing context-free grammars is Backus-Naur form. In Backus-Naur form, the name of the element is placed on the left side of the expression and its definition on the right. The element is separated from its definition by the :: = symbol. As in Prolog clauses, only one object can appear on the left side of a definition.

The definition of a language element consists of some number of terminals and non-terminals which can be separated by commas. As with Prolog's conjunction operator, each of the objects in the definition must be present in order for the statement to parse correctly.

Definitions can also be separated by the vertical bar. This indicates that the language element being defined can take one of the forms given in the definition, much as multiple clauses in Prolog can have the same head.

Finally, some objects are enclosed in square brackets and separated by a vertical bar. The vertical bar can be read as ''or.'' One or the other object within the square brackets must be present. This is like the disjunction operator in Prolog.

The grammar for arithmetic expressions can be defined with only a few rules. The first grammar rule states that an arithmetic expression can consist of a term followed by a plus sign or a minus sign followed by an expression, or an expression can be a term. In Backus-Naur form, this is written:

```
expression :: =
      term, [ + | - ], expression
    | term
```

A term can be defined as a number, followed by a multiplication or division operator, followed by a term; or a term can be a number.

```
term :: =
      number [ * | / ] term
    | number
```

A number can be a plus or minus sign followed by a number, or it can be a digit.

```
number :: =
      [ + | - ] number
    | digit
```

Finally, a digit is any of the terminals 0 through 9.

digit :: =
    [0 | 1 | 2 | 3 | 4 | 5 | 6 | 7 | 8 | 9]

The syntax of a DCG is similar to that of Backus-Naur form. The name of the language element being defined is on the left side of the expression. The :: = operator is replaced with the -- > operator. A language element can be defined in terms of terminals or non-terminals.

The arithmetic expression grammar can be written in DCG notation like this:

```
expr -- > term, [ + ], expr.
expr -- > term, [ - ], expr.
expr -- > term.

term -- > number, [*], term.
term -- > number, [/], term.
term -- > number.

number -- > [ + ], number.
number -- > [ - ], number.
number -- > [N].
```

This grammar uses the DCG notation to write a context-free grammar. However, DCGs can extend the context-free grammar in two important ways:

- DCGs can pass information between definitions as arguments. In this way, DCGs need not define context-free grammars. The various parts of a language statement can communicate things such as tense, person, and gender.

- The DCG can contain executable goals that are not part of the grammar itself but that are executed whenever a statement in the language is parsed. In this way, the grammar can also produce side-effects or results. Executable goals are placed inside curly braces.

At this point, you may have begun to get a sense of what these definitions mean procedurally. First, they are recursive. All three language elements are defined in terms of themselves. That is, an expression can contain an expression, a term can contain a term, and a number can contain a number. Also, as in Backus-Naur form, parsing a complete DCG expression must begin with the top-level definition. The previous example begins with the *expr* definition. It, in turn, calls the *term* definition, which calls the *number* definition. This suggests the tree structure in figure 7-3.

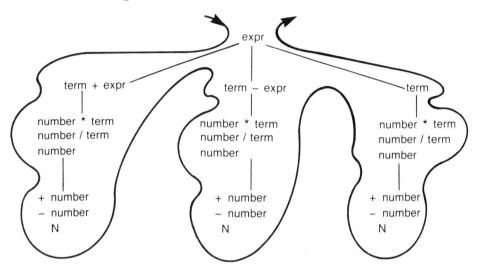

Figure 7-3: A Grammar for Arithmetic Expressions

If you follow the tree to parse an expression like *7 – 8 / 2*, you can see that a lot of backtracking occurs. The parser must go all the way down to the number level and back to the top level before it finds out that the *7* is not followed by a plus sign. Again, the parser has to backtrack when it finds out that the *7 – 8* is not followed by a multiplication operator.

This excessive amount of backtracking is the major drawback of DCGs. By taking care in the grammar definition, however, you can ensure that Prolog parses the language as efficiently as possible. In the next example, the grammar is written in a slightly different way to dramatically cut down on the amount of backtracking that can occur.

In this definition, an expression consists of a term followed by the rest of the expression. The rest of the expression consists of a plus sign followed by an expression, a minus sign followed by an expression, or an empty list to indicate the end of the expression. *Cuts* can even be added to further ensure that no backtracking occurs.

    expr --> term, restexp.

```
restexp --> [ + ], !, expr.
restexp --> [ - ], !, expr.
restexp --> [].
```

A term consists of a number followed by the rest of the term. The rest of the term consists of a multiplication sign followed by a term, a division sign followed by a term, or the empty list to indicate the end of the term.

```
term --> number, restterm.

restterm --> [*], term.
restterm --> [/], term.
restterm --> [].
```

A number consists of a plus sign followed by a number, a minus sign followed by a number, or an unsigned number.

```
number --> [ + ], number.
number --> [ - ], number.
number --> [C].
```

Although this grammar contains as many calls to *expr* and *term* as the previous grammar, the calls are not recursive. Instead, a second level of predicate is created that begins with a terminal. The terminal determines much earlier in the parsing process whether the call should be made. As a result, this grammar generates a much smaller tree, as shown in figure 7-4.

If the first token is not a number, the parser fails at the end of the first branch of the tree. If the token is not followed by the multiplication or division operator or by the empty list, then the parser fails at the end of the second branch. At each node, the parser knows that it has correctly parsed the previous token and that it will not have to backtrack over the previous branch of the tree.

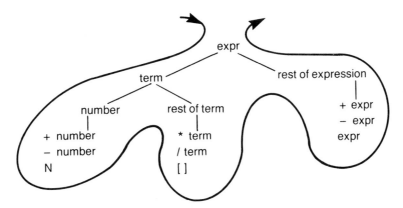

Figure 7-4: A More Efficient Grammar

Converting DCGs into Prolog Clauses

The $-->$ symbol is a standard Prolog operator. It is defined to convert DCG clauses into regular Prolog clauses. During the translation, two arguments are added to the clause. The first argument is the list of tokens being parsed; the second is the list of tokens remaining when the clause has executed. Each clause parses the token at the head of the list and passes the remaining list to the next clause.

For example, the *expr* clause is translated into a clause having two goals. The first goal calls *term* to find a term in A and return the list of remaining tokens to C. The second goal calls *restexp* to find the rest of the expression in C and return the list of remaining tokens to B.

```
expr(A,B) :-
    term(A,C),
    restexp(C,B).
```

The *term* definition is also translated into a clause having two goals. The first calls *number* to find a number in A and return the remaining tokens to C. The second calls *restterm* to find the rest of the term in C and return the remaining tokens to B.

```
term(A,B) :-
    number(A,C),
    restterm(C,B).
```

The *number* predicate looks for the plus or minus sign at the head of the list. If it is found, it calls itself to look for the number in the next position in the list. It returns the remaining tokens through the *B* argument.

```
number([ + |A],B) :-
    number(A,B).
number([ - |A],B) :-
    number(A,B).
number([A|B],B).
```

The *restterm* clause looks for the multiplication and division operators at the head of the list, followed by a term. If neither operator is found, *restterm* returns the entire list.

```
restterm([*|A],B) :-
    term(A,B).
restterm([/|A],B) :-
    term(A,B).
restterm(A,A).
```

The *restexp* predicate looks for the addition and subtraction operators at the head of the list. If they are found, it calls *expr* to find another expression. Otherwise, it returns the entire list.

```
restexp([ + |A],B) :-
    expr(A,B).
restexp([ - |A],B) :-
    expr(A,B).
restexp(A,A).
```

If a well-formed arithmetic expression is passed to *expr*, it should return the empty list to the second argument. Otherwise, *expr* returns that portion of the list that it was unable to parse. For example, the following expression is parsed completely and *expr* returns the empty list to the second argument:

```
?- expr([5, + ,2,*,4],X).

X = []
```

Adding Arguments

One of the things that a parser can produce is a parse tree. The parse tree shows the relationship between the elements of the statement. A parse tree for an arithmetic expression would show how the arguments relate to the operators and the order in which the subexpressions are evaluated. For example, the expression *1 + 2 * 3* can be represented by the parse tree:

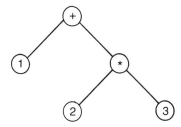

Because trees are evaluated from the bottom up, *2 * 3* is evaluated before it is added to *1*. Another way to represent this tree is with the following Prolog term:

+(1,*(2,3)).

You can write a DCG to return a parse tree as a Prolog term by adding arguments to the DCG. As tokens are removed from the token list, they are added to the tree. When building the parse tree, *expr* locates the left side of the tree with the *term* definition and passes the left side to *restexp*, which will return the complete parse tree to *E*.

expr(E) --> term(L), restexp(L,E).

Given the left side of the tree, *restexp* looks for a plus or minus sign and calls *expr* to return the right side of the tree. The right side can then be added as an argument to the plus or minus operator in the tree, along with the left side of the tree. The tree is complete when the empty list is found. The left side of the tree is passed back to *expr* unchanged.

restexp(L, +(L,R)) --> [+], expr(R).
restexp(L, –(L,R)) --> [–], expr(R).
restexp(L,L) --> [].

A term also has a left side and a right side. The left side contains a number and the right side contains the rest of the term. The left and right side of the term are also passed between clauses as arguments.

```
term(T) --> number(L), restterm(L,T).
```

Restterm is passed the left side of the term and it locates the right side, which consists of a multiplication or division operator followed by a term. When the empty list is found, then the entire term has been parsed and the left side of the tree is returned to *term* unchanged.

```
restterm(L,*(L,R)) --> [*], term(R).
restterm(L,/(L,R)) --> [/], term(R).
restterm(L,L) --> [].
```

Finally, the *number* definition returns N if the number is preceded by the plus sign, it returns $-N$ if the number is preceded by a minus sign, and it returns an unsigned number unchanged.

```
number(N) --> [+], number(N).
number(-N) --> [-], number(N).
number(C) --> [C].
```

In this way, the parse tree is built from the bottom up. Terms involving the unary plus and minus operators are added to the tree first, terms involving the multiplication and division operators are added to the tree next, and terms involving addition and subtraction are added to the tree last.

When Prolog translates this DCG into Prolog clauses, additional arguments are placed before the input and output token lists. Therefore, the parse tree is returned to the first argument, the input list is given in the second argument, and the remaining list is returned to the third argument.

```
expr(A,B,C) :-
    term(D,B,E),
    restexp(D,A,E,C).

restexp(A, +(A,B),[+|C],D) :-
    expr(B,C,D).
restexp(A, -(A,B),[-|C],D) :-
```

```
        expr(B,C,D).
    restexp(A,A,B,B).

    term(A,B,C) :-
        number(D,B,E),
        restterm(D,A,E,C).

    restterm(A,*(A,B),[*|C],D) :-
        term(B,C,D).
    restterm(A,/(A,B),[/|C],D) :-
        term(B,C,D).
    restterm(A,A,B,B).

    number(A,[ + |B],C) :-
        number(A,B,C).
    number( – A,[ – |B],C) :-
        number(A,B,C).
    number(A,[A|B],B).
```

You can now call *expr* like this:

```
?- expr(X,[5, + ,2,*,6],Y).

X  =  5  +  2  *  6
Y  =  []
```

Often, as in this example, the parse tree is an executable statement. The parse tree returned by this DCG can be used as an argument to the *is* evaluable predicate to return the result of the arithmetic expression. Other language processors may optimize parse trees to make them execute more efficiently.

Earlier, it was mentioned that the DCG extends the context-free grammar so that the parser can communicate information about the tense, number, or gender of the various parts of a natural language sentence. This kind of information is also communicated through additional arguments to the DCG. For example, parsing the sentence ''The boy runs to school,'' may involve checking that the person of the noun phrase agrees with the person of the verb phrase.

The parse tree in figure 7-5 shows how number agreement would be communicated through the different parts of the sentence. The *noun__phrase*, *verb__phrase*, *noun*, and *verb* definitions have an additional argument. The terminals *boy* and *runs* also have additional arguments defining these words as referring to the third person. When the parser locates these terminals, the arguments to *noun__phrase* and *verb__phrase* will be instantiated and Prolog will check that their values match.

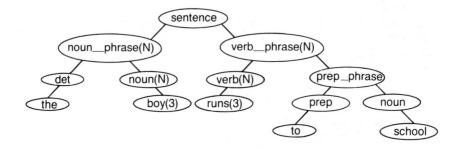

Figure 7-5: Parse Tree to Check Number Agreement

A more complete natural language system will be described in chapter 8.

Executing Goals within a DCG

Goals can be executed from within a DCG by placing the goals inside curly braces. When Prolog reads the DCG, it performs no translation on the goals, placing them in the clause unchanged. For example, the answer to the arithmetic expression can be calculated by using the parse tree as an argument to the *is* evaluable predicate.

    expr(A) --> term(L), restexp(L,E), { A is E } .

When Prolog reads this definition, the extra argument to hold the result is placed first in the argument list and the goal within braces is added to the clause unchanged.

    expr(A,B,C) :-
        term(D,B,E),
        restexp(D,F,E,C),
        A is F.

The rest of the DCG remains the same:

    restexp(L, +(L,R)) --> [+], expr(R).

```
restexp(L, –(L,R)) --> [ – ], expr(R).
restexp(L,L) --> [].

term(T) --> number(L), restterm(L,T).

restterm(L,*(L,R)) --> [*], term(R).
restterm(L,/(L,R)) --> [/], term(R).
restterm(L,L) --> [].

number(N) --> [ + ], number(N).
number( – N) --> [ – ], number(N).
number(C) --> [C].
```

With this new version of *expr*, you can return the result of the calculation, like this:

```
?- expr(X,[1, + ,2,*,3],__).
```

X = 7

An Arithmetic Calculator

There are almost enough pieces now to write an arithmetic calculator. To make the calculator more application-like, one more piece is needed — a simple predicate to read characters from the keyboard until a carriage return is typed and to create a character string from that stream of input:

```
edit(Curr,New) :-
    get0(C),
    update(C,Curr,New).

update(13,Curr,Curr).
update(C,Curr,New) :-
    append(Curr,[C],X),
    edit(X,New).
```

Be careful using *edit*, however, because it does not handle non-printing characters correctly. For example, if the user presses the backspace key, the ASCII code 8 will be added to the input stream and the character will not be removed from the string. You can expand this predicate to check for the backspace. Then it removes the last character from the string. Other special keys would be handled by their own clauses.

```
update(13,Curr,Curr).
update(8,Curr,New) :-
     remove_last(Curr,[],X),
     edit(X,New).
update(C,Curr,New) :-
     append(Curr,[C],X),
     edit(X,New).

remove_last([H|[[]][]],X,X).
remove_last([H|T],X,Y) :-
     append(X,[H],N),
     remove_last(T,N,Y).
```

The *edit* predicate, the tokenizer, and the DCG that returns the result can now be put together to form a calculator. The output from the *edit* predicate is used as input to the *tokenize* predicate; the output from *tokenize* can be used as the input to *expr*. The arithmetic calculator consists of three goals:

```
calculator(X) :-
     edit(L),
     tokenize(L,__,I),
     expr(X,I,__).
```

When *calculator* is run, the user supplies a variable to which the predicate can return the answer. For example:

```
?- calculator(X).
 − 4 + 5 * 6

X = 26
```

In this example *edit* reads in the string [45,52,32,43,32,53,32,42,32,54]. *Tokenize* converts the string to the list [− ,4, + ,5,*,6]. *Calculator* then passes the string of tokens to *expr*, which processes the expression and returns the answer.

Summary

When computers process language, they follow many of the same steps regardless of the language. They separate a statement into tokens and then analyze the sentence for grammar and meaning. Finally, the statement is converted to an internal form. These stages are called tokenization, syntax and semantic analysis, and code generation. This chapter concentrated on tokenization and syntax analysis, or ''parsing.''

Two methods for parsing language are built into Prolog. The Prolog reader parses Prolog terms and operators extend Prolog syntax. With the reader and operator definitions, Prolog can parse well-defined languages, such as a database query language or an expert system development language.

Definite clause grammar notation (DCGs) can parse more complex grammars. Although DCG notation can define context-free grammars, it extends these grammars in two ways. First, the DCG can pass context information between parts of the statement. This allows the grammar to check for agreement among the different parts of a statement. Second, the DCG can execute goals directly as part of the grammar. This allows the grammar to produce results, such as parse trees or the results of arithmetic computations, as shown in this chapter.

Definite clause grammars have been used successfully for parsing much more demanding languages than the arithmetic expression grammar in this chapter has demonstrated. In the next chapter, DCGs are used for understanding natural language queries and for returning natural language responses.

8

Natural Language Processing

Even though the term "natural language" implies communication as easy as conversing with your next-door neighbor, it is not that simple. People often confuse "natural language" with "human language" and computers simply are not yet adequate for human interaction. To be able to understand human language, a computer would need to possess the kind of knowledge about the language that humans possess. There are many reasons why they cannot possess this kind of information at this time.

A grammar for human language ensures that the parts of the sentence agree in tense, person, and so on. This is referred to as "context" information. Chapter 7 explained that context-free grammars are not able to handle context information but that definite clause grammars (DCGs) can. Therefore, when built with DCGs, natural languages can imitate human language.

However, in human language conversation, the context extends beyond a single sentence. Many different topics weave in and out of a conversation and the participants may refer to the various topics in ambiguous ways. Maintaining the context of an entire conversation is a very difficult programming problem. Although there are programs that can scan books or papers and pick out the main topics, this book will stick to much simpler language processing problems.

Beyond their complexity, human languages are too large for computers to handle. To carry on a conversation in human language, a computer would have to store the definitions of thousands of words and all the possible ways in which those words can be combined. It is an interesting fact that a two year old child knows more about the family kitchen than the largest supercomputer can hold.

If this is so, it will be a while before computers can store enough information to understand human language.

Even though the size and complexity of human languages cannot be handled by the current technology, useful but more limited "natural" language systems can be developed. If the system is limited so that it handles only one statement at a time, the grammar is less complex. This makes it possible to build a system using well-known techniques, such as definite clause grammars. If the topics about which the system can converse are also limited, the grammar is kept small.

Yet even with these constraints, there are still problems. Human languages allow anomalies that natural languages cannot allow. For example, "The fox runs through the woods" can be a complete sentence but it can also be part of a larger sentence. Here, "fox" is used as a noun. In the sentence "The fox runs through the woods were easy for the hounds to follow," "fox" is used as an adjective. You cannot discover the intended meaning of "fox runs" until you have read the entire sentence. Sentences like these are called "garden path" sentences. Garden path sentences are difficult for a natural language system to parse because the system needs to know all the different ways in which phrases like "fox runs" can be used. There is no way to parse such a sentence efficiently. The system must choose one interpretation of the phrase without knowing if it is going to be the correct interpretation. It may have to backtrack and start the parsing process again.

Another anomaly that human languages allow is the ambiguous reference. For example, in the sentence "The ice cream is in the freezer and it is cold," you need to decide whether "it" refers to the ice cream or to the freezer. We can usually guess what "it," "this," and "that" refer to, simply by context. These rules for guessing are not easily translated into grammar rules.

Where words like "it," "this," and "that" alert us to ambiguous references, other ambiguous references are less obvious to see. Consider the sentence, "I know a man with a wooden leg named Smith." We know that the man is named Smith, not the leg. However, the natural language system would need to know that people have names and that wooden legs probably do not.

In human language, various parts of a sentence can be arranged in different ways and still produce the same meaning. For example, "What time does the train leave?" and "The train leaves at what time?" both mean the same thing. However, each form requires its own grammar definition.

A natural language system that could handle all of these situations would still be unreasonably large and complex. Natural language systems must not only limit the grammar to single sentences, they must also make assumptions about the types of sentences the user will enter. When designing a natural language system, you must decide which sentence forms your system will recognize and what those sentences will mean. Often within a well-defined subject area, you can choose a limited number of sentence structures to handle most of the user's needs.

Choosing a Topic

To keep the size and complexity of a natural language system within reasonable bounds, the topic about which the system can converse must be limited. A suitable topic should deal with only a few kinds of objects. For example, information kept in a rolodex is limited to names, companies, addresses, and phone numbers. A successful natural language system could be built around this kind of information.

This chapter describes a simple natural language system that processes questions and statements about airline flight schedules. The application of natural language to airline flight schedules is based on the thesis by W.A. Woods titled "Semantics for a Question-Answering System." (Rep. NSF-19, Harvard University Computation Laboratory, 1967; available from NTIS as PB-176-548). (See also Woods, W.A. "Semantics and Quantification in Natural Language Question Answering," in *Advances in Computers*, Vol. 17, Academic Press, 1978.)

Airline flight schedules can be handled adequately by a natural language system because there are only a few things that a person needs to know about a flight. In this example, the system keeps information about the flight number, the airline for the flight, the cities that the flight connects, and the regions in which those cities are located.

The application ties a natural language system into a database containing the Prolog facts:

```
flight(79).
flight(89).
flight(45).
flight(99).
```

```
airline(79,branniff).
airline(89,branniff).
airline(45,usair).
airline(99,usair).

connects(79,phi,la).
connects(89,phi,ny).
connects(45,phi,bos).
connects(99,bos,ny).

city(la).
city(phi).
city(ny).
city(bos).

region(la,west__coast).
region(phi,east__coast).
region(bos,east__coast).
region(ny,east__coast).
```

You can expand the system by adding more flight information to the database. This makes the database larger but it does not make the natural language system more complex.

Defining the Natural Language

To keep the language from becoming too large and complex, you must also limit the sentence structures that the system will recognize. Often with a well-defined subject area you can predict what types of questions will meet most people's needs. In an airline flight schedule system, for example, people will probably want to ask questions about specific flights and airlines. They may also want to ask general questions about flight patterns or make general and specific statements about flights and airlines. Therefore, this system will handle three types of sentences.

Users can ask for specific flights from one city or region to another city or region. Examples of specific questions include:

Does flight number 19 fly to bos?
Does Branniff flight 79 from la go to the east__coast?
Do any flights go to la?
Does any airline have a flight to ny?
Do some flights from ny go to bos?
Do any flights from a west__coast city go to ny?
Does branniff have a flight to la?

Users can also ask general questions rather than questions about specific flights. These questions determine trends in the flights that are stored in the database. For example:

Do all west__coast flights go to la?
Does every branniff flight fly from phi?
Do all west__coast flights fly from the east__coast?

The difference between these two types of questions is in the number, or quantity, of answers that need to be found in the database. Words like "any," "some," "a," or "the" indicate that only one instance must be found in the database to satisfy the question. These words will be referred to as "simple quantifiers." Words like "all," "each," or "every" indicate that all instances of a database query must satisfy certain conditions. These words will be referred to as "existential quantifiers."

Finally, the user can make statements. Like questions, statements can be specific or general, as in:

All usair flights go to bos.
Flight 79 flies to ny from bos.
Usair has a flight to ny.

As you determine the types of sentences the system can understand, you also determine the vocabulary that the system will require. Table 8-1 shows the vocabulary required for the airline flight schedule application. It lists four classes of words. Nouns and verbs define the objects and actions that the system understands. Quantifiers determine whether the user wants information about specific flights (using simple quantifiers) or whether the user wants general information (using existential quantifiers). Auxiliaries indicate whether the sentence is a question or a statement.

Table 8-1: Airline Flight Schedule Vocabulary

Nouns	Quantifiers	Verbs	Auxiliaries	Prepositions
flight	any	fly	do	to
flights	some	flies	does	from
plane	the	go		
planes	a	goes		
airline	every	have		
airlines	all	has		
city	each			
cities				
region				
regions				

The vocabulary is stored in the database as Prolog facts.

```
noun(airline,airline).
noun(airlines,airline).
noun(flight,flight).
noun(flights,flight).
noun(plane,flight).
noun(planes,flight).
noun(number,number).
noun(city,city).
noun(cities,city).

verb(fly,intrans).
verb(flies,intrans).
verb(go,intrans).
verb(goes,intrans).
verb(connects,intrans).
verb(has,trans).
verb(have,trans).

is__aux(do).
is__aux(does).

is__quant(every,every).
is__quant(all,every).
is__quant(each,every).
```

is＿quant(some,some).
is＿quant(any,some).
is＿quant(the,some).
is＿quant(a,some).

Writing a Natural Language Parser

Once you have determined the vocabulary and sentence structures your system requires, you can write the grammar rules for each valid sentence type. The technique you use depends on the requirements of the language. If the grammar will need to pass information between the parts of the sentence, then you must use context-sensitive parsing techniques. The parser described here uses DCGs because they are built into Prolog.

Remember from chapter 6 that DCGs assume that a list of tokens is the input to a grammar definition. The definition can check that the element at the beginning of the list is a valid token followed by some recognizable list of tokens. This part of the grammar notation is very similar to defining a grammar in Backus-Naur form.

As the grammar checks that a list of tokens conforms to the definition of a valid sentence, it will also build an appropriate database query for the sentence. To build the query, the parser must pass information between the parts of a sentence as additional arguments to the DCG. The additional arguments supply information regarding the following items:

- The variables over which the sentence is quantified. This is important for sentences that contain existential quantifiers.
- The arguments that are currently instantiated. It is important that variables shared between a noun and a verb phrase have the same values. A structure is passed between all parts of a sentence so that as values become known to one part of the sentence, they also become known to the rest. The argument structure has the following form:

args(N,O,D,A)

flight origin destination airline

- The ambiguity of the sentence. Ambiguity arises when an object from one table can appear in more than one position within a sentence and when it is not clear which position the user intends. In the airline application, references to a city or region can be ambiguous if they do not appear within a prepositional phrase. For example, the noun phrase "a ny flight" could mean that the flight is going to New York or that it is coming from New York. The parser must wait until more information is available before deciding which is the correct meaning. References to flights or airlines will never be ambiguous because they can be used in only one way within a sentence. In addition, there can be only one origin and one destination in a sentence. These constraints make it possible to resolve ambiguities with relative ease. The greater the number of arguments that can be ambiguous and the number of ways in which they can be used ambiguously, the more difficult it becomes to resolve references.

The Top Level of the Grammar

The top level of the grammar tests to see whether the sentence is a question or a statement. The queries built from questions are returned as a structure with the name *test*; the queries built from statements are returned as a structure with the name *assert*. If the system cannot parse the sentence, then an error message is issued and the program exits with a *cut* and *fail*.

```
semantic(test(Sent)) -->
     aux, sentence(Sent), !.
semantic(assert(Sent)) -->
     sentence(Sent), !.
semantic(_) -->
     { write('Cannot understand your question.'),
       nl, !, fail
     }.
```

```
aux --> [X], { is_aux(X) }.
```

Existentially quantified sentences are translated into *for_each* expressions.

```
sentence(for_each V : (Prec --> Ante)) -->
     quant(every),
     nounphrase(Prec,V,Args,Amb),
```

```
        { var(V),
          pass_args(V,Args,Newargs)
        },
        verbphrase(Ante,Newargs,Amb).

quant(Quant) --> [X], { is_quant(X,Quant) }.
quant(some) --> [].

pass_args(V,args(X,Y,Z,W),args(X,Y1,Z1,W1)) :-
    ( V == X ; V == W ), !.
pass_args(_,_,args(X,Y,Z,W)).
```

Statements that are not existentially quantified are translated into a list of goals, where the noun phrase builds one part of the list and the verb phrase builds another. These two lists are appended to form the complete list of goals for the query.

```
sentence(Conjuncts) -->
    quant(some),
    nounphrase(Conj1,V,Args,Amb),
    verbphrase(Conj2,Args,Amb),
    { append_conj(Conj1,Conj2,Conjuncts) }.

append_conj([], B, B).
append_conj([A|B], C, D) :-
    append_conj(B,C,D), member(A,D), !.
append_conj([A|B], C, [A|D]) :-
    append_conj(B,C,D).
```

A noun phrase can be a single *nphrase* or an *nphrase* followed by a prepositional phrase.

```
nounphrase(Preds, V, Args, Amb) -->
    nphrase(Preds,V,Args,Amb).
nounphrase(Preds, V, Args, Amb) -->
    nphrase(Preds1,V,Args,Amb),
    pp(Preds2,Args,Amb),
    { append_conj(Preds1,Preds2,Preds) }.
```

The verb phrase specifies to and from which cities or regions the requested flights travel. The first *verbphrase* definition below lets the user ask questions such as "Does an airline fly to the west__coast." The second definition lets you ask questions like "Does branniff have a flight to any west__coast city." The second contains the quantifier "any" as part of the verb phrase. However, the quantifier of a prepositional phrase cannot be an existential quantifier like "all" or "every." This means that the user cannot ask the question, "Does branniff have a flight to every west__coast city."

```
verbphrase(Conj, Args, Amb) -->
     [V], { verb(V,intrans) },
     pp(Conj,Args,Amb).
verbphrase(Conj, Args, Amb1) -->
     [V], { verb(V,trans) },
     quant(some),
     nounphrase(Conj1,__,Args,Amb2),
     { pass__amb(Amb1,Amb2,Amb) },
     pp(Conj2,Args,Amb),
     { append__conj(Conj1,Conj2,Conj) }.
```

The verb phrase must pass ambiguity information to any prepositional phrase that it may encounter. The *pass__amb* predicate is called within curly braces to check whether any variable was ambiguous when the verb phrase was entered and whether any ambiguity was encountered while parsing the verb phrase. The *pass__amb* predicate checks the two ambiguity arguments *A1* and *A2*. If *A1* is ambiguous, it is passed to the prepositional phrase. Otherwise, the ambiguity argument *A2* is passed to the prepositional phrase. The atom *not__amb* indicates that no ambiguous references have been detected.

```
pass__amb(A1,A2,A1) :- ambiguous(A1), !.
pass__amb(A1,A2,A2).
```

```
ambiguous(A) :- A \ == not__amb.
```

One easy modification to the DCG that you can make would allow questions like "What flights go to ny?" To add this to the DCG, you need to add the word "what" to the vocabulary as a quantifier having the same meaning as "any." Because this type of question does not begin with either "do" or "does," the DCG treats it as a statement rather than a question. Therefore, the query produced by the question is returned as an *assert* structure.

Parsing Unambiguous Sentences

References to flights and airlines are unambiguous if no city or region is part of the phrase. Table 8-2 gives some examples of unambiguous noun phrases and the goals that the parser produces for each phrase.

Table 8-2: Translation of Noun Phrases into Prolog Goals

Clause Number	Noun Phrase	Prolog Goals
[1]	flight 79	flight(79)
[2]	branniff flight 79	flight(79), airline(79,branniff)
[3]	usair flights	flight(X),airline(X,usair)
[4]	airline	airline(X,Y)
[5]	flights	flight(X)
[6]	branniff	flight(X),airline(X,branniff)

Each noun phrase must have its own definition in the DCG. The *nphrase* definitions translate the noun phrase into a list of one or more goals. The known values within the goals are placed in the *args* structure, and the valid variable over which the query can be existentially quantified is defined. The clause numbers to the left of each definition below correspond to the clause numbers in the left column of table 8-2.

```
[1] nphrase([flight(Num)], Num, args(Num,X,Y,Z), not_amb) -->
        flight,
        flight_no(Num).
[2] nphrase([flight(Num), airline(Num,Air)], Num, args(Num,Y,Z,Air),
    not_amb) -->
        airlinename(Air),
        flight,
        flight_no(Num).
[3] nphrase([flight(X), airline(X,Air)], X, args(X,Y,Z,Air), not_amb) -->
        airlinename(Air),
        flight.
[4] nphrase([airline(X,A)], A, args(X,Y,Z,A), not_amb) -->
        [N], { noun(N,airline) }.
```

[5] nphrase([flight(X)], X, args(X,Y,Z,A), not__amb) -->
      flight.
[6] nphrase([airline(X,Airline)], Airline, args(X,Y,Z,Airline), not__amb) -->
      airlinename(Airline).

    flight --> [X], { noun(X,flight) }.

    flight__no(Num) --> [X], { noun(X,number) }, number(Num).
    flight__no(Num) --> number(Num).

    number(Num) --> [Num], { integer(Num) }.

    airlinename(X) --> [X], { is__airline(X) }.

Prepositional phrases tell the sources and destinations of the requested flights. The source and destination for a flight can be a city, a region, or a combination of the two. In an unambiguous prepositional phrase, both the origin and destination are known. Each of the valid forms of a prepositional phrase are shown in table 8-3 with the Prolog goals that the parser produces for the phrase.

Table 8-3: Translation of Prepositional Phrases into Prolog Goals

Clause	Sample Sentence	Prolog Goals
[1]	from phi to ny	connects(X,phi,ny)
[2]	to la from phi	connects(X,phi,la)
[3]	from the east__coast to the west__coast	connects(X,Y,Z), region(Y,east__coast), region(X,west__coast)
[4]	from the west__coast to ny	connects(X,Y,ny), region(Y,west__coast)
[5]	to the west__coast from phi	connects(X,phi,Z), region(Z,west__coast)

The DCG defines each of these forms of prepositional phrase. The clause numbers are included here to show how they correspond to the goals in table 8-3.

[1] pp([connects(X,Y,Z)], args(X,Y,Z,A), Amb) -->
    { noambiguity(Amb) },
    from__to(Y,city,Z,Place),
    { Place == city; Place == [] }.
[2] pp([connects(X,Y,Z)], args(X,Y,Z,A), Amb) -->
    { noambiguity(Amb) },
    from__to(Y,Place,Z,city),
    { Place == city ; Place == [] }.
[3] pp([connects(X,Y,Z), region(Y,R1), region(Z,R2)], args(X,Y,Z,A), Amb) -->
    { noambiguity(Amb) },
    from__to(R1,region,R2,region).
[4] pp([connects(X,Y,Z), region(Y,R)], args(X,Y,Z,A), Amb) -->
    { noambiguity(Amb) },
    from__to(R,region,Z,Place),
    { Place == city ; Place == [] }.
[5] pp([connects(X,Y,Z), region(Z,R)], args(X,Y,Z,A), Amb) -->
    { noambiguity(Amb) },
    from__to(Y,Place,R,region),
    { Place == city ; Place == [] }.

The *pp* definitions rely on *from__to* to determine which argument within a *connects* goal is instantiated to the origin and which is instantiated to the destination.

    from__to(X,Y,Z,W) --> from(X,Y), to(Z,W).
    from__to(X,Y,Z,W) --> to(Z,W), from(X,Y).
    from__to(X,Y,Z,[]) --> from(X,Y).
    from__to(X,[],Z,W) --> to(Z,W).

    from(X,Y) --> prep(from), place(X,Y).
    to(X,Y) --> prep(to), place(X,Y).

    prep(Y) --> [X], { is__prep(X,Y) }.

    place(X,city) --> [X], { city(X) }.
    place(X,region) --> quant(some), [X], { regionname(X) }.
    place(X,region) -->
        quant(some),
        [X], { regionname(X) },
        [Y], { noun(Y,city) }.

    noambiguity(Amb) :- Amb == not__amb.

Parsing Ambiguous Sentences

Ambiguous sentences contain a reference to a city or region that is not part of a prepositional phrase. For example, in the sentence "Does ny have any flights to la," the parser cannot tell whether New York is the origin or the destination until it reaches the end of the sentence. It can then assume that New York is the origin and Los Angeles is the destination. The parser deals with ambiguity by passing the ambiguous argument between the parts of the sentence until enough information becomes available.

The parser may also encounter a sentence in which the ambiguity is not cleared up. For example, the question "Does branniff have any west_coast flights" never indicates whether the west coast is the origin or the destination. It is up to you, the system designer, to choose how to interpret this kind of question. This system will assume that the west coast is the destination.

Table 8-4 shows the kinds of noun phrases that are ambiguous.

Table 8-4: Ambiguous Noun Phrases

Noun Phrase	Prolog Goals	Ambiguity
ny flights	flight(X), connects(X,Y,Z)	Y or Z may become instantiated to ny
west_coast flights	flight(X), connects(X,Y,Z), region(*,west_coast)	* may be instantiated to Y or Z
east_coast city	city(X), connects(Y,Z), region(*,east_coast)	* may be instantiated to Y or Z

In an ambiguous noun phrase, the parser cannot assign a value to the origin or destination cities. The *nphrase* definition assigns the ambiguous value to the last argument of the DCG. This value is passed along to the *pp* definition.

```
nphrase([flight(X), connects(X,Y,Q)], X, args(X,Y,Q,Z), City) -->
    place(City,city),
    flight.
nphrase([flight(X), connects(X,Y,Z1), city(Z), region(Z,Region)],
X, args(X,Y,Z1,A),Z) -->
    place(Region,region),
    flight.
nphrase([city(City), region(City,Region)], City, args(X,Y,Z,A), City) -->
```

```
        place(Region,region),
        [C],
        { noun(C,city) }.
nphrase([city(City)], City, args(X,Y,Z,A), City) -->
        place(City,city).
```

Ambiguity is resolved by the prepositional phrase. The *pp* definitions place the ambiguous value in the proper position within a *connects* goal. The last *pp* definition handles those situations when the ambiguity cannot be resolved. In this case, the ambiguous value is placed in the destination position within the *connects* goal.

```
pp([connects(X,Y,Z)], args(X,Y,Z1,A), Z) -->
        { ambiguous(Z) },
        from(Y,city),
        { Z = Z1 }.
pp([connects(X,Y,Z), region(Y,Region)], args(X,Y,Z1,A), Z) -->
        { ambiguous(Z) },
        from(Region,region),
        { Z = Z1 }.
pp([connects(X,Y,Z), region(Z,Region)], args(X,Y1,Z,A), Y) -->
        { ambiguous(Y) },
        to(Region,region),
        { Y = Y1 }.
pp([connects(X,Y,Z)], args(X,Y1,Z,A), Y) -->
        { ambiguous(Y) },
        to(Z,City),
        { Y = Y1 }.
pp([connects(X,Y,Amb)], args(X,Y,Amb,A), Amb) -->
        { ambiguous(Amb) }.
```

Executing Queries

The DCG translates sentences into an intermediate form. When you call the top level of the DCG (*semantic*) with the list of tokens that make up a sentence, it returns either a *test* or an *assert* structure. *Test* structures are created for sentences that begin with an auxiliary (these are questions). *Assert* structures are created for sentences that do not begin with an auxiliary (these are statements). The first decision that must be made is how to interpret these two types of statement.

When the system encounters a question, it should query the database. When the system encounters a statement, it could do one of two things: it could add the new piece of information to the database if it does not already exist or it could treat the statement as a question. When adding information to the database, the system would have to be careful not to add incomplete information or information that would conflict with existing information. When adding information, therefore, the first step is to treat the statement as a question. This will show whether the information already exists or whether it conflicts. This is as far as the example system will go.

Sentences that contain a simple quantifier are returned as a list of goals. Here are some examples of the way that *semantic* translates questions:

```
?- semantic(S,[do,any,flights,go,to,la],[]).
S = test([flight(X), connects(X,Y,la)])

?- semantic(S,[does,any,airline,fly,to,bos],[]).
S = test([airline(X,Y), connects(X,Z,bos)])

?- semantic(S,[does,any,airline,have,a,flight,to,ny],[]).
S = test([airline(X,Y), connects(X,Z,ny)])

?- semantic(S,[some,flights,from,ny,go,to,bos],[]).
S = assert([flight(X), connects(X,ny,bos)])

?- semantic(S,[do,any,flights,from,a,west__coast,city,go,to,ny,[]).
S = test([flight(X), connects(X,Y,ny), region(Y,west__coast)])
```

Sentences that contain an existential quantifier are returned as *for__each* expressions. A *for__each* expression contains two lists of goals separated by the -- > operator. The first list defines the goals over which the expression is quantified; the second contains the conditions that are being tested. Here are some examples of the way that *semantic* translates existentially quantified sentences:

```
?- semantic(S,[do,all,west__coast,flights,go,to,la],[]).
S = test(for__each X : ([flight(X)] --> [connects(X,Y,la)])).

?- semantic(S,[does,every,branniff,flight,fly,from,phi],[]).
S = test(for__each X : ([flight(X), airline(X,branniff)] -->
          [connects(X,phi,Y)])).
```

```
?- semantic(S,[all,usair,flights,go,to,bos],[]).
S  =  assert(for__each X : ([flight(X), airline(X,usair)] -->
          [connects(X,Y,bos)]])).
```

```
?- semantic(S,[do,all,west__coast,flights,fly,from,the,east__coast],[]).
S  =  test(for__each X : ([flight(X), connects(X,Y,Z),
          region(Z,west__coast)] -->
          [connects(X,A,B), region(A,east__coast)]])).
```

Existential quantification requires the definition of two operators. The
for__each operator and the colon operator that it uses must be defined as follows:

```
:- op(900,fx,for__each).
:- op(800,xfy,:).
```

The precedence of these operators is based on 1200. For Prolog systems
that base precedence on 256, the operators can be defined as:

```
:- op(250,fx,for__each).
:- op(200,xfy,:).
```

Before it can be executed, the goal must be converted from its intermediate
form to an executable clause. The first step is performed by the *execute* predicate, which strips off the functor (either *test* or *assert*). It is at this point that the
system can no longer distinguish between a question and a statement. If you
are going to expand the system to add new data to the database, you would expand the *execute* predicate at this point in the program.

```
execute(test(X)) :- construct(X).
execute(assert(X)) :- construct(X).
```

Execute passes the goals to a predicate called *construct*. *Construct* can recognize the two forms that the goals may take. For a *for__each* expression, it must
construct two clauses. One corresponds to the list of goals to the left of the -->
operator and the other corresponds to the list of goals to the right of the -->
operator. For conjunctions, *construct* produces only one clause.

251

```
construct(for__each X : (P --> Q)) :-
        !, make__clause__fe(P,C1), make__clause__fe(Q,C2),
        for__each(C1,C2,P,Q).
construct([H|T]) :-
        make__clause(T,H,Clause),
        gen(Clause,[H|T]).
```

The *make__clause__fe* and *make__clause* predicates recursively add each goal to the executable clause.

```
make__clause__fe([H|T],Clause) :-
        make__clause(T,H,Clause).
```

```
make__clause([],Temp,Temp).
make__clause([H|T],Temp,X) :-
        make__clause(T,(Temp,H),X).
```

Construct also controls the execution of these clauses. Existentially quantified statements are passed to the *for__each* predicate; regular conjunctions are passed to the *gen* predicate. These two predicates use different schemes for executing clauses.

For conjunctions, the clause can be called within a fail loop to find all the answers in the database. At this point, *gen* will simply write each result on a separate line.

```
gen(Clause) :-
        call(Clause),
        write(Clause), nl,
        fail.
gen(__).
```

Existentially quantified goals must be executed differently. For each instance in the database that satisfies the first clause, the second clause must also be proved. The *for__each* test can be handled by the following predicate. Again, the result's appearance will be simplified for now.

```
for__each(C1,C2) :-
        not(( C1, not C2)),
        write('for__each succeeded'), nl.
```

This predicate checks that there is no instance of *C1* for which there is not also an instance of *C2*. It does this by first finding an instance of *C1*. If one is found, it then finds an instance of *C2*. If an instance of *C2* is also found, then *not C2* fails. When *not C2* fails, *for__each* looks for the next instance of *C1* and tests *C2* again. If an instance of *C2* cannot be found, then *not C2* succeeds. Now *C1* and *not C2* are both true. This causes the outermost *not* to fail. The outermost *not* also fails when no instance of *C1* can be found.

It may be easier to understand how *for__each* works by looking at a few examples. The question "Do all west__coast flights go to la?" should succeed because the database contains only one flight to the west coast, and it goes to Los Angeles. When this sentence is given to *semantic*, it returns a *for__each* expression.

```
?- semantic(S,[do,all,west__coast,flights,go,to,la],[]).
S = test(for__each X : ([flight(X), connects(X,Y,Z),
region(Z,west__coast)] --> [connects(X,A,la)])).
```

The *execute* predicate removes the *test* functor from the structure and passes the argument to *construct*. *Construct* finds that this is a *for__each* statement, so it makes two clauses; one for the left side of the expression and one for the right. When both calls to *make__clause__fe* are completed, two sets of goals are returned to the *C1* and *C2* arguments. These two clauses are as follows:

```
C1 = (flight(X), connects(X,Y,Z), region(Z,west__coast))
C2 = (connects(X,A,la))
```

C1 and *C2* are passed to *for__each*. *For__each* first locates a flight, the cities it connects, and tests whether the destination city is on the west coast:

```
flight(79),connects(79,phi,la),region(la,west__coast)
```

Because *C1* succeeded, *for__each* tries the second goal:

```
not(connects(79,phi,la))
```

Flight 79 does connect Philadelphia and Los Angeles, so the *not* fails. This causes *for__each* to look for the next instance of *C1* in the database:

```
flight(89),connects(89,phi,ny),region(ny,west__coast)
```

This instance of *C1* fails because New York is not on the west coast. *For__each* then looks for the next instance of *C1*:

flight(45),connects(45,phi,pit),region(pit,west__coast)

Again, this clause fails. *For__each* will continue to look for an instance of *C1*. When one is found, then it looks for an instance of *C2*. When no more instances of *C1* are found, then the search is stopped and *for__each* exits successfully. That is, no instances of *C1* were found for which an instance of *C2* was not also found.

Consider now what happens when there is no matching *C2* clause for *C1*, as in the question "Do all flights go to the west__coast?" *Semantic* parses the sentence and returns a *for__each* expression:

?- semantic(S,[do,all,flights,go,to,the,west__coast],[]).
S = test(for__each X : ([flight(X)] --> [connects(X,Y,Z),
region(Z,west__coast)]))

The *execute* predicate strips off the *test* functor and *construct* produces two goals:

C1 = flight(X)
C2 = connects(X,Y,Z), region(Z,west__coast)

For__each must first find a flight in the database:

flight(79)

It then looks for the cities that the flight connects and checks that the destination city is on the west coast:

not(connects(79,phi,la), region(la,west__coast))

For flight 79, both goals succeed. This makes the inner *not* fail. *For__each* then looks for another flight number for *C1*.

flight(89)

It looks for the cities that flight 89 connects and checks to see if the destination city is on the west coast. However, this time, the *not* succeeds because New York is not on the west coast.

```
not(connects(89,phi,ny), region(ny,west__coast))
```

Because the second goal succeeds, no more flights are tried. The predicate stops searching the database at this point and fails.

Generating Natural Language Responses

Often, it is desirable for a system that understands natural language to respond in natural language, too. However, as many issues surround natural language generation as surround natural language understanding. When parsing a natural language sentence, you have to make assumptions about the types of questions the user may want to ask. When executing queries produced from the questions, you have to make assumptions about what those queries mean. When generating a response to a query, you must make assumptions about the types of responses that are appropriate. Most important, as you build answers, you must try to make them reflect the intent of the user's question.

When someone asks a question like "Do any flights fly to ny?" they probably want more than a "yes" or "no" answer. They probably want to know which flights fly to New York and where the flights originate. Other information, such as the name of the airline or the region, should be included if they are part of the question. For conjunctions, therefore, the airline flight schedule system will generate answers like this:

```
Question:  do any flights fly to la
  Answer:  flight 79 flies from phi to la

Question:  do any flights fly to ny
  Answer:  flight 89 flies to ny
           flight 99 flies to ny
```

The system must not only generate answers to questions for which it can find an answer, it must also generate answers to questions for which it cannot find an answer. When a conjunction of goals fails, the system will respond with answers such as this:

Question: do any flights fly from la
Answer: no flights fly from la

Existentially quantified questions require a different sort of answer. The person asking a question probably does not care about any specific flight. This system simply prints a statement regarding the truth of the question.

Question: do all branniff flights fly from phi
Answer: all branniff flights fly from phi

Negative answers to existentially quantified questions are a little more difficult. Consider the question:

Question: do all flights from la go to the east_coast

If the system were to answer this question with a simple "no," it would be misleading. Do some flights from Los Angeles fly to the west coast? Or do no flights fly from Los Angeles at all? The following answers to negative queries involving existential quantifiers attempt to explain the reason why the question failed:

Question: do all flights from la go to ny
Answer: no flights fly from la

Question: do all flights fly to the east_coast
Answer: flight 79 does not fly to the east_coast

A good natural language system should try to determine what assumptions the users make when they ask a particular type of question and it should make sure that its responses address those assumptions.

Natural language responses can be generated by DCGs, just as the user's questions were parsed by a DCG. This process is exactly the reverse of the parsing process performed by *semantic*. Rather than accepting tokens that make up the sentence, the language generator will accept the list of goals that make up the query. Each part of an answer will be returned as a list of words which the system appends to the other parts of the response. All possible combinations of goals are defined by the DCG to match the possible combinations defined by *semantic*.

Answering Successful Conjunctions of Goals

During semantic analysis, the system converts a large number of possible sentence forms into a smaller number of query forms. For example, although prepositional phrases can be written in many different ways, the parser generates only four kinds of query. That is, a prepositional phrase will translate into one of the following:

```
    connects(X,Y,Z)
    connects(X,Y,Z), region(Y,Region)
    connects(X,Y,Z), region(Z,Region)
or  connects(X,Y,Z), region(Y,Region1), region(Z,Region2)
```

The system also defines synonyms. For example, "flight," "flights," "plane," and "planes" are synonyms. This means that the number of possible questions is considerably larger than the number of forms that the answer to a question can take.

For conjunctions, an answer can consist of a flight number followed by a connect statement, as in the query *flight(79), connects(79,phi,la)*. The answer is constructed by appending the words "flight" and the flight number to the answer returned by the connect statement.

```
    ans(Ans) -->
        flight(Num),
        connect(B),
        { append([flight,Num],B,Ans) }.

    flight(Num) --> [flight(Num)].
```

A connect statement can take one of three forms:

- Both the origin and destination may be regions.
- The origin may be a region and the destination a city, or the origin may be a city and the destination a region.
- Both the origin and the destination may be cities.

In all cases, the DCG finds the origin and destination cities and returns them to the phrase *[flies,from, Y,to,Z]*.

```
connect([flies,from,Y,to,Z,'.']) -->
    [connects(X,Y,Z)],
    region(_),
    region(_).
connect([flies,from,Y,to,Z,'.']) -->
    [connects(X,Y,Z)],
    region(R).
connect([flies,from,Y,to,Z,'.']) -->
    [connects(X,Y,Z)],
    region(_).
connect([flies,from,Y,to,Z,'.']) -->
    [connects(X,Y,Z)].

    region(R) --> [region(X,R)].
```

An answer may consist of a city statement followed by a flight, followed by a connect statement.

```
ans(Ans) -->
    city,
    flight(Num),
    connect(B),
    { append([flight,Num],B,Ans) }.

city --> [city(X)].
```

An answer may also consist of an airline statement followed by a connect statement, where an airline statement returns both the flight number and the airline name. For example, the query *airline(79, branniff), connects(79, phi, la)* would be handled by this definition.

```
ans(Ans) -->
    airline(A),
    connect(B),
    { append(A,B,Ans) }.

airline([Airline,flight,Num]) -->
    [airline(Num,Airline)].
```

An answer may consist of a flight followed by an airline statement followed by a connect statement, as in *flight(79), airline(79, branniff), connect(79, phi, la)*.

```
ans(Ans) -->
     flight(__),
     airline(A),
     connect(B),
     { append(A,B,Ans) }.
```

An answer can be made from an airline statement, followed by a flight, followed by a connect statement, or it can be made from an airline statement followed by a flight, followed by a city and a connect statement.

```
ans(Ans) -->
     airline(A),
     flight(__),
     connect(B),
     { append(A,B,Ans) }.
ans(Ans) -->
     airline(A),
     flight(__),
     city,
     connect(C),
     { append(A,C,Ans) }.
```

Finally, the answer may consist of a flight followed by a region followed by a connect statement, as in *flight(79), region(la, west__coast), connect(79, phi, la), region(phi, east__coast)*.

```
ans(Ans) -->
     flight(Num),
     region(R),
     connect(C),
     { append([R,flight,Num],C,Ans) }.
```

A call to *ans* can replace the *write* statement within the *gen* predicate. However, *gen* now needs an additional argument containing the list from which the clause was made. The clause argument is used to find the answers to the query; the list argument is used to generate the answer. Because the clause was created directly from the list, both arguments share variables. Therefore, each time *gen* calls the clause, the variables within the list are instantiated to the same values as the variables within the clause. *Gen* passes the instantiated list to *ans*, which returns the answer as a list of words. The answer is then passed to a simple output routine.

```
gen(Clause,List) :-
    call(Clause),
    ans(Answer,List,[]),
    output(Answer),
    fail.
gen(__,__).

output([]).
output(['.'|T]) :- !, write('.'), nl, output(T).
output([H|T]) :- tab(1), write(H), output(T).
```

Negative Answers to Conjunctions

For all possible combinations of goals that can appear in a conjunction, a corresponding negative answer must be defined. The *no__ans* DCG defines how a conjunction of goals is translated into a negative answer. For example, the first definition looks for a flight statement in which the flight number is uninstantiated, followed by a connects statement. This form of conjunction produces an answer such as ''No flights fly from ny to bos.''

```
no__ans(Ans) --&gt;
    no__flight(Num),
    { var(Num) },
    no__connect(B),
    { append([no,flights],B,Ans) }.
no__ans(Ans) --&gt;
    no__flight(Num),
    { nonvar(Num) },
    no__connect(B),
    { append([flight,number,Num,does,not],B,Ans) }.
no__ans(Ans) --&gt;
    no__airline(A),
    no__connect(B),
    { append(A,B,Ans) }.
no__ans(Ans) --&gt;
    no__flight(__),
    no__airline(A),
```

```
        no__connect(B),
        { append(A,B,Ans) }.
no__ans(Ans) -->
        no__airline(A),
        no__flight(__),
        no__connect(B),
        { append(A,B,Ans) }.
no__ans(Ans) -->
        no__flight(__),
        no__region(R),
        no__connect(C),
        { append([no,R,flights],C,Ans) }.

no__flight(Num) --> [flight(Num)].

no__connect([fly,from,the,R1,to,the,R2,'.']) -->
        [connects(X,Y,Z)],
        no__region(R1),
        no__region(R2).
no__connect(Ans) -->
        [connects(X,Y,Z)],
        no__region(connects(X,Y,Z),Ans).
no__connect([fly,from,City,'.']) -->
        [connects(X,City,Z)], { var(Z) }.
no__connect([fly,to,City,'.']) -->
        [connects(X,Y,City)], { var(Y) }.
no__connect([fly,from,Y,to,Z,'.']) -->
        [connects(X,Y,Z)].

no__region(R) -->
        [region(X,R)].
no__region(connects(X,Y,Z),[fly,from,the,R,'.']) -->
        [region(Y,R)], { Y \ == Z, var(Z) }.
no__region(connects(X,Y,Z),[fly,to,the,R,'.']) -->
        [region(Z,R)], { Y \ == Z, var(Y) }.
no__region(connects(X,Y,Z),[fly,from,the,R,to,Z,'.']) -->
        [region(Y,R)], { Y \ == Z, nonvar(Z) }.
no__region(connects(X,Y,Z),[fly,to,the,R,from,Y,'.']) -->
        [region(Z,R)], { Y \ == Z, nonvar(Y) }.

no__airline([no,Airline,flights]) -->
        [airline(Num,Airline)].
```

A new predicate, called *check__for__negative*, needs to be defined. It calls the clause once. If the clause fails, *check__for__negative* passes the list of goals to *no__ans*. Checking for a negative answer to a conjunction of goals must be done before calling *gen*.

```
construct([H|T]) :-
      make__clause(T,H,Clause),
      check__for__negative(Clause,[H|T]),
      gen(Clause,[H|T]).

check__for__negative(Clause,[H|T]) :-
      not(call(Clause)),
      no__ans(Ans,[H|T],[]),
      output(Ans),
      !, fail.
check__for__negative(__,__).
```

Answering Successful For__Each Goals

When someone wants to know whether all flights go to the west coast, they may be less interested in knowing which flights are involved and more interested in a simple confirmation that they all fly to the west coast. This is the assumption that this system will make.

An existentially quantified statement is translated into two clauses. When generating an answer, the first clause is treated as the noun phrase for the answer; the second is treated as the verb phrase. For example, the question "Do all usair flights fly to bos" is translated into the two goals:

```
(flight(X), airline(X,usair)) --> (connects(X,Y,bos)).
```

If, in fact, all Usair flights fly to Boston, the DCG will convert the first clause to the phrase "All usair flights" and the second clause to the phrase "fly to bos."

```
ex__np([all,A,flights]) -->
      ex__flight,
      ex__airline(A).
ex__np([all,CorR,flights]) -->
      ex__flight,
      ex__connect(CorR).
```

```
ex__np([all,flights]) -->
    ex__flight.
ex__np([all,airlines]) -->
    ex__airline(__).

ex__flight -->
    [flight(Num)].

ex__airline(A) -->
    [airline(__,A)].

ex__connect(City) -->
    [connects(X,Y,City)],
    { var(Y) }.
ex__connect(City) -->
    [connects(X,City,Z)],
    { var(Z) }.
ex__connect(Region) -->
    [connects(X,Y,Z)],
    ex__region(Region).

ex__region(Region) -->
    [region(X,Region)].
```

The verb phrase states either where the flight originates, where it lands, or both. The *ex__vp* definitions must determine which parts of the verb phrase need to be included in the answer and which should not be included. This is done by checking whether certain variables are uninstantiated.

```
ex__vp([go,to,City,'.']) -->
    [connects(X,Y,City)],
    { var(Y) }.
ex__vp([fly,from,City,'.']) -->
    [connects(X,City,Z)],
    { var(Z) }.
ex__vp([go,from,the,Region,'.']) -->
    [connects(X,Y,Z)],
    ex__region(Region),
    { var(Y) }.
```

```
ex_vp([fly,to,the,Region,'.']) -->
    [connects(X,Y,Z)],
    ex_region(Region),
    { var(Z) }.
ex_vp([fly,from,the,R1,to,the,R2,'.']) -->
    [connects(X,Y,Z)],
    [region(Y,R1)],
    [region(Z,R2)].
```

Now the *for_each* predicate can be rewritten so that it returns natural language responses. The lists from which the clauses were built are added as arguments to the predicate. These lists are used by *ex_np* and *ex_vp* to construct the answer. Each answer is printed by the *output* predicate.

```
for_each(C1,C2,P,Q) :-
    not(( C1, not C2 )),
    ex_np(A1,P,[]), output(A1),
    ex_vp(A2,Q,[]), output(A2).
```

Negative Answers to For_Each Goals

When someone asks a question involving an existential quantifier, the answer may be negative for a reason other than what the user may think. For example, a questions such as "Do all west_coast flights fly from ny" may be negative because some west coast flights come from Philadelphia or because the New York airports are closed for the day and no flights are originating from New York to any location. In the first case it would be appropriate to respond "There are no flights to the west_coast from ny." The second case should generate a more precise answer such as, "There are no flights from ny."

How does the system know when one answer is more appropriate than the other? An existentially quantified question relies on two clauses, both of which must succeed for the entire statement to be true. For example, the question "Do all flights from la go to the east_coast" translates into the two clauses:

```
flight(X), connects(X,Y,Z), region(Y,east_coast)
```
and
```
connects(X,Y,la)
```

If the first clause fails on its first attempt, then no flights fly from Los Angeles to anywhere. If the second clause fails or if the first fails on a subsequent attempt, then there are flights from Los Angeles to regions other than the east coast. These two situations require two different answers. In the first case, to let the user know that the original assumption is incorrect. In the second case, to tell the user the reason why the query failed, perhaps by stating which flight did not conform to the question.

For those *for_each* expressions in which the first clause fails, you do not need to write a new DCG. The *no_ans* grammar can generate an appropriate response. In the same way that *construct* checked for a negative response for conjunctions, it can test the first clause in the *for_each* expression:

```
construct(for_each X : (P --> Q)) :-
    !, make_clause_fe(P,C1),
    make_clause_fe(Q,C2),
    check_for_negative(C1,P),
    for_each(C1,C2,P,Q).
```

To generate negative answers when some but not all conditions exist in the database, a new DCG is needed. As in successful *for_each* answers, the first clause in negative answers is used for building the noun phrase and the second clause is used for building the verb phrase.

```
not_ex_np([A,flight,Num]) -->
    not_ex_flight(Num),
    not_ex_airline(A).
not_ex_np([CorR,flight,Num]) -->
    not_ex_flight(Num),
    ex_connect(CorR).
not_ex_np([flight,Num]) -->
    not_ex_flight(Num).
not_ex_np([A,flight,Num]) -->
    not_ex_airline(Num,A).

not_ex_flight(Num) --> [flight(Num)].
not_ex_airline(A) --> [airline(_,A)].

not_ex_vp([does,not,go,to,City,'.']) -->
    [connects(X,Y,City)], { var(Y) }.
not_ex_vp([does,not,fly,from,City,'.']) -->
```

```
            [connects(X,City,Z)], { var(Z) }.
    not_ex_vp(VP) -->
            [connects(X,Y,Z)],
            not_ex_region(connects(X,Y,Z),R),
            { append([does,not,fly],R,VP) }.


    not_ex_region(connects(X,Y,Z),[from,the,Region,'.']) -->
            [region(Y,Region)],
            { Y \ == Z, var(Z) }.
    not_ex_region(connects(X,Y,Z),[to,the,Region,'.']) -->
            [region(Z,Region)],
            { Y \ == Z, var(Y) }.
    not_ex_region(connect(X,Y,Z),[from,the,Region,to,Z,'.']) -->
            [region(Y,Region)],
            { Y \ == Z, nonvar(Z) }.
    not_ex_region(connects(X,Y,Z),[to,the,Region,from,Y,'.']) -->
            [region(Z,Region)],
            { Y \ == Z, nonvar(Y) }.
```

A few changes need to be made to *for_each* for it to generate these negative answers. Each time the *not* tests are made to the clauses, both the clauses and the lists are instantiated to new values. Therefore, it is possible to record which instance of the query caused the question to fail. Two goals are added to the *not* goal to record what caused the question to fail.

```
    for_each(C1,C2,P,Q) :-
            not(( C1, not C2, recordz(p,P,_),recordz(q,Q,_) )),
            ex_np(A1,P,[]), output(A1),
            ex_vp(A2,Q,[]), output(A2).
```

A second *for_each* clause retrieves the clauses stored in the database and passes them to *not_ex_np* and *not_ex_vp* to generate the answer. Then, *p* and *q* are removed from the database.

```
    for_each(_,_,_,_) :-
            recorded(p,X,_), recorded(q,Y,_),
            not_ex_np(A1,X,[]), not_ex_vp(A2,Y,[]),
            output(A1), output(A2),
            eraseall(p), eraseall(q).
    for_each(_,_,_,_).
```

The Application

Using the tokenizer of chapter 7 and the pieces that have been built in this chapter, you can now build the airline flight schedule application. Within a repeat/fail loop, the application prints a prompt, reads a list of characters from the keyboard, tokenizes the list, parses the list of tokens, and executes the queries.

```
airport :-
    repeat,
    nl,
    write('air > '),
    read(Question),
    tokenize(Question,[],List),
    semantic(Queries,List,__),
    execute(Queries),
    fail.
```

The application is invoked by the top-level predicate called *airport*. Here are some examples of its use:

```
?- airport.

air > "does branniff have any flights to la".
branniff flight 79 flies from phi to la.

air > "do any flights fly to ny".
flight 89 flies to ny.
flight 99 flies to ny.

air > "do all flights from la go to ny".
no flights fly from la.

air > ^C
```

Summary

There are still many problems to be overcome before true natural language systems can be developed. Beyond the problems involved in understanding discourse, even single sentences can be difficult to parse. Garden path sentences impact the solution space of the parsing problem. Rules must be written for each of the possible ways in which a phrase may be used. Ambiguous references also impact the complexity of the parsing program. Additional information must be passed between the parts of the sentence. The parser must be ready to recognize when an ambiguous reference has been cleared up and to take appropriate actions. Finally, each sentence form must have its own definition, even if the meaning of the different forms is the same. This can affect the size of the parser.

All these issues must be considered during the system design phase. They impact the development of natural language systems by placing constraints on the types of applications that can be developed and on the sophistication that those systems can achieve. Until new techniques are found, you must choose small, well-defined subject areas and you must choose a subset of sentence structures that the system can recognize.

This chapter showed an airline flight schedule application. The application used natural language to accept sentences from the user. The system generated database queries for those sentences and then executed the queries. Finally, the system generated natural language responses.

In all phases of natural language development, you must make assumptions. When building the parser, you must guess what types of statements that the user will want to make. For example, the parser in this chapter handled simple and existential quantifiers, but not negative statements, garden path sentences, and so on. When generating the queries, you must decide what the meaning of the sentence will have within the context of the database. For example, a statement was treated as a question and not as a way to add information to the database. When generating responses to queries, you must make assumptions about the intent of the user's question in order to return appropriate responses. For example, an existentially quantified statement failed for one of two reasons. The system had to let the user know which reason caused the failure.

Unfortunately, the term ''natural language'' raises unrealistically high expectations for the user. Perhaps the most important thing that the user must understand is that ''natural language'' does not mean ''human language.'' Because they are highly constrained, natural language systems will not meet everyone's needs. However, if the right constraints are chosen, they should meet most people's needs.

A
Summary of Arity/Prolog

Prolog was originally implemented as an interpreted language. In an interpreted environment, program statements are parsed and executable code is generated at run time. An interpreted environment is highly interactive. You can enter some lines of code and find out immediately whether they behave as expected. However, interpreted code cannot be as efficient as compiled code.

In a compiled environment, a program is parsed and machine code is produced for an entire application at one time. The program is then linked, with fixed memory addresses assigned to the code. Because a compiler can see an entire program at once, rather than one statement at a time, it can perform optimizations that an interpreter cannot perform. Thus, compiled programs are faster and more efficient.

Arity/Prolog supplies both an interpreter and a compiler for Prolog. This means that you can build your applications incrementally, test each module within the interpreted environment, and compile the modules as they become stable.

Arity/Prolog runs on the IBM PC, XT, AT, and compatibles. It is a superset of the version of Prolog described by Clocksin and Mellish in their book, *Programming in Prolog*, because Arity/Prolog provides a number of features beyond those described in that book.

Arity/Prolog provides a virtual database of up to 1 gigabyte in size. This built-in database makes use of disk space as well as memory. In addition, the virtual database allows you to define multiple partitions, or worlds. By partitioning your program among different worlds, you can create databases of unlimited size.

Arity/Prolog lets you interface to other programming languages. Your Prolog programs can call routines written in other languages and you can link modules written in other languages into your Prolog application. Arity/Prolog also lets your applications interface to programming tools, such as the Arity/SQL and Arity/Expert development packages. These tools allow you to build the capabilities of an SQL or expert system into your Prolog application.

There are many additional evaluable predicates defined in Arity/Prolog that are not defined in Clocksin and Mellish. These additional predicates provide greater flexibility in a number of areas:

- Database access. Arity/Prolog provides b-tree and hashing storage and access methods into the database. It also provides database primitives with which to build other access methods.

- Screen layout. Arity/Prolog provides a set of text mode primitives that let you access attribute bytes on the IBM color or monochrome screen. These primitives allow you to write to specific locations of the screen, and to shade or scroll areas of the screen. With these primitives, it is possible to write special-purpose screen-handling packages.

- Counters. Arity/Prolog defines 32 built-in counters and a set of predicates to set, increment, decrement, or return the value of any of these counters.

- Floating-point support. Arity/Prolog's floating-point support conforms to the IEEE floating-point standard. This package uses the 8087 chip, if possible, but this chip is not required.

The sections that follow describe the evaluable predicates and operators of Arity/Prolog. Those that are in the regular typeface are ''standard'' predicates that can be found in many, or most, implementations of Prolog. Those that are in italics are predicates that are not commonly found or that are exclusive to Arity/Prolog.

Program Control

P , P	Specifies a conjunction of goals.
P ; P	Specifies a disjunction of goals.
!	The cut symbol, controls and limits searches.
[! P !]	*The snip symbol, delimits a group of goals to be skipped during backtracking.*
\ + P	Succeeds if the goal P fails; fails if P succeeds.
T1 = T2	Attempts to unify T1 and T2.
T1 \ = T2	Fails if T1 unifies with T2.
abort	Aborts the current program.
break	Suspends execution of a program. Resume the program by typing: "end_of_file."
call(P)	Calls a goal P if P is instantiated; fails if P is uninstantiated.
case([A1 --> B1, A2 --> B2, ... |C])	*Executes B1 if A1 succeeds; executes B2 if A2 succeeds; executes C if none of the cases succeed. That is, C is the default action.*
case([A1 --> B1, A2 --> B2, ...])	*Similar to the previous use of case, but no default action C is defined.*
end_of_file	*Ends a break situation.*
fail	Always fails.

ifthen(P, Q)	*If P succeeds, then Q is executed.*
ifthenelse(P, Q, R)	*If P succeeds, then Q is executed; otherwise, R is executed.*
not(P)	Fails if the goal P can be satisfied; succeeds if not.
repeat	Causes a series of goals to be executed until a certain condition is detected.
true	Always succeeds.

Standard Operator Definitions

Arity/Prolog operator definitions differ from those listed in Clocksin and Mellish. Arity/Prolog operator definitions are defined with numbers from 1 to 1200.

Operator	Associativity	Precedence
: – -->	xfx	1200
: – ? –	fx	1200
mode public	fy	1150
extrn visible module	fy	1150
;	xfy	110
,	xfy	1000
case	fx	900
spy nospy	fy	900
not \ +	fy	900
-->	xfy	800*
= is =.. \= == \==	xfx	700
@< @=< @> @>=	xfx	700
=\= < > =< >= =:=	xfx	700
+ – /\ \/	yfx	500
:	xfy	500
+ –	fx	500
* / >> << //	yfx	400
mod	xfx	300
*	xfy	200

*In Arity/Prolog, the – > operator is used within the *case* statement to signify possible execution paths. The – > operator is used differently in some other Prolog implementations.

Arithmetic Functions

In the following table, X and Y are operands of an arithmetic expression.

Expression	Operation
X + Y	Addition
X − Y	Subtraction
X * Y	Multiplication
X / Y	Division
X // Y	Integer division
X ^ Y	Exponentiation
− X	Unary minus (negation)
X /\ Y	Bitwise Conjunction (AND)
X \/ Y	Bitwise Disjunction (OR)
\(X)	Bitwise negation (NOT)
X << Y	Bitwise shift left X by Y places
X >> Y	Bitwise shift right X by Y places
[X]	Evaluates to X if X is an integer
X mod Y	*Remainder of X divided by Y*
abs(X)	*Absolute value of X*
acos(X)	*Arc cosine of X*
asin(X)	*Arc sine of X*
atan(X)	*Arc tangent of X*
cos(X)	*Cosine of X*
exp(X)	*e raised to the value of X*
ln(X)	*Logarithm base e*
log(X)	*Logarithm base 10*
sin(X)	*Sine of X*
sqrt(X)	*Square root of X*
tan(X)	*Tangent of X*
round(X, N)	*X rounded to N decimal places*

Arithmetic Evaluable Predicates

In the following descriptions, E1 and E2 are arithmetic expressions as described earlier under "Standard Operator Definitions."

E1 > E2	Determines whether the value of E1 is greater than the value of E2.
E1 < E2	Determines whether the value of E1 is less than E2.
E1 >= E2	Determines whether the value of E1 is greater than or equal to the value of E2.
E1 =< E2	Determines whether the value of E1 is less than or equal to the value of E2.
E1 =:= E2	Determines whether the values of E1 and E2 are equal.
E1 =\= E2	Determines whether the values of E1 and E2 are not equal.
dec(N,X)	*Decrements by 1 the number N to the value X.*
inc(N,X)	*Increments by 1 the number N to the value X.*
X is E	Evaluates E and unifies the value with X.

Comparing Terms

Terms are compared according to the "standard" ordering of terms, as follows, from lowest to highest:

- Variables, in an arbitrary order.
- Integers and floating-point numbers, from −infinity to +infinity.
- Atoms and strings, in alphabetic order.
- Complex terms, ordered first by arity, next by functor, and recursively by their arguments.

In the following, T1 and T2 are Prolog terms.

T1 == T2	Determines whether terms T1 and T2 are equivalent.
T1 \== T2	Determines whether terms T1 and T2 are not equivalent.
T1 @< T2	Determines whether T1 is before T2.
T1 @=< T2	Determines whether T1 is before or equal to T2.
T1 @> T2	Determines whether T1 is after T2.
T1 @>= T2	Determines whether T1 is after or equal to T2.
compare(Op,T1,T2)	Compares terms T1 and T2 in the standard order and unifies Op with a comparison value. Comparison values are: =, <, and >.
eq(X, Y)	*Determines whether X and Y are the same data object and stored at the same address.*
keysort(L1,L2)	Sorts the list L1 in the standard order. Elements of the list must have the form: Key-Value. Duplicates are not merged. The sorted list is returned in L2.
sort(L1,L2)	Sorts the list L1 in the standard order, merging duplicates, and returns the sorted list in L2.

Converting Terms

Struct =.. List	Referred to as "univ." Converts a structure to a list, or a list to a structure.
arg(N,Term,X)	Unifies X with the value of the Nth argument of a term. (Arguments are numbered upward from 1.)
arg0(N,Term,X)	Unifies X with the value of the N + 1th argument of a term. (Arguments are numbered upward from 0.)

argrep(Term, N, Arg, New Term)
> *Replaces the nth argument of a term with the value of Arg and returns the new term to New Term.*

functor(Struct,Name,Arity)
> Returns a structure's name and arity.

length(L,N)
> Returns the length, N, of a character list or atom.

name(Atom,List)
> Converts a list to an atom or converts an atom or integer to a list.

Classifying Terms

atom(X)
> Determines whether X is an atom.

atomic(X)
> Determines whether X is an atomic data type.

float(X)
> *Determines whether X is a floating-point number.*

integer(X)
> Determines whether X is an integer.

nonvar(X)
> Determines whether X is instantiated.

number(X)
> *Determines whether X is an integer or floating-point number.*

string(X)
> *Determines whether X is a string.*

system(P)
> Determines whether P is an evaluable predicate.

var(X)
> Determines whether X is an uninstantiated variable.

Collecting Terms

bagof(X,P,Bag)
> Collects all instances of X where the goal P is satisfiable and returns these instances of X in an unordered list (Bag).

findall(X,P,Set)   Collects all instances of X where the goal P is satisfiable and returns those instances in an unsorted list containing duplicates (Set).

setof(X,P,Set)   Collects all instances of X where the goal P is satisfiable and returns those instances in an ordered list without duplicates (Set).

String Operations

The Arity/Prolog string data type is used for large textual objects. Strings are more efficient for text manipulation than are atoms or lists for a number of reasons. They can be accessed more quickly than atoms or lists, they take up less storage space, and they can be easily manipulated by the evaluable predicates supplied with the product.

atom__string(Atom, String)
Converts an atom to a string or a string to an atom.

concat(String1, String2, Result) or concat([String1, String2, ...], Result)
Concatenates two or more strings and returns the new string to Result.

float__text(Float, Text, Format)
Converts a floating-point number to a string according to a Format specification or it converts a string to a floating-point number.

int__text(Integer, AtomString)
Converts an integer to a string or a string to an integer.

list__text(List, AtomString)
Converts a list of characters to an atom (if the atom already exists) or to a string, or converts an atom or string to a list of characters.

nth__char(N, String, Char)
Returns the ASCII code of a character at offset N from the beginning of the string.

string__length(String, Length)
> Returns the length of the string.

string__search(SubString, String, Offset)
> Searches a string for the substring and returns the offset of the substring. This predicate can backtrack.

string__term(String, Term)
> Converts the string to a term.

substring(InString, N, Length, OutString)
> Extracts a substring from a string.

Controlling the Database

abolish(Name/Arity)
: Removes from the database all clauses with the specified name and arity.

assert(Clause)
: Adds a clause to the end of a predicate.

asserta(Clause)
: Adds a clause to the beginning of a predicate.

assertz(Clause)
: Adds a clause to the end of a predicate.

clause(Head, Body)
: Returns the goals associated with a given head.

current__predicate(Predicate)
: Returns through backtracking the predicates that are currently defined in the database.

erase(Ref)
: Removes the term stored under the given reference number.

eraseall(Key)
: Removes all terms stored under the key.

instance(Ref, Term)
> Returns the term associated with the reference number.

key(Key, Ref)	*Returns the reference number for the key.*
Keys(Name/Arity)	*Returns, through backtracking, the name and arity of all keys stored in the database.*
listing	Writes to standard output all the predicates in the database.
listing(Name)	Writes to standard output all the predicates in the database stored under the given name with any arity.

listing(Name/Arity) or listing([Name/Arity,Name/Arity])

> Writes to standard output all the clauses for the specified predicate or list of predicates.

nref(Ref, Next)	*Returns the reference number of the next term in the chain of terms having the same key.*
nth__ref(Key, N, Ref)	*Returns the reference number for the term some number of positions from the top of a chain of terms.*
pref(Ref, Prev)	*Returns the reference number for the previous term in a chain of terms.*

record__after(Ref, Term, Newref)

> *Adds a term after Ref and returns the new reference number for that term.*

recorda(Key, Term, Ref)

> Adds a term to the beginning of a chain of terms having the same key, and returns the reference number assigned to the term.

recordb(Tree, Key, Term)	*Adds a term to a b-tree under the specified key.*

recorded(Key, Term, Ref)

> Returns through backtracking the terms and associated reference numbers stored under a given key.

recordh(Table, Key, Term)   *Adds a term to a hash table under the specified key.*

recordz(Key, Term, Ref)

Adds a term to the end of a chain of terms having the same key and returns the reference number assigned to the term.

ref(X)   *Determines whether X is a reference number.*

removeallb(Tree)   *Deletes all the terms stored in a tree.*

removeallh(Table)   *Deletes all the terms stored in a hash table.*

replace(Ref, Term)

Replaces the term having the specified reference number with the term given by the Term argument. The new term must not be larger than the term that it is replacing.

retract(Clause)   Removes the clause from the database.

retrieveb(Tree, Key, Term)   *Returns a term from a b-tree stored under a given key.*

retrieveh(Table, Key, Term)   *Returns a term from a hash table stored under a given key.*

Managing Worlds

code_world(Old, New)   *Unifies the current code world with Old and changes to New.*

create_world(Name)   *Creates a new world.*

data_world(Old, New)   *Unifies the current data world with Old and changes to New.*

default_world(X)   *Unifies the default world with X.*

delete__world(Name)   *Erases a world.*

what__worlds(Name)   *Returns through the backtracking the names of the worlds that*
                             are currently defined.

Standard I/O

current__op(Prec,Assoc,Op)
                             Returns through backtracking the operator definitions
                             currently in the database.

display(Term)   Writes a term in Prefix Polish form to the standard
                             output device.

flush   Removes all characters in the type-ahead buffer.

get(Char)   Reads the next character from the standard input de-
                             vice, skipping non-printing characters, and unifies the
                             ASCII value with Char.

get0(Char)   Reads the next character from the standard input de-
                             vice and unifies the ASCII value with Char. Get0
                             does not skip non-printing characters.

get0__noecho(Char)   Reads the next character from the standard input de-
                             vice and unifies the ASCII value with Char.
                             Get0__noecho does not echo the character to the stan-
                             dard output device.

keyb(Ascii,Scan)   *Reads the next character from the standard input device and*
                             returns the character's ASCII and Scan codes.

nl   Writes a newline to the standard output device.

op(Prec,Assoc,Op)   Defines or returns the precedence, position, and asso-
                             ciativity of an operator.

put(Char)	Writes the character to the standard output device.
read(Term)	Reads a term from the standard input device.
read__string(MaxLength, String)	*Reads a string from the standard input device.*
reset__op	Returns the operator definitions to their default values.
skip(Char)	Reads and skips characters from the standard input device until the character is found.
tab(N)	Writes a given number of spaces to the standard output device.
write(Term)	Writes the term to the standard output device.
writeq(Term)	Writes the term to the standard output device and quotes atoms and functors as necessary for the term to be readable as a Prolog term.

File I/O

close(Handle)	*Closes the file specified by the handle.*
create(Handle, Filespec)	*Creates and opens a new file and returns the file's handle.*
display(Handle, Term)	*Writes a term in Prefix Polish form to a file.*
dup(Handlein, HandleOut)	*Assigns a second handle to an open file.*
get(Handle, Char)	*Reads the next printing character from the file and unifies the ASCII value with Char.*

get0(Handle, Char)	*Reads the next character from the file and unifies the ASCII value with Char.*
nl(Handle)	*Writes a new line to the specified file.*
open(Handle, Filespec, Access)	*Opens an existing file.*
put(Handle, Char)	*Writes the character to a file.*
read(Handle, Term)	*Reads a term from the specified file.*
read__line(Handle, Line)	*Reads a string from a file until a carriage return is encountered.*
read__string(Handle, MaxLength, String)	*Reads the string from the file.*
see(X)	Opens a file for reading as the standard input device.
seeing(X)	Returns the name of the file opened by see.
seek(Handle, Offset, Method, NewLoc),	*Moves the internal file pointer to a specific location within a file.*
seen	Closes the currently opened file and returns the standard input device to the terminal keyboard.
skip(Handle, Char)	*Reads and skips characters from a file until the specified character is found.*
stdin(Filespec, Goal)	*Redirects standard input for the duration of the goal.*

stdinout(InFile, OutFile, Goal)

> Redirects the standard input and output for the duration of the goal.

stdout(Filename, Goal)   Redirects the standard output for the duration of the goal.

tab(Handle, N)   Writes a given number of spaces to the file.

tell(X)   Opens a file for writing as the standard output device.

telling(X)   Returns the name of the file currently opened by tell.

told   Closes the currently opened file and returns the standard output device to the terminal screen.

write(Handle, Term)   Writes the term to the specified file.

writeq(Handle, Term)   Writes the term to the file specified, and quotes atoms and functors as necessary for the term to be readable as a Prolog term.

Low-level I/O

in(Port, Byte)   Reads a byte from the specified port.

out(Port, Byte)   Writes a byte to the specified port.

Controlling the Terminal Screen

cls   Clears the screen and moves the cursor to the upper left corner.

region__c(N, String)   Reads N number of characters from the screen, beginning at the current cursor position, and returns the string.

region__ca(N, String)   Reads N number of characters and their attributes from the screen, beginning at the current cursor position, and returns the string.

tget(Row, Column)	*Returns the coordinates of the current cursor location.*
tmove(Row, Column)	*Moves the cursor to the specified coordinates.*
tscroll(Count, UL, LR)	*Scrolls the area defined by the upper left (UL) and lower right (LR) coordinates by the number of lines specified by Count.*
wa(Count, Attribute)	*Changes the attribute byte for the number of character positions specified by Count on the screen starting from the current cursor location.*
wc(Count, Char)	*Writes the number of copies of the character to the screen starting from the current cursor location.*
wca(Count, Char, Attribute)	*Writes to the standard output device a given number of copies of a character with the specified attribute.*

Managing Counters

ctr__dec(Ctr, X)	*Decrements a counter and returns the counter's previous value.*
ctr__inc(Ctr, X)	*Increments a counter and returns the counter's previous value.*
ctr__is(Ctr, X)	*Returns the current value of a counter.*
ctr__set(Ctr, X)	*Sets a counter to the specified value.*

Performing System Functions

[Filespec]	Reads clauses into the database from a file with the fast__consult predicate. + *Filespec uses the consult predicate;* − *Filespec uses the reconsult predicate.*
chdir(Path)	*Changes or returns the current directory.*
chmod(Filespec, Attributes)	*Changes or returns the attributes of a file.*

consult(Filespec)   Reads clauses into the database from a file.

command__string(X)   *Returns the command line argument with which the application was invoked.*

date(date(Year, Month, Day))
                           Sets the system clock to the date specified or returns the current date.

date__day(date(Year, Month, Day), WeekDay)
                           Returns the day of the week for a given date as an integer between 0 (Sunday) and 6 (Saturday).

delete(Filespec)   *Deletes the specified file.*

directory(Path, Name, Mode, Time, Date, Size)
                           Lists the directory files specified by Path.

disk(DiskName)   *Sets or returns the default disk drive to the letter specified.*

edit(Filename)   *Invokes an editor and opens the file. When the editor exits, the file is reconsulted into the database.*

errcode(Code)   *Returns the most recent syntax or file I/O error message code.*

fileerrors(Old, New)   *Enables or disables DOS I/O error messages or checks the current setting of these messages.*

gc(Amount)   Restores unused stack space.

halt   Exits from the interpreter or from the compiled application.

mkdir(Path)   *Creates a new directory.*

reconsult(Filespec)   Reads clauses into the database from a file, replacing any predicates that are already present in the database with those clauses that also occur in the file.

rename(Filespec, NewName)
　　　　　　　　　　　　Changes the name of a file.

restore(Name)　　　　Restores a program database.

rmdir(Path)　　　　　*Deletes a directory.*

save(Name)　　　　　Saves a program database.

shell　　　　　　　　*Allows you to enter the DOS environment while maintaining your current program state. Type "exit" from MS-DOS to return. This predicate always succeeds.*

shell(DOSCommand)　*Executes an MS-DOS command and succeeds.*

statistics　　　　　　Displays information about Arity/Prolog system usage.

statistics(Atom,Struct)　Returns the specified information about Arity/Prolog system usage.

syntaxerrors(Old,New)　*Enables or disables Arity/Prolog syntax errors or checks the current setting of these messages.*

time(time(Hours,Minutes,Seconds,Hundredths))
　　　　　　　　　　　Returns or sets the system clock.

Debugging

leash(mode)　　　　Sets the ports at which the debugger stops while creeping through a spy point. Modes are: full (all ports), tight (call, redo, and fail ports), half (call and redo ports), loose (call ports), or off (no ports).

nospy(Name/Arity)　Removes a spy point from the specified predicate.

notrace   Turns the debugger off.

spy(Name/Arity)   Specifies a predicate as a spy point for debugging.

trace   Turns the debugger on.

Debugging Options:

a	abort	b	break
c	creep	\<cr\>	creep
d	display goal	e	exit from Prolog
f	fail	h	help
l	leap	\<lf\>	leap
n	nodebug	q	quasi skip
s	skip	\<esc\>	skip
w	write goal	x	back to choice point
@	accept command	;	redo

DCGs

expand_term(Term,Newterm)

                Transforms a term using definite clause grammar notation into its equivalent Prolog term.

Interfacing to Other Languages

Three versions of each of the following routines are supplied with Arity/Prolog. The assembly language routines are named with the _a suffix; the C language functions are named with the _c suffix; the Pascal language functions are named with the _p suffix. Each differs in its calling conventions but they perform the same functions.

getint   *Passes a Prolog integer to the calling language.*

gettxt   *Passes a Prolog string or atom to the calling language.*

getflt   *Passes a Prolog floating-point number to the calling language.*

getfunctor   *Passes the name of a Prolog structure to the calling language.*

getfuncarg	*Passes one argument of a Prolog structure to the calling language.*
findtype	*Returns the data type of a Prolog object.*
putint	*Passes an integer value to Prolog.*
puttxt	*Passes a string to Prolog.*
putatm	*Passes an atom to Prolog.*
putflt	*Passes a floating-point number to Prolog.*
putfunctor	*Passes a structure name to Prolog.*

Arity/Prolog Compiler Directives

: – public(Name/Arity)	*Declares the predicate to be callable from any Prolog module.*
: – extrn(Name/Arity:Lang)	*Declares that the predicate is defined in another module and is written in the specified language.*
: – visible Name/Arity	*Declares that the compiled Prolog module can be called from "interpreted" code (code that is stored in the Prolog database).*
: – default(invisible)	*Directs the compiler to make all Arity/Prolog evaluable predicates invisible to interpreted code unless they are explicitly made visible. This can make the size of a compiled application smaller.*
: – module Name.	*Assigns a name to a Prolog object module.*

: − mode Name(Type-Specs)

    Declares which arguments to the named predicate are always going to be instantiated or always uninstantiated when the predicate is invoked. Mode declarations can cause the compiler to make certain optimizations that it could not make otherwise.

: − op(Prec, Assoc, Op):compiletime
: − op(Prec, Assoc, Op):runtime
: − op(Prec, Assoc, Op)

    Declares that an operator is to be in effect only at compile time, only at run time, or both at compile time and run time.

: − segment(Name)

    Places the Prolog module in a far code segment.

B
Listings of Selected Examples

Robbie the Robot

```
bag__supply(brown,1).
bag__supply(brown,2).
bag__supply(brown,3).
bag__supply(freezer,1).
bag__supply(freezer,2).

item(bread,bag,medium,notfrozen).
item(jelly,jar,small,notfrozen).
item(granola,box,large,notfrozen).
item(icecream,carton,medium,frozen).
item(pepsi__tm,bottle,large,notfrozen).
item(chips,bag,medium,notfrozen).
unbagged(chips).

unbagged(jelly).
unbagged(bread).
unbagged(icecream).
unbagged(granola).

robbie :-
    check__order(__), fail.
robbie :-
    unbagged(Item),
    check__order(Item), fail.
robbie.
```

```
check_order(_) :-
    unbagged(chips),
    not(unbagged(pepsi_tm)),
    write('Adding Pepsi (TM) to order.') , nl,
    assertz(unbagged(pepsi_tm)), !.

check_order(item(Item,bottle,large,_)) :-
    n_items(Bag),
    bag(Bag,Item), !.
check_order(item(Item,_,large,_)) :-
    n_items(Bag),
    bag(Bag,Item), !.

n_items(Num) :-
    ctr_set(0,0),
    bag_supply(_,Num),
    count(Num),
    ctr_is(0,N), !.

count(Bag) :-
    ctr_inc(0,_),
    bagged(Bag,_),
    fail.
count(Bag).

fresh_bag(Bag) :-
    bag_supply(_,Bag), not(bagged(Bag,_)), !.

check_order(item(Item,_,medium,frozen)) :-
    not(bagged(frozen,Item)),
    bag(freezer,Item), fail.
check_order(item(Item,_,medium,_)) :-
    medium(Bag),
    n_items(Bag),
    bag(Bag,Item), !.

medium(Bag) :-
    bag_supply(_,Bag),
```

```
    ( fresh__bag(Bag) ;
          bagged(Bag,Item),
          item(Item,__,medium,__)
    ), !.
check__order(item(Item,__,small,__)) :-
    bag__supply(__,Bag),
    small(Bag),
    n__items(Bag),
    bag(Bag,Item), !.
check__order(item(Item,__,small,__)) :-
    n__items(Bag),
    bag(Bag,Item), !.

small(Bag) :-
    bagged(Bag,Item),
    item(Item,bottle,__,__),
    !, fail.
small(Bag).

check__order(__) :-
    bag__supply(Type,Bag), nl,
    write('Bag': (Type,Bag)), nl,
    list__rest(Bag),
    fail.
check__order(__).

list__rest(Bag) :-
    bagged(Bag,Item),
    tab(4), write(Item), nl.
list__rest(__).

bag(freezer,Item) :-
    assertz(bagged(freezer,Item)), !.
bag(Bag,Item) :-
    assertz(bagged(Bag,Item)),
    retract((unbagged(Item))), !.
```

CFO Advisor

cfo__frame([interest : Interest,
        revenues : Revenues,
        expenses : Expenses,
        risk : Risk,
        term : Term,
    investment : Investment]).

valdef(expenses,'Exceed budget (by more than 10%)', +).
valdef(expenses,'Under budget (by more than 10%)', –).
valdef(expenses,'Unchanged', =).

valdef(revenues,'Exceed expected (by more than 10%)', +).
valdef(revenues,'Shortfall (by more than 10%)', –).
valdef(revenues,'Unchanged', =).

valdef(interest,'Up',up).
valdef(interest,'Unchanged',unchanged).
valdef(interest,'Down',down).

valdef(risk,'Low',low).
valdef(risk,'Low-Medium',low – medium).
valdef(risk,'Medium-High',medium – high).
valdef(risk,'High',high).

valdef(investment,'U.S. Government & Treasury Securities',usgov).
valdef(investment,'Offshore Banks or Eurodollars',offshore).
valdef(investment,'Unrated Corporate Bonds or CDs of Savings &
Loans',unrated).
valdef(investment,'Obligations of large Banks or Corporations', obligs).

valdef(term,'Short (1-3 mos.)',short).
valdef(term,'Medium (3-6 mos.)',medium).
valdef(term,'Long (6-12 mos.)',long).

question(interest,
    'What do you expect interest rates to do within the next year? ').

question(expenses,
    'How much might your expenditures diverge from expectations? ').
question(revenues,
    'How much might your revenues diverge from expectations? ').
question(risk, 'What is your tolerance for risk? ').

rule(term:short,[interest:[down],revenues:[–],expenses:[+ , =]]).
rule(term:medium,[interest:[down],revenues:[–],expenses:[–]]).
rule(term:medium,[interest:[down],revenues:[=],expenses:[+]]).
rule(term:long,[interest:[down],revenues:[=],expenses:[– , =]]).
rule(term:long,[interest:[down],revenues:[+],expenses:[+ , = , –]]).
rule(term:short,[interest:[up],revenues:[+ , = , –],expenses:[+ , = , –]]).
rule(term:short,[interest:[unchanged],revenues:[–],expenses:[– , + , =]]).
rule(term:medium,[interest:[unchanged],revenues:[=],expenses:[= , –]]).
rule(term:short,[interest:[unchanged],revenues:[=],expenses:[+]]).
rule(term:long,[interest:[unchanged],revenues:[+],expenses:[= , –]]).
rule(term:medium,[interest:[unchanged],revenues:[+],expenses:[+]]).

rule(investment:usgov,[risk:[low],term:[medium,long]]).
rule(investment:obligs,[risk:[low],term:[short]]).
rule(investment:obligs,[risk:[low-medium],term:[medium,long]]).
rule(investment:offshore,[risk:[low-medium],term:[short]]).
rule(investment:offshore,[risk:[medium-high],term:[short,medium,long]]).
rule(investment:unrated,[risk:[high],term:[short,medium,long]]).

cfo :-
    cfo__frame([Interest,Revenues,Expenses,Risk,Term,Investment]),
    bind__all([Interest,Revenues,Expenses,Risk]),
    apply__rules(Term,[Interest,Revenues,Expenses]),
    apply__rules(Investment,[Risk,Term]).

bind__all([ ]).
bind__all([S:V|Slots]):-
    first__unbound__slot([S:V|Slots]),
    user__choose__value([S:V|Slots]),
    bind__all(Slots).

first__unbound__slot([Slot:Val|Slots]) :- var(Val), !.

```
first_unbound_slot([_|Slots]) :- first_unbound_slot(Slots).
user_choose_value([S:V|Slots]) :-
    question(S,Q),
    write(Q),
    get_ans(S,V,Q),
    !.

get_ans(Slot,Ans,Q) :-
    read(Ans),
    valdef(Slot,_,Ans), !.
get_ans(Slot,Ans,Q) :-
    write('Valid values for slot':Slot), nl,
    get_ans_aux(Slot,Q),
    get_ans(Slot,Ans,Q).

get_ans_aux(Slot,Q) :-
    valdef(Slot,Prompt,Def),
    tab(4), write(Prompt:Def), nl, fail.
get_ans_aux(Slot,Q) :-
    nl, write(Q).

apply_rules(Trole:Tval, Froles) :-
    rule(Trole:Tval, FRole_list),
    unify(Froles,FRole_list).

unify([],[]).
unify([H:Val|T],[H1:Val1|T1]) :-
    member(Val,Val1),
    unify(T,T1).
```

An Expert System Shell

Rule Compiler

```
rule_consult(File) :-
    open(H, File, r),
    repeat,
    read(H,X),
```

```
          rule__consult__p(X),
          close(H),
          !,
          rule__consult__epilog.
rule__consult__p(end__of__file).
rule__consult__p(question(Name, Legalvals) = Question) :-
          NameTerm = .. [Name,X,CF],
          assertz((NameTerm:-question(Question, Legalvals, X, CF))),
          recordz(rule__consulted, Name, __),
          !, fail.
rule__consult__p(Goal = Obj) :-
          GoalTerm = .. [Goal,X,CF],
          ObjTerm = .. [Obj,X,CF],
          assertz((GoalTerm:-ObjTerm)),
          recordz(rule__consulted, Goal, __),
          !, fail.
rule__consult__p((Antecedents—>Conclusions)) :-
          xlat__ante(Antecedents, P__Ante, CF),
          xlat__conc(Conclusions, P__Ante, CF),
          !, fail.

xlat__ante((A1,A2), (P__A1,P__A2), CF) :- !,
          xlat__one__ante(A1, P__A1, Out),
          xlat__rest__ante(A2, P__A2, Out, CF).
xlat__ante(A, P__A, CF) :-
          xlat__one__ante(A, P__A, CF).

xlat__rest__ante((A1,A2), (P__A1,Temp2 is In*Temp1,P__A2), In, Out) :- !,
          xlat__one__ante(A1, P__A1, Temp1),
          xlat__rest__ante(A2, P__A2, Temp2, Out).
xlat__rest__ante(A, (P__A,Out is In*Temp), In, Out) :-
          xlat__one__ante(A, P__A, Temp).

xlat__one__ante((A1;A2), (P__A1;P__A2), Out) :- !,
          xlat__ante(A1, P__A1, Out),
          xlat__ante(A2, P__A2, Out).
xlat__one__ante(Term, find(Atom,Val,Out), Out) :-
          Term = .. [Atom, Val].
```

```
xlat_conc((C1,C2), P_A, Out) :-
    xlat_one_conc(C1, P_A, Out),
    xlat_conc(C2, P_A, Out).
xlat_conc(C, P_A, Out) :-
    xlat_one_conc(C, P_A, Out).

xlat_one_conc(Term/CF, P_A, Out) :- !,
    Term  =.. [H,Val],
    RealTerm  =.. [H,Val,Out1],
    assertz((RealTerm :- P_A, Out1 is Out*CF)),
    recordatom(H).
xlat_one_conc(Term, P_A, Out) :-
    Term  =.. [H,Val],
    RealTerm  =.. [H,Val,Out],
    assertz((RealTerm:-P_A)),
    recordatom(H).

recordatom(Atom) :- recorded(rule_consulted, Atom, _), !.
recordatom(Atom) :- recordz(rule_consulted, Atom, _).

rule_consult_epilog :-
    create(H, 'rules.out'),
    dup(H, 1),
    output_goalpreds,
    listing(findaux/3),
    close(H),
    open(H1, con, w),
    dup(H1, 1).

output_goalpreds :-
    recorded(rule_consulted, Atom, _),
    Goal  =.. [Atom,Value,CF],
    assertz((findaux(Atom,Value,CF) :- Goal)),
    listing(Atom/2),
    nl,
    fail.
output_goalpreds.
```

Inference Engine

```
go :-
    find(goal, Value, Conf),
    nl, write(value  =  Value), nl,
    write(confidence  =  Conf), nl,
    fail.
go.

question(Question, Legalvals, X, CF) :-
    write(Question),
    tab(1),
    read(Y),
    goodanswer(Y, Legalvals), !,
    allanswers(Y, X, CF).
question(Question, Legalvals, X, CF) :-
    write('All values must be in '),
    write(Legalvals),
    nl,
    question(Question, Legalvals, X, CF).

goodanswer((A,B), Legalvals) :- !,
    goodanswer(A, Legalvals),
    goodanswer(B, Legalvals).
goodanswer(Y/__, Legalvals) :- !,
    goodanswer(Y, Legalvals).
goodanswer(Y, Legalvals) :-
    (
        member(Y, Legalvals)
    ;
        Y  =  unknown
    ),
    !.

allanswers((A,B), X, CF) :- !,
    (
        allanswers(A, X, CF)
```

```
        ;
            allanswers(B, X, CF)
        ).
allanswers(X/CF, X, CF) :- !.
allanswers(X, X, 1.0).

member(X, [X|__]).
member(X, [__|Y]) :- member(X, Y).

find(Atom, Value, CF) :-
    key(Atom, __),
    !,
    recorded(Atom, found(Value,CF), __).
find(Atom, Value, CF) :-
    findaux(Atom, V, CFTemp),
    add__evidence(Atom, V, CFTemp),
    fail.
find(Atom, Value, CF) :-
    key(Atom, __),
    !,
    recorded(Atom, found(Value,CF), __).
find(Atom, unknown, 1.0) :-
    recordz(Atom, found(unknown,1.0), __).

add__evidence(Atom, Value, CFNew) :-
    recorded(Atom, found(Value,CFOld), Ref), !,
    CFMerge is CFOld  +  CFNew * (1.0 — CFOld),
    replace(Ref, found(Value,CFMerge)).
add__evidence(Atom, Value, CFNew) :-
    recordz(Atom, found(Value,CFNew), __).

reinit :-
    recorded(rule__consulted,X,__),
    eraseall(X),
    fail.
reinit.
```

Tokenizer

```
tokenize([H|T],List,L) :-
    digit(H), !,
    get_rest_num(T,[H],Num,Rem),
    append(List,[Num],NewList),
    tokenize(Rem,NewList,L).
tokenize([H|T],List,L) :-
    letter(H,Letter), !,
    get_rest_word(T,[Letter],Word,Rem),
    append(List,[Word],NewList),
    tokenize(Rem,NewList,L).
tokenize([H|T],List,L) :-
    token(H,Token), !,
    append(List,[Token],NewList),
    tokenize(T,NewList,L).
tokenize([32|T],List,L) :-
    !, tokenize(T,List,L).
tokenize([],List,List).

get_rest_num([H|T],List,Num,X) :-
    digit(H), !,
    append(List,[H],Nlist),
    get_rest_num(T,Nlist,Num,X).
get_rest_num([32|T],List,Num,T) :-
    name(Num,List), !.
get_rest_num([H|T], List, Num, [H|T]) :-
    token(H,_),
    name(Num,List), !.
get_rest_num([],List,Num,[]) :-
    !, name(Num,List).
get_rest_num([H|T],List,Num,X) :-
    get_rest_num(T,List,Num,X).

get_rest_word([H|T],List,Word,X) :-
    identifier(H,Id), !,
    append(List,[Id],Nlist),
    get_rest_word(T,Nlist,Word,X).
```

get__rest__word([32|T],List,Word,T) :-
    name(Word,List), !.
get__rest__word([],List,Word,[]) :-
    !, name(Word,List).

token(' + , +).
token(' - , -).
token('*,*).
token('/,/).

digit(C) :-
    C >= '0, C =< '9.

letter(C,D) :-
    C >= 'A, C =< 'Z,
    D is C + 32.
letter(C,C) :-
    C >= 'a, C =< 'z.

identifier(C,C) :- digit(C).
identifier(C,D) :- letter(C,D).
identifier('__,'__).
identifier('#,'#).
identifier('@,'@).
identifier('$,'$).

Arithmetic Expression Grammar

expr(A) --> term(L), restexp(L,E), { A is E }.

restexp(L,L + R) --> [+], expr(R).
restexp(L,L - R) --> [-], expr(R).
restexp(L,L) --> [].

term(T) --> number(L), restterm(L,T).

restterm(L,L * R) --> [*], term(R).
restterm(L,L / R) --> [/], term(R).

```
restterm(L,L) --> [].
number(N) --> [+], number(N).
number(-N) --> [-], number(N).
number(C) --> [C].
```

Airline Flight Schedule System

Main Predicate and Query Executor

```
main :-
     repeat,
     eraseall(p), eraseall(q),
     nl,
     write('air> '),
     airport,
     fail.

airport :-
     read(Question),
     tokenize(Question,[],List),
     semantic(Queries,List,_),
     execute(Queries).

execute(test(X)) :- construct(X).
execute(assert(X)) :- construct(X).
execute(_).

construct(for_each X : (P --> Q)) :-
     make_clause_fe(P,C1), make_clause_fe(Q,C2),
     check_for_negative(C1,P), !,
     for_each(C1,C2,P,Q).
construct([H|T]) :-
     make_clause(T,H,Clause),
     check_for_negative(Clause,[H|T]),
     gen(Clause,[H|T]).

check_for_negative(Clause,[H|T]) :-
     not(call(Clause)), no_ans(Ans,[H|T],[]),
```

```
        output(Ans),
        !, fail.
check_for_negative(_,_).

gen(Clause,L) :-
        call(Clause),
        ans(Answer,L,[]),
        output(Answer),
        fail.
gen(_,_).

output([]).
output(['.'|T]) :- !, write('.'), nl, output(T).
output([H|T]) :- tab(1), write(H), output(T).

make_clause_fe([H|T],Clause) :-
        make_clause(T,H,Clause).

make_clause([],Temp,Temp).
make_clause([H|T],Temp,X) :-
        make_clause(T,(Temp,H),X).

for_each(C1,C2,P,Q) :-
        not(( C1, not C2, recordz(p,P,_),recordz(q,Q,_) )),
        ex_np(A1,P,[]), output(A1),
        ex_vp(A2,Q,[]), output(A2).
for_each(_,_,_,_) :-
        recorded(p,X,_), recorded(q,Y,_),
        not_ex_np(A1,X,[]), not_ex_vp(A2,Y,[]),
        output(A1), output(A2).
        eraseall(p), eraseall(q).
for_each(_,_,_,_).

append([],L,L).
append([H|T],L,[H|T1]) :- append(T,L,T1).
```

The Parser

```
:- op(900,fx,for_each).
:- op(800,xfy,:).
```

```
semantic(test(Sent)) -->
    aux, sentence(Sent), !.
semantic(assert(Sent)) -->
    sentence(Sent), !.
semantic(__) --> { write('Cannot understand your question.'), nl, !, fail }.


sentence(for__each V : (Prec --> Ante)) -->
    quant(every),
    nounphrase(Prec,V,Args,Amb),
    { var(V),
    pass__args(V,Args,Newargs)
    },
    verbphrase(Ante,Newargs,Amb).
sentence(Conjuncts) -->
    quant(some),
    nounphrase(Conj1,V,Args,Amb),
    verbphrase(Conj2,Args,Amb),
    { append__conj(Conj1,Conj2,Conjuncts) }.


nounphrase(Preds,V,Args,Amb) -->
    nphrase(Preds,V,Args,Amb).
nounphrase(Preds,V,Args,Amb) -->
    nphrase(Preds1,V,Args,Amb),
    pp(Preds2,Args,Amb),
    { append__conj(Preds1,Preds2,Preds) }.


nphrase([flight(Num)],Num,args(Num,X,Y,Z), not__amb) -->
    flight,
    flight__no(Num).
nphrase([flight(Num),airline(Num,Air)],Num,args(Num,Y,Z,Air),not__amb)
-->
    airlinename(Air),
    flight,
    flight__no(Num).
nphrase([flight(X),airline(X,Air)],X,args(X,Y,Z,Air),not__amb) -->
    airlinename(Air),
    flight.
```

nphrase([airline(X,A)],A,args(X,Y,Z,A),not_amb) -->
    [N], { noun(N,airline) }.
nphrase([flight(X)],X,args(X,Y,Z,A),not_amb) -->
    flight.
nphrase([airline(X,Airline)],Airline,args(X,Y,Z,Airline),not_amb) -->
    airlinename(Airline).
nphrase([flight(X),connects(X,Y,Q)],X,args(X,Y,Q,Z),City) -->
    place(City,city),
    flight.
nphrase([flight(X),connects(X,Y,Z1),city(Z),region(Z,Region)],X,args(X,Y,Z1,A),Z)
-->
    place(Region,region),
    flight.
nphrase([city(City),region(City,Region)],City,args(X,Y,Z,A),City) -->
    place(Region,region),
    [C],
    { noun(C,city) }.

nphrase([city(City)],City,args(X,Y,Z,A),City) -->
    place(City,city).

pp([connects(X,Y,Z)], args(X,Y,Z,A), Amb) -->
    { noambiguity(Amb) },
    from_to(Y,city,Z,Place),
    { Place == city; Place == [] }.
pp([connects(X,Y,Z)],args(X,Y,Z,A),Amb) -->
    { noambiguity(Amb) },
    from_to(Y,Place,Z,city),
    { Place == city ; Place == [] }.
pp([connects(X,Y,Z), region(Y,R1),region(Z,R2)],args(X,Y,Z,A),Amb) -->
    { noambiguity(Amb) },
    from_to(R1,region,R2,region).
pp([connects(X,Y,Z), region(Y,R)],args(X,Y,Z,A),Amb) -->
    { noambiguity(Amb) },
    from_to(R,region,Z,Place),
    { Place == city ; Place == [] }.

pp([connects(X,Y,Z),region(Z,R)],args(X,Y,Z,A),Amb) -->
    { noambiguity(Amb) },
    from__to(Y,Place,R,region),
    { Place == city ; Place == [] }.
pp([connects(X,Y,Z)],args(X,Y,Z1,A),Z) -->
    { ambiguous(Z) },
    from(Y,city),
    { Z = Z1 }.
pp([connects(X,Y,Z),region(Y,Region)],args(X,Y,Z1,A),Z) -->
    { ambiguous(Z) },
    from(Region,region),
    { Z = Z1 }.
pp([connects(X,Y,Z),region(Z,Region)],args(X,Y1,Z,A),Y) -->
    { ambiguous(Y) },
    to(Region,region),
    { Y = Y1 }.
pp([connects(X,Y,Z)],args(X,Y1,Z,A),Y) -->
    { ambiguous(Y) },
    to(Z,City),
    { Y = Y1 }.
pp([connects(X,Y,Amb)], args(X,Y,Amb,A), Amb) -->
    { ambiguous(Amb) }.

from__to(X,Y,Z,W) --> from(X,Y), to(Z,W).
from__to(X,Y,Z,W) --> to(Z,W), from(X,Y).
from__to(X,Y,Z,[]) --> from(X,Y).
from__to(X,[],Z,W) --> to(Z,W).

from(X,Y) --> prep(from), place(X,Y).
to(X,Y) --> prep(to), place(X,Y).

place(X,city) --> [X], { city(X) }.
place(X,region) --> quant(some), [X], { regionname(X) }.
place(X,region) -->
    quant(some),
    [X], { regionname(X) },
    [Y], { noun(Y,city) }.

```
prep(Y) --> [X], { is_prep(X,Y) }.

is_prep(to,to).
is_prep(from,from).

noambiguity(Amb) :- Amb == not_amb.

verbphrase(Conj,Args,Amb) -->
    [V], { verb(V,intrans) },
    pp(Conj,Args,Amb).
verbphrase(Conj,Args,Amb1) -->
    [V], { verb(V,trans) },
    quant(some),
    nounphrase(Conj1,_,Args,Amb2),
    { pass_amb(Amb1,Amb2,Amb) },
    pp(Conj2,Args,Amb),
    { append_conj(Conj1,Conj2,Conj) }.

verb(flies,intrans).
verb(goes,intrans).
verb(go,intrans).
verb(fly,intrans).
verb(connects,intrans).
verb(have,trans).
verb(has,trans).

city(la).
city(phi).
city(ny).
city(pit).

regionname(east_coast).
regionname(west_coast).

region(la,west_coast).
region(phi,east_coast).
region(pit,east_coast).
region(ny,east_coast).
```

airlinename(X) --> [X], {is__airline(X) }.

is__airline(branniff).
is__airline(usair).

flight(79).
flight(89).
flight(45).
flight(99).

airline(79,branniff).
airline(89,branniff).
airline(45,usair).
airline(99,usair).

connects(79,phi,la).
connects(89,phi,ny).
connects(45,phi,pit).
connects(99,pit,ny).

flight --> [X], { noun(X,flight) }.

noun(airlines,airline).
noun(airline,airline).
noun(flight,flight).
noun(flights,flight).
noun(plane,flight).
noun(planes,flight).
noun(number,number).
noun(city,city).

current__city(pit).

flight__no(Num) --> [X], {noun(X,number) }, number(Num).
flight__no(Num) --> number(Num).
number(Num) --> [Num], { integer(Num) }.

quant(Quant) --> [X], { is__quant(X,Quant) }.
quant(some) --> [].

is__quant(all,every).
is__quant(every,every).
is__quant(each,every).
is__quant(any,some).
is__quant(some,some).
is__quant(the,some).
is__quant(a,some).
is__quant(what,some).

aux --> [X], {is__aux(X) }.

is__aux(do).
is__aux(does).

pass__args(V,args(X,Y,Z,W),args(X,Y1,Z1,W1)) :-
    (V == X ; V == W), !.
pass__args(__,__,args(X,Y,Z,W)).

append__conj([],B,B).
append__conj([A|B],C,D) :-
    append__conj(B,C,D), member(A,D), !.
append__conj([A|B],C,[A|D]) :-
    append__conj(B,C,D).

member(A,[]) :- !,fail.
member(A,[B|Rest]) :- (A == B ; member(A,Rest)).

pass__amb(A1,A2,A1) :- ambiguous(A1), !.
pass__amb(A1,A2,A2).

ambiguous(Z) :- Z \== not__amb.

The Response Generator

```
ans(Ans) --->
    city,
    flight(Num),
    connect(B),
    { append([flight,Num],B,Ans) }.
ans(Ans) --->
    flight(Num),
    connect(B),
    { append([flight,Num],B,Ans) }.
ans(Ans) --->
    airline(A),
    connect(B),
    { append(A,B,Ans) }.
ans(Ans) --->
    flight(_),
    airline(A),
    connect(B),
    { append(A,B,Ans) }.
ans(Ans) --->
    airline(A),
    flight(_),
    connect(B),
    { append(A,B,Ans) }.
ans(Ans) --->
    flight(Num),
    region(R),
    connect(C),
    { append([R,flight,Num],C,Ans) }.
ans(Ans) --->
    airline(A),
    flight(_),
    city,
    connect(C),
    { append(A,C,Ans) }.

flight(Num) ---> [flight(Num)].
```

airline([Airline,flight,Num]) -->
    [airline(Num,Airline)].

city --> [city(X)].

connect([flies,from,Y,to,Z,'.']) -->
    [connects(X,Y,Z)],
    region(__),
    region(__).
connect([flies,from,Y,to,Z,'.']) -->
    [connects(X,Y,Z)],
    region(R).
connect([flies,from,Y,to,Z,'.']) -->
    region(__),
    [connects(X,Y,Z)].
connect([flies,from,Y,to,Z,'.']) -->
    [connects(X,Y,Z)].

region(R) --> [region(X,R)].

% % % % no answers % % % % %

no__ans(Ans) -->
    no__flight(Num),
    { var(Num) },
    no__connect(B),
    { append([no,flights],B,Ans) }.
no__ans(Ans) -->
    no__flight(Num),
    { nonvar(Num) },
    no__connect(B),
    { append([flight,number,Num,does,not],B,Ans) }.
no__ans(Ans) -->
    no__airline(A),
    no__connect(B),
    { append(A,B,Ans) }.
no__ans(Ans) -->
    no__flight(__),

```
        no__airline(A),
        no__connect(B),
        { append(A,B,Ans) }.
no__ans(Ans) -->
        no__airline(A),
        no__flight(__),
        no__connect(B),
        { append(A,B,Ans) }.
no__ans(Ans) -->
        no__flight(__),
        no__region(R),
        no__connect(C),
        { append([no,R,flights],C,Ans) }.

no__flight(Num) --> [flight(Num)].
no__airline([no,Airline,flights]) -->
        [airline(Num,Airline)].

no__connect([fly,from,the,R1,to,the,R2,'.']) -->
        [connects(X,Y,Z)],
        no__region(R1),
        no__region(R2).
no__connect(Ans) -->
        [connects(X,Y,Z)],
        no__region(connects(X,Y,Z),Ans).
no__connect([fly,from,City,'.']) -->
        [connects(X,City,Z)], { var(Z) }.
no__connect([fly,to,City,'.']) -->
        [connects(X,Y,City)], { var(Y) }.
no__connect([fly,from,Y,to,Z,'.']) -->
        [connects(X,Y,Z)].

no__region(R) -->
        [region(X,R)].
no__region(connects(X,Y,Z),[fly,from,the,R,'.']) -->
        [region(Y,R)], { Y \== Z, var(Z) }.
no__region(connects(X,Y,Z),[fly,to,the,R,'.']) -->
        [region(Z,R)], { Y \== Z, var(Y) }.
```

```
no__region(connects(X,Y,Z),[fly,from,the,R,to,Z,'.']) -->
    [region(Y,R)], { Y \== Z, nonvar(Z) }.
no__region(connects(X,Y,Z),[fly,to,the,R,from,Y,'.']) -->
    [region(Z,R)], { Y \== Z, nonvar(Y) }.
```

%%%%% existential answers are formed in two parts (np + vp)

```
ex__np([all,A,flights]) -->
    ex__flight,
    ex__airline(A).
ex__np([all,CorR,flights]) -->
    ex__flight,
    ex__connect(CorR).
ex__np([all,flights]) -->
    ex__flight.
ex__np([all,airlines]) -->
    ex__airline(__).

ex__flight -->
    [flight(Num)].
ex__airline(A) -->
    [airline(__,A)].

ex__connect(City) -->
    [connects(X,Y,City)],
    { var(Y) }.
ex__connect(City) -->
    [connects(X,City,Z)],
    { var(Z) }.
ex__connect(Region) -->
    [connects(X,Y,Z)],
    ex__region(Region).

ex__region(Region) -->
    [region(X,Region)].
```

```
ex__vp([go,to,City,'.']) -->
    [connects(X,Y,City)],
    { var(Y) }.
ex__vp([fly,from,City,'.']) -->
    [connects(X,City,Z)],
    { var(Z) }.
ex__vp([go,from,the,Region,'.']) -->
    [connects(X,Y,Z)],
    ex__region(Region),
    { var(Y) }.
ex__vp([fly,to,the,Region,'.']) -->
    [connects(X,Y,Z)],
    ex__region(Region),
    { var(Z) }.
ex__vp([fly,from,the,R1,to,the,R2,'.']) -->
    [connects(X,Y,Z)],
    [region(Y,R1)],
    [region(Z,R2)].


%%% negative existentials

not__ex__np([A,flight,Num]) -->
    not__ex__flight(Num),
    not__ex__airline(__,A).
not__ex__np([CorR,flight,Num]) -->
    not__ex__flight(Num),
    ex__connect(CorR).
not__ex__np([flight,Num]) -->
    not__ex__flight(Num).
not__ex__np([A,flight,Num]) -->
    not__ex__airline(Num,A).


not__ex__flight(Num) --> [flight(Num)].
not__ex__airline(F,A) --> [airline(F,A)].


not__ex__vp([does,not,go,to,City,'.']) -->
    [connects(X,Y,City)],
    { var(Y) }.
```

```
not__ex__vp([does,not,fly,from,City,'.']) --->
    [connects(X,City,Z)],
    { var(Z) }.
not__ex__vp(VP) --->
    [connects(X,Y,Z)],
    not__ex__region(connects(X,Y,Z),R),
    { append([does,not,fly],R,VP) }.

not__ex__region(connects(X,Y,Z),[from,the,Region,'.']) --->
    [region(Y,Region)], { Y \== Z, var(Z) }.
not__ex__region(connects(X,Y,Z),[to,the,Region,'.']) --->
    [region(Z,Region)], { Y \== Z, var(Y) }.
not__ex__region(connect(X,Y,Z),[from,the,Region,to,Z,'.']) --->
    [region(Y,Region)], { Y \== Z, nonvar(Z) }.
not__ex__region(connects(X,Y,Z),[to,the,Region,from,Y,'.']) --->
    [region(Z,Region)], { Y \== Z, nonvar(Y) }.
```

C
Bibliography

On the Prolog Language

Bratco, Ivan. *Prolog Programming for Artificial Intelligence*. Reading, MA: Addison-Wesley Publishing Company, 1986.

Campbell, J.A. *Implementations of Prolog*. West Sussex, England: Ellis Horwood, 1984.

Clark, K.L. and Tarnlund, S.A. *Logic Programming*. New York: Academic Press, 1982.

Clocksin, W.F. and Mellish, C.S. *Programming in Prolog,* second edition. New York: Springer-Verlag, 1984.

Kowalski, Robert. *Logic for Problem Solving*. New York: Elsevier North Holland, 1979.

Lloyd, J.W. *Foundations of Logic Programming*. New York: Springer-Verlag, 1984.

On Relational Databases

Date, C.J. *A Guide to DB2*. Reading, MA: Addison-Wesley Publishing Company, 1984.

Date, C.J. *An Introduction to Database Systems*, vol. 1. Reading, MA: Addison-Wesley Publishing Company, 1981.

Date, C.J. *An Introduction to Database Systems*, vol. 2. Reading, MA: Addison-Wesley Publishing Company, 1983.

Date, C.J. *Relational Databases, Selected Writings*. Reading, MA: Addison-Wesley Publishing Company, 1986.

Gray, Peter. *Logic, Algebra and Databases*. New York: John Wiley & Sons, 1984.

Li, Deyi. *A Prolog Database System*. Letchworth, England: Research Studies Press, 1984.

On Expert Systems

Buchanan, Bruce G. and Shortliffe, Edward H. *Rule-Based Expert Systems.* Reading, MA: Addison-Wesley Publishing Company, 1984.

Harmon, Paul and King, David. *Expert Systems: Artificial Intelligence in Business.* New York: John Wiley & Sons, 1985.

Hayes-Roth, Frederick, Waterman, Donald A., Lenat, Douglas B. *Building Expert Systems.* Reading, MA: Addison-Wesley Publishing Company, 1983.

Weiss, Sholom M., Kulikowski, Casimir A. *A Practical Guide to Designing Expert Systems.* Totowa, NJ: Rowman & Allanheld, 1984.

On Natural Language

Dahl, Veronica and Patrick Saint-Dizier, eds. *Natural Language Understanding and Logic Programming.* New York: Elsevier Science Publishing Company, 1985.

Mellish, C.S. *Computer Interpretation of Natural Language.* West Sussex, England: Ellis Horwood, 1985.

Sager, Naomi. *Natural Language Information Processing.* Reading, MA: Addison-Wesley Publishing Company, 1981.

Wallace, Mark. *Communicating with Databases in Natural Language.* West Sussex, England: Ellis Horwood, 1984.

Winograd, Terry. *Language as a Cognitive Process*, vol. 1. Reading, MA: Addison-Wesley Publishing Company, 1983.

On Artificial Intelligence

Barr, Avron and Edward A. Feigenbaum. *The Handbook of Artificial Intelligence*, vols 1, 2, and 3. Los Altos: William Kaufmann, 1981.

Nilsson, Nils J. *Principles of Artificial Intelligence.* Palo Alto, CA: Tioga Publishing, 1980.

Winston, Patrick Henry. *Artificial Intelligence*, second edition. Reading, MA: Addison-Wesley Publishing Company, 1984.

Index